Level **G** ⟩ **Mathematics**

Measuring Up®

™

to the

Pennsylvania Academic Standards

and Success Strategies for the PSSA

Mathematics

This book is customized for Pennsylvania and the lessons
match the **Pennsylvania Academic Standards**.
The Measuring Up® program includes comprehensive worktexts plus
Measuring Up® e-Path online assessments and print and
Pennsylvania Diagnostic Practice Tests, which are available separately.

800-822-1080
www.PeoplesEducation.com

Peoples Education
Your partner in student success

Executive Vice President and Chief Creative Officer: Diane Miller

Vice President, Product Development: Steven Jay Griffel

Assistant Vice President, Editorial Director: Eugene McCormick

Editorial Development: Gramercy Book Services, Inc.

Mathematics Director: April Barth

Executive Mathematics Editor: Martha Torn

Editors: Jane Books, Mark D. Perry

Editorial Assistants: Joseph Schwab

Director of Editorial Service: Lee Shenkman

Supervising Copy Editor: Lee Laddy

Copy Editors: Dee Josephson, Josh Gillenson Katy Leclerq

Vice President of Production and Manufacturing: Doreen Smith

Production Director: Nicole Dawson

Project Manager: Julio Espin

Senior Book Coordinator: Sharon MacGregor

Production Editor: Eileen Turano

Vice President of Marketing: Melissa Dubno Geller

Designer: Jodi Notowitz

Permissions Manager: Kristine Liebman

Photo Researcher: Robert E. Lee

Technical Art: Sharon MacGregor

Cover Design: Cynthia Mackowicz, Michele Sakow, Chris Kennedy

Pennsylvania Advisory Panel

Mrs. Barbara E. Davis, Tulpehocken Area School District
Bernville, PA

John Holland , School Mathematics Consultant

Your partner in student success™

Copyright © 2007

Peoples Education, Inc.
299 Market Street
Saddle Brook, New Jersey 07663

ISBN 978-1-56256-342-4

Printed in the United States of America.

 10 9 8 7 6 5 4 3

Contents

This section provides test-taking tips and strategies for answering
multiple-choice and open-ended items. You will also learn how to
build endurance and confidence to answer those really tough questions
that require higher-order thinking.

Part 1 Number and Operations, Algebra, Ratio and Proportion 1

Chapter 1 Whole Numbers and Decimals

Chapter 2 Fractions

Chapter 3 Integers

Chapter 4   Algebraic Concepts

Chapter 5   Ratio, Proportions, and Percents

Chapter 6   Measurement

Chapter 7 Perimeter, Circumference, and Area

Chapter 8   Geometry

Chapter 9 Statistics and Data Analysis

Chapter 10 Probability

Standard	Assessment Anchors & Eligible Content
2.4.8.B, 2.7.5.E, 2.7.5.G, 2.7.5.J, 2.7.8.E	M7.E.3.1.1; M7.E.3.1.2
2.7.8.B, 2.7.8.D, 2.7.8.E	M7.E.3.1.3 M7.E.4.1.1
2.4.8.B, 2.7.5.E, 2.7.5.G, 2.7.5.J, 2.7.8.E	M7.E.3.1.1; M7.E.3.1.2; M7.E.3.1.3

For a quick review of concepts, review the glossary of terms. If you are having difficulty with a concept, review that lesson again.

Pennsylvania Assessment Anchors and Eligible Content		Lessons
M7.A	**Numbers and Operations**	
M7.A.1	**Demonstrate an understanding of numbers, ways of representing numbers, relationships among numbers and number systems.**	
M7.A.1.1	**Express numbers in equivalent forms.**	
M7.A.1.1.1	Convert between fractions, decimals and/or percents (e.g., 20% = 0.2 = 1/5) (terminating decimals only).	8, 9, 10, 33, Ch. 2 BS, Ch. 5 BS
M7.A.1.2	**Compare quantities and/or magnitudes of numbers.**	
M7.A.1.2.1	Compare and/or order integers, mixed numbers, fractions and decimals (fractions and decimals may be mixed— no more than 5 numbers in a set to be ordered).	1, 9, 10, Ch. 1 BS, Ch. 2 BS
M7.A.1.2.2	Locate/identify decimals, fractions, mixed numbers and/ or integers on a number line (a mix of these number forms may be on the same number line).	10, 15, 16, 18, Ch. 3 BS
M7.A.2	**Understand the meanings of operations, use operations and understand how they relate to each other.**	
M7.A.2.1	**Complete calculations by applying the order of operations.**	
M7.A.2.1.1	Use the order of operations to simplify numerical expressions (may use parentheses, brackets, $+, -, \times, \div$, squares up to 10^2 and cubes up to 4^3; whole numbers only).	21, Ch. 4 BS
M7.A.2.2	**Solve problems using ratios, proportions, percents and/or rates**	
M7.A.2.2.1	Write ratios to compare quantities (e.g., ratio of boys to girls).	28, 31, 32, Ch. 5 BS
M7.A.2.2.2	Solve for a variable in a given proportion.	30, 31, 32, Ch. 5 BS
M7.A.2.2.3	Use proportions to determine if two quantities are equivalent (e.g., similar figures, prices of different sized items, etc).	29, 30, Ch. 5 BS
M7.A.2.2.4	Calculate and/or apply unit rates or unit prices (terminating decimals through the hundredth place only).	29, Ch. 5 BS
M7.A.2.2.5	Select and/or use ratios or proportions to solve problems.	30, 31, 32, Ch. 5 BS
M7.A.2.2.6	Use proportions to find the missing length of a side in similar figures.	47, 49, Ch. 8 BS

Ch. = Chapter   BS = **Building Stamina**®

Pennsylvania Assessment Anchors and Eligible Content		Lessons
M7.A.3	**Compute accurately and fluently and make reasonable estimates.**	
M7.A.3.1	**Apply estimation strategies to a variety of problems.**	
M7.A.3.1.1	Estimate answers to problems involving whole numbers, decimals, fractions or mixed numbers.	3, 6, 14, Ch. 1 BS, Ch. 2 BS
M7.A.3.2	**Compute accurately with and without use of a calculator.**	
M7.A.3.2.1	Solve problems involving operations ($+, -, \times, \div$) of whole numbers, decimals, fractions, or mixed numbers (straight computation or word problems).	2, 4, 5, 7, 11, 12, 13, 14, 19, Ch. 1 BS, Ch. 2 BS, Ch. 3 BS
M7.A.3.2.2	Solve problems involving addition and subtraction of integers.	17, 18, 19, Ch. 3 BS
M7.B.1	**Demonstrate an understanding of measurable attributes of objects and figures, and the units, systems and processes of measurement.**	
M7.B.1.1	**Add, subtract, or convert measurements.**	
M7.B.1.1.1	Add, subtract, or convert measurements, using only the units below, with and without regrouping (e.g., 4 ft − 2 ft 5 in. = 1 ft 7 in.). Answer should be converted to the largest whole unit (e.g., 37 oz = 2 lb 5 oz or 39 in. = 1 yd 3 in. Conversion chart provided on the reference sheet. • in. ft, yd • fl oz, cup, pint, quart, gallon • oz, lb • sec, min, hours, days • metric units including milli, centi and kilo (m, g or L)	35, 36, 37, 38, Ch. 6 BS
M7.B.2	**Apply appropriate techniques, tools and formulas to determine measurements.**	
M7.B.2.1	**Develop, use and/or describe strategies to find the measure of length, perimeter, circumference, area or volume.**	
M7.B.2.1.1	Develop and/or use strategies to find the perimeter and/or area of compound figures (compound figures should only include quadrilaterals and triangles). Area formulas provided on the reference sheet.	41, 43, Ch. 7 BS
M7.B.2.1.2	Find the circumference and/or area of circles (formulas provided on the reference sheet).	42, 43, Ch. 7 BS

Ch. = Chapter   BS = **Building Stamina**®

Pennsylvania Assessment Anchors and Eligible Content		Lessons
M7.B.2.1.3	Find the area of triangles and/or all types of parallelograms (formulas provided on the reference sheet).	39, 40, 43, Ch. 7 BS
M7.B.2.2	**Construct, interpret and/or use scale drawings to solve real-world problems.**	
M7.B.2.2.1	Interpret and/or apply scales shown on maps, blueprints, models, etc.	31, 32, Ch. 5 BS
M7.B.2.2.2	Determine and/or apply an appropriate scale for reduction or enlargement.	32, Ch. 5 BS
M7.C.1	**Analyze characteristics and properties of two- and three-dimensional geometric shapes and demonstrate understanding of geometric relationships.**	
M7.C.1.1	**Define and/or apply basic properties of two- and three-dimensional geometric shapes.**	
M7.C.1.1.1	Identify, describe and/or define diameter, radius, chord and/or circumference in circles.	42, 44, Ch. 7 BS, Ch. 8 BS
M7.C.1.1.2	Solve problems involving the relationship between the radius and diameter of the same circle.	44, Ch. 8 BS
M7.C.1.1.3	Identify parallel, perpendicular and/or skew line segments within three-dimensional figures.	45, Ch. 8 BS
M7.C.1.2	**Identify congruence and/or similarity in polygons.**	
M7.C.1.2.1	Identify and/or use polygons that are similar and/or congruent, given either measurements or tic and angle marks.	46, 47, 49, Ch. 8 BS
M7.C.1.2.2	Identify corresponding sides and/or angles of congruent or similar polygons.	46, 47, 49, Ch. 8 BS
M7.C.2	**Identify and/or apply concepts of transformations or symmetry.**	
	Not assessed at Grade 7	
M7.C.3	**Locate points or describe relationships using the coordinate plane.**	
M7.C.3.1	**Locate, plot and/or describe points on a coordinate plane.**	
M7.C.3.1.1	Plot and/or identify ordered pairs on a coordinate plane (all four quadrants).	48, Ch. 8 BS

Ch. = Chapter   BS = **Building Stamina®**

Pennsylvania Assessment Anchors and Eligible Content		Lessons
M7.C.3.1.2	Identify Quadrants I, II, III, IV, the *x*- & *y*-axes and the origin on a coordinate plane.	48, Ch. 8 BS
M7.D.1	**Demonstrate an understanding of patterns, relations and functions.**	
M7.D.1.1	**Recognize, reproduce, extend and/or describe patterns.**	
M7.D.1.1.1	Describe, extend or find a missing element of a pattern (show 3 repetitions of the pattern) • fractions or decimals - may use only one operation from +, − or × • whole numbers – may use only one operation from +, −, ×, ÷ or squares	26, 27, Ch. 4 BS
M7.D.2	**Represent and/or analyze mathematical situations using numbers, symbols, words, tables and/or graphs.**	
M7.D.2.1	**Select and/or use appropriate strategies to solve or represent equations or expressions.**	
M7.D.2.1.1	Select and/or use appropriate strategies to solve one-step equations (no negative numbers).	24, 25, Pt. 1 BS
M7.D.2.1.2	Use substitution of one and/or two variables to simplify expressions (whole numbers only — use order of operations).	21, 22, 27, Ch. 4 BS
M7.D.2.2	**Create and/or interpret expressions, equations or inequalities that model problem situations.**	
M7.D.2.2.1	Identify expressions, equations or inequalities that model mathematical situations (using whole numbers or decimals, no more than two operations and one variable).	20, 21, 22, 23, 24, 25, Ch. 4 BS
M7.D.3	**Analyze change in various contexts.**	
M7.D.3.1	**Describe the relationship between two variables (e.g., time, temperature).**	
M7.D.3.1.1	Solve problems involving a constant rate of change (e.g., word problems, graphs or data tables).	34, Ch. 5 BS
M7.D.3.1.2	Describe and/or use the relationship of data displayed on a rate of change graph (e.g., how does the *x*-axis data relate to the *y*-axis data).	34, Ch. 5 BS
M7.D.4	**Describe or use models to represent quantitative relationships.**	

Ch. = Chapter   BS = **Building Stamina**®

Pennsylvania Assessment Anchors and Eligible Content		Lessons
	Not assessed at Grade 7	
M7.E.1	Formulate or answer questions that can be addressed with data and/or organize, display, interpret or analyze data.	
M7.E.1.1	Interpret data shown in complex data displays.	
M7.E.1.1.1	Analyze data and/or answer questions pertaining to data represented in histograms, double bar graphs, multiple line graphs or stem-and-leaf plots.	52, 53, 54, 55, Ch. 9 BS
M7.E.2	Select and/or use appropriate statistical methods to analyze data.	
M7.E.2.1	Describe, compare and/or contrast data using measures of mean, median, mode or range.	
M7.E.2.1.1	Identify/calculate the mean (average), median, mode or range of a set of data.	50, 51, Ch. 9 BS
M7.E.2.1.2	Decide/choose which measure of central tendency (mean, median, mode or range) would be most appropriate for a given situation.	51, Ch. 9 BS
M7.E.3	Understand and/or apply basic concepts of probability or outcomes.	
M7.E.3.1	Determine theoretical or experimental probability.	
M7.E.3.1.1	Find the theoretical probability of a simple and/or compound event (answer written as a fraction in lowest terms — any compound events should be independent).	56, 58, Ch. 10 BS
M7.E.3.1.2	Find the theoretical probability of an event not occurring (e.g., what is the probability of not rolling a 1 on a number cube).	56, 58, Ch. 10 BS
M7.E.3.1.3	Use data displayed in charts, graphs or tallies to find experimental probability.	57, 58, Ch. 10 BS
M7.E.4	Develop and/or evaluate inferences and predictions or draw conclusions based on data or data displays.	
M7.E.4.1	Draw conclusions and/or make predictions based on data displays.	
M7.E.4.1.1	Formulate predictions and/or draw conclusions based on data displays (bar graphs, circle graphs or line graphs) or probability.	52, Ch. 9 BS

Ch. = Chapter   BS = **Building Stamina**®

Pennsylvania Academic Standards	Lessons
2.1 **Numbers, Number Systems and Number Relationships**	
2.1.8 **Pennsylvania's public schools shall teach, challenge and support every student to realize his or her maximum potential and to acquire the knowledge and skills to:**	
A. Represent and use numbers in equivalent forms (e.g., integers, fractions, decimals, percents, exponents, scientific notation, square roots).	1, 7, 8, 9, 10, 33, 34
B. Simplify numerical expressions involving exponents, scientific notation and using order of operations.	21, 22
C. Distinguish between and order rational and irrational numbers.	1
D. Apply ratio and proportion to mathematical problem situations involving distance, rate, time and similar triangles.	28, 29, 30
E. Simplify and expand algebraic expressions using exponential forms.	21, 22, 26, 27
F. Use the number line model to demonstrate integers and their applications.	1, 15, 16, 17, 18, 19
G. Use the inverse relationships between addition, subtraction, multiplication, division, exponentiation and root extraction to determine unknown quantities in equations.	24, 25
2.2 **Computation and Estimation**	
2.2.8 **Pennsylvania's public schools shall teach, challenge and support every student to realize his or her maximum potential and to acquire the knowledge and skills needed to:**	
A. Complete calculations by applying the order of operations.	Level H Lessons 7, 18
B. Add, subtract, multiply and divide different kinds and forms of rational numbers including integers, decimal fractions, percents and proper and improper fractions.	2, 4, 5, 6, 10, 11, 12, 13, 17, 18, 19
C. Estimate the value of irrational numbers.	Level H Lesson 17
D. Estimate amount of tips and discounts using ratios, proportions and percents.	Level H Lesson 30
E. Determine the appropriateness of overestimating or underestimating in computation.	3, 14
F. Identify the difference between exact value and approximation and determine which is appropriate for a given situation.	3, 14, 42

Pennsylvania Academic Standards		Lessons
2.3	**Measurement and Estimation**	
2.3.8	**Pennsylvania's public schools shall teach, challenge and support every student to realize his or her maximum potential and to acquire the knowledge and skills to:**	
A.	Develop formulas and procedures for determining measurements (e.g., area, volume, distance).	39, 40, 41, 42, 43
B.	Solve rate problems (e.g., rate × time = distance, principal × interest rate = interest).	29, 30, 34
C.	Measure angles in degrees and determine relations of angles.	Level H Lessons 42, 50, 51
D.	Estimate, use and describe measures of distance, rate, perimeter, volume, weight, mass and angles.	28, 29, 35, 36, area, 37, 38, 39, 40, 41, 42, 43
E.	Describe how a change in linear dimension of an object affects its perimeter, area and volume.	Level H Lesson 49
F.	Use scale measurements to interpret maps or drawings.	31
G.	Create and use scale models.	32
2.4	**Mathematical Reasoning and Connections**	
2.4.8	**Pennsylvania's public schools shall teach, challenge and support every student to realize his or her maximum potential and to acquire the knowledge and skills to:**	
A.	Make conjectures based on logical reasoning and test conjectures by using counter-examples.	Level H Lesson 10
B.	Combine numeric relationships to arrive at a conclusion.	10, 17, 18, 19, 35, 36, 37, 38, 56, 58
C.	Use if...then statements to construct simple, valid arguments.	Level H Lesson 57
D.	Construct, use and explain algorithmic procedures for computing and estimating with whole numbers, fractions, decimals and integers.	2, 3, 4, 5, 6, 11 12, 13, 14, 17, 18, 19
E.	Distinguish between inductive and deductive reasoning.	Level H Lesson 57
F.	Use measurements and statistics to quantify issues (e.g., in family, consumer science situations).	52, 53, 54, 55

Lesson Correlation to the Pennsylvania Mathematics Grade 8 Academic Standards

Pennsylvania Academic Standards		Lessons
2.5	**Mathematical Problem Solving and Communication**	
2.5.8	**Pennsylvania's public schools shall teach, challenge and support every student to realize his or her maximum potential and to acquire the knowledge and skills to:**	
A.	Invent, select, use and justify the appropriate methods, materials and strategies to solve problems.	7, 29, 30, 34, 50, 51
B.	Verify and interpret results using precise mathematical language, notation and representations, including numerical tables and equations, simple algebraic equations and formulas, charts, graphs and diagrams.	Level H Lesson 21
C.	Justify strategies and defend approaches used and conclusions reached.	Level H Lessons 19, 20, 22, 66
D.	Determine pertinent information in problem situations and whether any further information is needed for solution.	29, 30, 34
2.6	**Statistics and Data Analysis**	
2.6.8	**Pennsylvania's public schools shall teach, challenge and support every student to realize his or her maximum potential and to acquire the knowledge and skills to:**	
A.	Compare and contrast different plots of data using values of mean, median, mode, quartiles and range.	50, 51
B.	Explain effects of sampling procedures and missing or incorrect information on reliability.	Level H Lesson 66
C.	Fit a line to the scatter plot of two quantities and describe any correlation of the variables.	Level H Lesson 65
D.	Design and carry out a random sampling procedure.	Level H Lesson 66
E.	Analyze and display data in stem-and-leaf and box-and-whisker plots.	Level H Lesson 61
F.	Use scientific and graphing calculators and computer spreadsheets to organize and analyze data.	52, 53, 54, 55
2.7	**Probability and Predictions**	
2.7.8	**Pennsylvania's public schools shall teach, challenge and support every student to realize his or her maximum potential and to acquire the knowledge and skills to:**	

Pennsylvania Academic Standards		Lessons
A.	Determine the number of combinations and permutations for an event.	Level H Lesson 59
B.	Present the results of an experiment using visual representations (e.g., tables, charts, graphs).	57
C.	Analyze predictions (e.g., election polls).	Level H Lesson 66
D.	Compare and contrast results from observations and mathematical models.	57
E.	Make valid inferences, predictions and arguments based on probability.	56, 57, 58
2.8	**Algebra and Functions**	
2.8.8	**Pennsylvania's public schools shall teach, challenge and support every student to realize his or her maximum potential and to acquire the knowledge and skills to:**	
A.	Apply simple algebraic patterns to basic number theory and to spatial relations.	26, 27
B.	Discover, describe and generalize patterns, including linear, exponential and simple quadratic relationships.	26, 27
C.	Create and interpret expressions, equations or inequalities that model problem situations.	20, 21, 22, 23, 24, 25
D.	Use concrete objects to model algebraic concepts.	24
E.	Select and use a strategy to solve an equation or inequality, explain the solution and check the solution for accuracy.	24, 25
F.	Solve and graph equations and inequalities using scientific and graphing calculators and computer spreadsheets.	Level H Lessons 22, 34
G.	Represent relationships with tables or graphs in the coordinate plane and verbal or symbolic rules.	Level H Lesson 33
H.	Graph a linear function from a rule or table.	Level H Lesson 34
I.	Generate a table or graph from a function and use graphing calculators and computer spreadsheets to graph and analyze functions.	Level H Lesson 33
J.	Show that an equality relationship between two quantities remains the same as long as the same change is made to both quantities; explain how a change in one quantity determines another quantity in a functional relationship.	24, 25

Lesson Correlation to the Pennsylvania Mathematics Grade 8 Academic Standards

Pennsylvania Academic Standards		Lessons
2.9	**Geometry**	
2.9.8	**Pennsylvania's public schools shall teach, challenge and support every student to realize his or her maximum potential and to acquire the knowledge and skills to:**	
A.	Construct figures incorporating perpendicular and parallel lines, the perpendicular bisector of a line segment and an angle bisector using computer software.	45
B.	Draw, label, measure and list the properties of complementary, supplementary and vertical angles.	Level H Lesson 50
C.	Classify familiar polygons as regular or irregular up to a decagon.	45
D.	Identify, name, draw and list all properties of squares, cubes, pyramids, parallelograms, quadrilaterals, trapezoids, polygons, rectangles, rhombi, circles, spheres, triangles, prisms and cylinders.	39, 40, 41, 42, 44
E.	Construct parallel lines, draw a transversal and measure and compare angles formed (e.g., alternate interior and exterior angles).	45
F.	Distinguish between similar and congruent polygons.	46, 47, 49
G.	Approximate the value of π (pi) through experimentation.	42
H.	Use simple geometric figures (e.g., triangles, squares) to create, through rotation, transformational figures in three dimensions.	Level H Lesson 56
I.	Generate transformations using computer software.	Level H Lessons 36, 37
J.	Analyze geometric patterns (e.g., tessellations, sequences of shapes) and develop descriptions of the patterns.	Level H Lesson 23
K.	Analyze objects to determine whether they illustrate tessellations, symmetry, congruence, similarity and scale.	46, 47, 49
2.10	**Trigonometry**	
2.10.8	**Pennsylvania's public schools shall teach, challenge and support every student to realize his or her maximum potential and to acquire the knowledge and skills to:**	
A.	Compute measures of sides and angles using proportions, the Pythagorean Theorem and right triangle relationships.	Level H Lesson 53
B.	Solve problems requiring indirect measurement for lengths of sides of triangles.	Level H Lesson 53, 55

Pennsylvania Academic Standards	Lessons
2.11 Concepts of Calculus	
2.11.8 Pennsylvania's public schools shall teach, challenge and support every student to realize his or her maximum potential and to acquire the knowledge and skills to:	
A. Analyze graphs of related quantities for minimum and maximum values and justify the findings.	Level H Lesson 33
B. Describe the concept of unit rate, ratio and slope in the context of rate of change.	Level H Lesson 34
C. Continue a pattern of numbers or objects that could be extended infinitely.	Level H Lesson 23

Lesson Correlation to the Pennsylvania Mathematics Grade 5 Academic Standards

Pennsylvania Academic Standards		Lessons
2.1	**Numbers, Number Systems and Number Relationships**	
2.1.5	**Pennsylvania's public schools shall teach, challenge and support every student to realize his or her maximum potential and to acquire the knowledge and skills to:**	
A.	Use expanded notation to represent whole numbers or decimals.	Level E, Lessons 1, 13
B.	Apply number theory concepts to rename a number quantity (e.g., six, 6, $\frac{12}{2}$, 3×2, 10 - 4).	Level E, Lesson 5
C.	Demonstrate that mathematical operations can represent a variety of problem situations.	Level E, Lesson 28
D.	Use models to represent fractions and decimals.	Level E, Lessons 21, 23, 24, 25
E.	Explain the concepts of prime and composite numbers.	Level E, Lesson 5
F.	Use simple concepts of negative numbers (e.g., on a number line, in counting, in temperature).	Level E, Lessons 6, 37
G.	Develop and apply number theory concepts (e.g., primes, factors, multiples, composites) to represent numbers in various ways.	Level E, Lessons 4, 5
2.2	**Computation and Estimation**	
2.2.5	**Pennsylvania's public schools shall teach, challenge and support every student to realize his or her maximum potential and to acquire the knowledge and skills to:**	
A.	Create and solve word problems involving addition, subtraction, multiplication and division of whole numbers.	Level E, Lessons 8, 9, 10, 20
B.	Develop and apply algorithms to solve word problems that involve addition, subtraction, and/or multiplication with decimals with and without regrouping.	Level E, Lessons 15, 17, 20
C.	Develop and apply algorithms to solve word problems that involve addition, subtraction, and/or multiplication with fractions and mixed numbers that include like and unlike denominators.	Level E, Lessons 23, 24, 25, 26
D.	Demonstrate the ability to round numbers.	Level E, Lessons 3, 8, 16
E.	Determine through estimations the reasonableness of answers to problems involving addition, subtraction, multiplication and division of whole numbers.	Level E, Lessons 8, 11, 19
F.	Demonstrate skills for using fraction calculators to verify conjectures, confirm computations and explore complex problem-solving situations.	Level E, Lesson 26

Pennsylvania Academic Standards		Lessons
G.	Apply estimation strategies to a variety of problems including time and money.	Level E, Lessons 16, 19
H.	Explain multiplication and division algorithms.	Level E, Lessons 9, 10, 18
I.	Select a method for computation and explain why it is appropriate.	Level E, Lesson 20
2.3	**Measurement and Estimation**	
2.3.5	**Pennsylvania's public schools shall teach, challenge and support every student to realize his or her maximum potential and to acquire the knowledge and skills to:**	
A.	Select and use appropriate instruments and units for measuring quantities (e.g., perimeter, volume, area, weight, time, temperature).	Level E, Lessons 33, 34, 35, 36, 37, 38, 40, 42
B.	Select and use standard tools to measure the size of figures with specified accuracy, including length, width, perimeter and area.	Level E, Lessons 33, 34, 38
C.	Estimate, refine and verify specified measurements of objects.	Level E, Lessons 33, 34, 35, 36
D.	Convert linear measurements within the same system.	35, 36, 37
E.	Add and subtract measurements.	Level E, Lessons 34, 35, 36, 37, 38
2.4	**Mathematical Reasoning and Connections**	
2.4.5	**Pennsylvania's public schools shall teach, challenge and support every student to realize his or her maximum potential and to acquire the knowledge and skills to:**	
A.	Compare quantities and magnitudes of numbers.	Level E, Lessons 2, 14, 22
B.	Use models, number facts, properties and relationships to check and verify predictions and explain reasoning.	Level E, Lesson 7
C.	Draw inductive and deductive conclusions within mathematical contexts.	Level E, Lesson 58
D.	Distinguish between relevant and irrelevant information in a mathematical problem.	Level E, Lesson 7
E.	Interpret statements made with precise language of logic (e.g., "all", "or", "every", "none", "some", "or", "many").	Level E, Lesson 58
F.	Use statistics to quantify issues (e.g., in social studies, in science).	Level E, Lesson 54

Pennsylvania Academic Standards		Lessons
2.5	**Mathematical Problem Solving and Communication**	
2.5.5	**Pennsylvania's public schools shall teach, challenge and support every student to realize his or her maximum potential and to acquire the knowledge and skills to:**	
A.	Develop a plan to analyze a problem, identify the information needed to solve the problem, carry out the plan, check whether an answer makes sense and explain how the problem was solved.	Level E, Lessons 7, 12
B.	Use appropriate mathematical terms, vocabulary, language symbols and graphs to explain clearly and logically solutions to problems.	Level E, Lesson 7
C.	Show ideas in a variety of ways, including words, numbers, symbols, pictures, charts, graphs, tables, diagrams and models.	Level E, Lessons 53, 55, 56, 57, 58
D.	Connect, extend and generalize problem solutions to other concepts, problems and circumstances in mathematics.	Level E, Lessons 7, 27, 32
E.	Select, use and justify the methods, materials and strategies used to solve problems.	Level E, Lesson 12
F.	Use appropriate problem-solving strategies (e.g., solving a simpler problem, drawing a picture or diagram).	Level E, Lesson 27
2.6	**Statistics and Data Analysis**	
2.6.5	**Pennsylvania's public schools shall teach, challenge and support every student to realize his or her maximum potential and to acquire the knowledge and skills to:**	
A.	Organize and display data using pictures, tallies, tables, charts, bar graphs and circle graphs.	Level E, Lessons 53, 55, 56, 57
B.	Describe data sets using mean, median, mode and range.	Level E, Lesson 54
C.	Sort data using Venn diagrams.	Level E, Lesson 58
D.	Predict the likely number of times a condition will occur based on analyzed data.	Level E, Lesson 59
E.	Construct and defend simple conclusions based on data.	Level E, Lessons 55, 56, 57
2.7	**Probability and Predictions**	
2.7.5	**Pennsylvania's public schools shall teach, challenge and support every student to realize his or her maximum potential and to acquire the knowledge and skills to:**	
A.	Perform simulations with concrete devices (e.g., dice, spinner) to predict the chance of an event occurring.	Level E, Lesson 61

Pennsylvania Academic Standards		Lessons
B.	Determine the fairness of the design of a spinner.	Level E, Lesson 59
C.	Express probabilities as fractions and decimals.	Level E, Lessons 60, 62
D.	Compare predictions based on theoretical probability and experimental results.	Level E, Lesson 61
E.	Calculate the probability of a simple event.	56, 58
F.	Determine patterns generated as a result of an experiment.	Level E, Lessons 61, 64
G.	Determine the probability of an event involving "and", "or" or "not".	56, 58
H.	Predict and determine why some outcomes are certain, more likely, less likely, equally likely or impossible.	Level E, Lesson 59
I.	Find all possible combinations and arrangements involving a limited number of variables.	Level E, Lessons 63, 64
J.	Develop a tree diagram and list the elements.	56, 58
2.8	**Algebra and Functions**	
2.8.5	**Pennsylvania's public schools shall teach, challenge and support every student to realize his or her maximum potential and to acquire the knowledge and skills to:**	
A.	Recognize, reproduce, extend, create and describe patterns, sequences and relationships verbally, numerically, symbolically and graphically, using a variety of materials.	Level E, Lesson 27
B.	Connect patterns to geometric relations and basic number skills.	Level E, Lesson 27
C.	Form rules based on patterns (e.g., an equation that relates pairs in a sequence).	Level E, Lesson 32
D.	Use concrete objects and combinations of symbols and numbers to create expressions that model mathematical situations	Level E, Lessons 28, 29
E.	Explain the use of combinations of symbols and numbers in expressions, equations and inequalities.	Level E, Lessons 28, 29, 30
F.	Describe a realistic situation using information given in equations, inequalities, tables or graphs	Level E, Lesson 28
G.	Select and use appropriate strategies, including concrete materials, to solve number sentences and explain the method of solution.	Level E, Lessons 29, 30
H.	Locate and identify points on a coordinate system.	48
I.	Generate functions from tables of data and relate data to corresponding graphs and functions.	Level E, Lesson 32

Pennsylvania Academic Standards	Lessons
2.9 **Geometry**	
2.9.5 Pennsylvania's public schools shall teach, challenge and support every student to realize his or her maximum potential and to acquire the knowledge and skills to:	
A. Give formal definitions of geometric figures.	Level E, Lessons 43, 44, 46
B. Classify and compare triangles and quadrilaterals according to sides or angles.	Level E, Lessons 45, 46
C. Identify and measure circles, their diameters and their radii.	Level E, Lesson 41
D. Describe in words how geometric shapes are constructed.	Level E, Lessons 43, 44, 46
E. Construct two- and three-dimensional shapes and figures using manipulatives, geoboards and computer software.	Level E, Lessons 45, 46
F. Find familiar solids in the environment and describe them.	Level E, Lesson 52
G. Create an original tessellation.	Level E, Lesson 44
H. Describe the relationship between the perimeter and area of triangles, quadrilaterals and circles.	Level E, Lessons 39, 41
I. Represent and use the concepts of line, point and plane.	Level E, Lesson 43
J. Define the basic properties of squares, pyramids, parallelograms, quadrilaterals, trapezoids, polygons, rectangles, rhombi, circles, triangles, cubes, prisms, spheres and cylinders.	Level E, Lessons 45, 46
K. Analyze simple transformations of geometric figures and rotations of line segments.	Level E, Lessons 49, 50, 51
L. Identify properties of geometric figures (e.g., parallel, perpendicular, similar, congruent, symmetrical).	Level E, Lessons 43, 46, 47, 48
2.10 **Trigonometry**	
2.10.5 Pennsylvania's public schools shall teach, challenge and support every student to realize his or her maximum potential and to acquire the knowledge and skills to:	
A. Identify and compare parts of right triangles, including right angles, acute angles, hypotenuses and legs.	Level E, Lesson 45
B. Create right triangles on a geoboard.	Level E, Lesson 45

Pennsylvania Academic Standards	Lessons
2.11 **Concepts of Calculus**	
2.11.5 Pennsylvania's public schools shall teach, challenge and support every student to realize his or her maximum potential and to acquire the knowledge and skills to:	
A. Make comparisons of numbers (e.g., more, less, same, least, most, greater than, less than).	Level E, Lessons 2, 14, 22
B. Identify least and greatest values represented in bar and circle graphs.	Level E, Lessons 55, 57
C. Identify maximum and minimum.	Level E, Lesson 54
D. Describe the relationship between rates of change and time.	Level E, Lesson 32
E. Estimate areas and volumes as the sums of areas of tiles and volumes of cubes.	Level E, Lessons 38, 40, 42
F. Describe the relationship between the size of the unit of measurement and the estimate of the areas and volumes.	Level E, Lessons 38, 42

What's Inside: A Lesson Guide

The lessons in this worktext first introduce individual assessment anchors/eligible content and content standards and then explain, apply, and assess the concepts and skills that are needed to meet those standards.

Focus on the Pennsylvania Academic Standards

Introduces the Assessment Anchors/Eligible Content, the Academic Content Standards and the important terms and concepts covered in the lesson. These terms are defined in a glossary at the end of the book.

Guided Instruction

Work with your teacher to learn the steps needed to solve different types of mathematical problems.

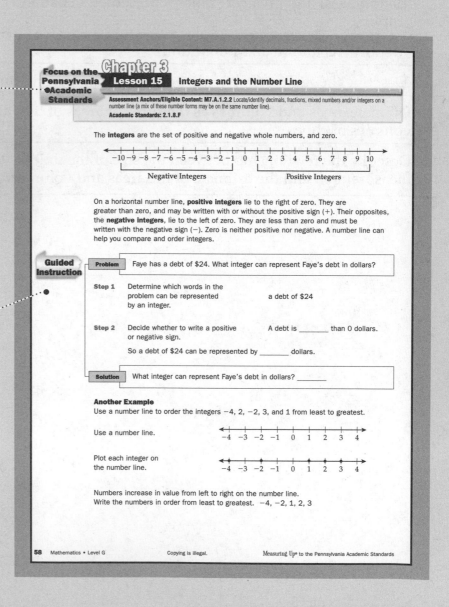

xxiv

Apply the Pennsylvania Standards

Provides practice for the important concepts and skills learned in the "Guided Instruction" section of the lesson.

 Apply the Pennsylvania Academic Standards

Write an integer to represent each situation.

1. a profit of $7 selling T-shirts

_____

2. a temperature 11 degrees Fahrenheit below zero

_____

3. 250 feet above sea level

_____

4. a 3-foot drop

_____

Use the number line below to order the integers from least to greatest.

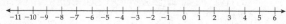

5. −10, −3, −7, −11, −9, 4

_____

6. 0, −4, 3, 2, 6, −2, −5

_____

Compare the integers. Use > or <.

7. −4 ◯ 4 **8.** 100 ◯ −99 **9.** −264 ◯ −265 **10.** 16 ◯ 19

11. 0 ◯ −5 **12.** −1 ◯ −24 **13.** −6 ◯ 2 **14.** −29 ◯ 30

Solve each problem.

15. What integer is neither negative *nor* positive? _____

16. If 5 represents 5 years from now, what does the opposite represent?

_____

17. Which of the following numbers are *not* integers? Explain.

−5, 2.6, −$\frac{3}{4}$, 7, −152

_____

_____

_____

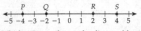 **PSSA Practice**

Directions: Read each question. Then circle the letter for the best answer.

1. Use the number line below to help answer the question.

If the integers 10, −25, 10, 25, and −1 are listed in order from **greatest** to **least**, which integer will come **first** in the list?

A −25

B −10

C 10

D 25

2. Look at the number line below.

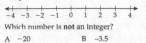

Which point on the number line could represent four feet below sea level?

A point *P*

B point *Q*

C point *R*

D point *S*

3. Use the number line below to help answer the question.

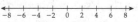

Which number is **not** an integer?

A −20   B −3.5

C 0   D 2

4. Which integer would come next in the pattern?

Hint: Use a number line to help you.

−7, −4, −1, 2, 5, . . .

A 12

B 10

C 8

D 6

Use the number line below to answer questions 5–6.

5. Which statement is **not** true?

A −1 is less than 0.

B −5 is less than −4.

C −6 is greater than −5.

D 2 is greater than −2.

6. Which list of integers is ordered from **least** to **greatest**?

A −2, −4, −7, −8

B 8, 7, 0, −5

C 2, 4, −7, −8

D −8, −7, 0, 5

PSSA Practice

Gives multiple-choice questions that will test understanding of the concepts and skills taught in the lesson.

XXV

Measuring Up®

to the
Pennsylvania Academic Standards
and Success Strategies for the PSSA

Dear Student,

How do you get better at anything you do? You practice! Just like with sports or other activities, the key to success in school is practice, practice, practice.

This book will help you review and practice mathematics strategies and skills. These are the strategies and skills you need to know to measure up to the Pennsylvania Academic Standards and Assessment Anchors for Mathematics. Practicing these skills and strategies now will help you do better in your work all year. Your skills practice will also help you score high on the PSSA, which you will take in the spring.

This Measuring Up® book has 10 chapters divided into two parts. Part 1 provides practice with whole numbers and decimals, fractions, integers, algebraic concepts, and ratio, proportion, and percent. Part 2 provides practice with measurement, perimeter, circumference, area, geometry, statistics, data analysis, and probability.

Each lesson has four main sections:

• **Focus on Pennsylvania Academic Standards** introduces the skills covered in the lesson. Important vocabulary is introduced to help you learn to speak mathematically as you communicate your understanding of math concepts.

• **Guided Instruction** shows you the steps and skills necessary to solve problems.

• **Apply the Pennsylvania Academic Standards** helps you practice important concepts and skills reviewed in the lesson.

• **PSSA Practice** gives you experience in responding to questions in the test format.

This book gives you many chances to practice your mathematics and test-taking skills. At the end of each chapter, the end of each part, and the end of the book is a **Building Stamina®** section. Each **Building Stamina®** section has both multiple-choice questions and open-ended questions. Many of these questions are more difficult and will help you prepare for taking the PSSA or other mathematics tests.

Taking the PSSA will be an important step forward. It will show how well you measure up to the Pennsylvania Academic Standards and Assessment Anchors. It is just one of the many important tests that you will take.

Have a great year!

Peoples Education™
Your partner in student success™

Measuring Up®

to the
Pennsylvania Academic Standards
and Success Strategies for the PSSA

To Parents and Families,

All students need mathematics skills to succeed. Pennsylvania educators have created grade-appropriate standards called the Pennsylvania Academic Standards and Assessment Anchors for Mathematics. These standards and anchors describe what all Pennsylvania students should know at each grade level. Students need to meet these standards, as measured by the *Pennsylvania System of School Assessment*, or *PSSA*, given in the spring.

The Pennsylvania Academic Standards, Assessment Anchors, and Eligible Content are directly related to the PSSA. They emphasize higher-level thinking skills. Students must learn to analyze, interpret, and generalize, as well as recall facts and operate with numbers.

Measuring Up® will help your child review the Pennsylvania Academic Standards and prepare for all mathematics exams. It contains:

- **Lessons** that focus on practicing the Pennsylvania Academic Standards;

- **Guided Instruction**, in which students are shown the steps and skills necessary to solve a variety of mathematical problems;

- **Apply the Pennsylvania Academic Standards**, which provides practice with concepts and skills reviewed in the lesson;

- **PSSA Practice**, which shows how individual standards can be understood through answering multiple-choice questions similar to those on the PSSA;

- **Building Stamina®**, which gives practice with multiple-choice and open-ended questions that require higher-level thinking.

For success in school and the real world, your child needs to be successful in mathematics. Get involved! Your involvement is crucial to your child's success. Here are some suggestions:

- Keep mathematics alive in your home. Involve your child in activities that use mathematics, such as mixing recipes, counting coins, telling time, and identifying geometric shapes and patterns.

- Look for ways mathematics is used when you are out with your family. Encourage your child to count your change after making a purchase, read the items and prices in a restaurant menu, identify shapes such as spheres and cubes in real objects, and add or subtract to find how many there are or how many are left in real-life situations.

- Ask your child to talk and write about what they have learned in mathematics. Always encourage them to use mathematical language.

- Encourage your child to take the time to review and check his or her homework. Finding a solution is just one part of solving a problem. Ask your child to tell why his or her answers are reasonable and make sense.

Work with us this year to ensure your child's success. Mathematics is essential not only for success in school but in the world as well.

Peoples Education™
Your partner in student success™

This book was created for Pennsylvania students like you. Each lesson, question, and problem will help you master the Pennsylvania Academic Standards and do well on the PSSA. It will also help you do well on other mathematics exams you take during the school year.

About the PSSA

Pennsylvania educators have developed standards for mathematics. They are called the Pennsylvania Academic Standards, Assessment Anchors, and Eligible Content. They spell out what all students at each grade level should know. Pennsylvania educators have also created the PSSA, a statewide test for mathematics. It shows how well students have mastered the standards and anchors.

Format of the PSSA

The PSSA has two types of test items, multiple-choice and open-ended questions.

Many questions include a picture, a graph, a number line, or another type of graphic which is used to solve the problem. Measuring Up® gives you practice in reading and using these types of graphics.

Measuring Up® on Multiple-Choice Questions

A multiple-choice question has two parts. The first part is the stem, or question.

The second part is made up of the answer choices. These choices have letters A–D in front of them. You will be asked to read each question and then circle the letter for the best answer.

Some of the multiple-choice questions have a graph or table. You will need to read information from the graph or table to solve the problem.

For example, in the question below, you will need to read the information in the table, select the answer choice that seems most reasonable, then circle the letter next to that answer.

1.   The table below shows the cost of flowers in a flower shop.

Number of Flowers	Cost
4	$1.00
5	$1.25
6	$1.50

How much does one flower cost?

A   10 cents

B   20 cents

C   25 cents

D   50 cents

By studying the pattern in the table, you can see that each flower costs 25 cents. So C is the correct answer. Notice how to mark your answer.

Here are some strategies for answering multiple-choice questions:

- Try to work the problem without looking at the answer choices. Once you have solved the problem, compare your answer with the answer choices.

- Eliminate answer choices you know are wrong. Then choose from the answers that are left.

- Some questions will be more difficult than others. The problem may require an extra step. Or, you may need to look for which answers do not apply.

- Even if you don't know the answer, you can make a good guess based on what you know and get the question right.

- Check and double-check your answers before you turn in the test. Be sure of your answers.

Measuring Up® **on Open-Ended Questions**

The PSSA for mathematics will have open-ended questions, which will require an answer and an explanation of how you solved the problem. These questions take about 10–15 minutes to answer. It is very important that you read the question carefully and completely before you begin to solve it. You must draw conclusions about mathematics, show your work and explain why and how you found your answers. Your answers on the PSSA will be scored according to the General Scoring Guidelines for Open-Ended Mathematics Items found on page 277.
Also, make sure you write your answer in the space provided.

Here are some things you can do to help you respond to open-ended items.

- Read the question carefully and completely. Make sure you understand what the question is asking. Think about what information you need to answer the question.

- Make a plan for solving the problem. Think about what strategies you can use.

- Check the directions to be sure that you are doing what is required, such as showing your work, explaining how you found your answer, or writing your answer in the correct form.

- Reread the question to make sure you are answering what is asked. This is especially important if the problem has more than one step.

- When you show your work, include labels such as measurement units. This helps you keep track of what you are doing and makes it easier to check your work when you are finished. When you explain how you found your answer or why you did each step, make the explanation complete, clear, and easy to understand.

- If you can't solve the whole problem, answer any parts that you can. Partial credit is usually given even if you don't explain everything. Explain everything that you can.

Here is an example of an open-ended item and its response.

10. Marco went walking last weekend. He walked 7 blocks east and 9 blocks south. He stopped to drink some water and eat his sandwich. Then he walked 4 blocks west and 10 blocks north. How many blocks is Marco from where he started? How many blocks did he walk in all? Draw a picture or diagram to help explain how you know.

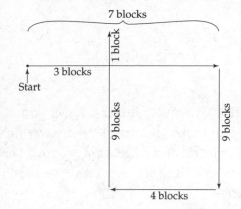

7 blocks
9 blocks
4 blocks
+ 10 blocks
───────────
30 blocks in all

3 blocks
+ 1 block
───────────
4 blocks from the start

My diagram shows that Marco walked 30 blocks. 7 + 9 + 4 + 10 = 30 blocks. I added each leg of his walk to find how many blocks he walked in all. According to my diagram, Marco ends up 3 blocks east and 1 block north of where he started. 3 + 1 = 4 blocks

- When you are finished, reread the question, your answer, and your explanation. Be sure you have answered all parts of the question and solved the problem completely and correctly.

- Check that your explanation is easy to understand. Will someone else understand what you wrote? Did you leave anything out? Use all the time you have left to check and recheck your work and your explanation.

For more examples and information about responding to open-ended items, see page 21, Lesson 7, entitled "Write a Response to an Open-Ended Item."

☆ Higher-Level Thinking Skills

Higher-level thinking skills are important on the PSSA. When you use higher-level thinking skills, you do more than just recall information. On the PSSA, some questions ask you to find and continue a pattern, understand and use information in a table or graph, or use a number line. Instead of adding or subtracting to solve a problem, you may need to solve a real-world problem and use more than one operation. In Measuring Up®, the higher-level thinking skills questions are starred.

Measuring Up® with Building Stamina®

A special feature of Measuring Up® is **Building Stamina**®. It was created to give you practice and build your confidence for taking hard tests. The more you practice answering hard questions, the more prepared you will be to succeed. At the end of each part and the end of the book is a longer **Building Stamina**®. These review the Pennsylvania Academic Standards and Assessment Anchors covered in the lessons.

Tips to Measure Up

There are some general test preparation strategies you can use to succeed. Here are a few useful tips:

- Start getting ready now. Spend a few minutes each day practicing answers to test questions. If you work hard, you will probably do well.

- Get a good night's sleep the night before the test.

- Eat a good breakfast.

- Think positively.

- Wear a watch. Keep track of time so that you finish the whole test.

You will learn a lot in Measuring Up®. You will review and practice the Pennsylvania Academic Standards. You will practice for the PSSA. Finally, you will build your stamina to answer tough questions. You will more than measure up. You'll be a smashing success!

Chapter 1 Whole Numbers and Decimals
In Chapter 1, you will study and practice:

- how to compare and order whole numbers and decimals;
- how to add and subtract whole numbers and decimals;
- how to estimate sums and differences;
- how to multiply and divide whole numbers and decimals;
- how to estimate products and quotients;
- how to write a response to an open-ended item.

★ **Building Stamina®:** This section gives you a chance to sharpen your skills with whole number and decimals, and to strengthen your test-taking ability.

Chapter 2 Fractions
In Chapter 2, you will study and practice:

- how to find equivalent fractions and mixed numbers;
- how to compare and relate fractions, mixed numbers, and decimals;
- how to add and subtract fractions and mixed numbers;
- how to multiply and divide fractions and mixed numbers;
- how to estimate to solve a problem.

★ **Building Stamina®:** This section gives you a chance to sharpen your skills with fractions and to strengthen your test-taking ability.

Chapter 3 Integers
In Chapter 3, you will study and practice:

- how to locate and place numbers on the number line;
- how to find the absolute value of a number;
- how to add and subtract integers;
- how to choose the correct operations.

★ **Building Stamina®:** This section gives you a chance to sharpen your skills with integers and to strengthen your test-taking ability.

Chapter 4 Algebraic Content

In Chapter 4, you will study and practice:

- how to write and evaluate expressions;
- how to use the order of operations;
- how to use properties to simplify expressions;
- how to write equations or inequalities;
- how to use models to solve equations;
- how to solve one-step equations;
- how to find and extend patterns, and solve problems using patterns.

★ **Building Stamina®:** This section gives you a chance to sharpen your algebraic skills and to strengthen your test-taking ability.

Chapter 5 Ratio, Proportions, and Percents

In Chapter 5, you will study and practice:

- how to use ratios and rates;
- how to use proportions and scaling to enlarge or reduce;
- how to understand percent;
- how to use proportional thinking to solve problems.

★ **Building Stamina®:** This section gives you a chance to sharpen your skills with ratios, proportions, and percents, and to strengthen your test-taking ability.

Focus on the **Chapter 1**
Pennsylvania
Academic **Lesson 1** **Compare and Order Whole Numbers and Decimals**
Standards

Assessment Anchors/Eligible Content: M7.A.1.2.1 Compare and/or order integers, mixed numbers, fractions and decimals (fractions and decimals may be mixed – no more than 5 numbers in a set to be ordered).
Academic Standards: 2.1.8.A, 2.1.8.C, 2.1.8.F

You can use a number line, models, or place value to compare and order numbers. Use the following symbols to compare two numbers: > means **is greater than,** < means **is less than,** and = means **is equal to.**

Guided Instruction

Problem

Brock is working on a homework problem. How can he list the numbers below in order from least to greatest?

| 3,472 | 2,374 | 3,427 | 2,743 |

Use place value to compare the digits from left to right.

Step 1 Align the whole numbers. Compare the numbers two at a time, beginning with the digits in the thousands place.

Since 2 < 3, the numbers with 2 in the thousands place are less than those with 3 in the thousands place.

<u>3</u>,472
<u>2</u>,374
<u>3</u>,427
<u>2</u>,743

Step 2 Compare 2,374 and 2,743. Since the digit in the thousands place is the same, compare the digits in the hundreds place.

3 hundreds ◯ 7 hundreds, so 2,374 ◯ 2,743.

Step 3 Compare 3,472 and 3,427. Since the digits in the thousands and hundreds places are the same, compare the digits in the tens place.

7 tens ◯ 2 tens, so 3,472 ◯ 3,427.

Step 4 Order the whole numbers.

2,374 < _____ < _____ < _____

Solution

How can Brock write the numbers in order from least to greatest?

_____

Another Example

List the decimals 0.25, 0.20, 0.28 and 0.23 in order from least to greatest. Locate the decimals on the number line below.

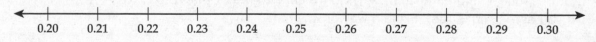

Compare: 0 hundredths is less than 3 hundredths: 0.20 < 0.23
3 hundredths is less than 5 hundredths: 0.23 < 0.25
5 hundredths is less than 8 hundredths: 0.25 < 0.28

The decimals 0.25, 0.20, 0.28 and 0.23 in order from least to greatest are 0.20, 0.23, 0.25, 0.28.

Apply the Pennsylvania Academic Standards

Compare. Write >, <, or =. Use the number line to help you.

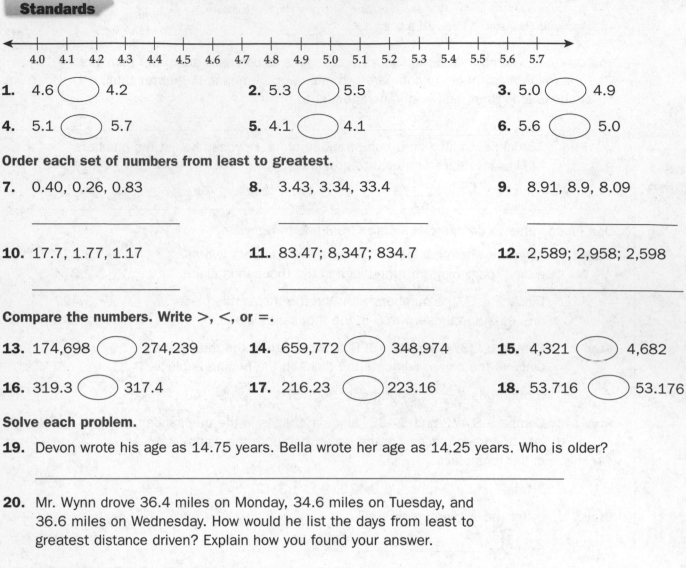

Number line: 4.0 4.1 4.2 4.3 4.4 4.5 4.6 4.7 4.8 4.9 5.0 5.1 5.2 5.3 5.4 5.5 5.6 5.7

1. 4.6 ◯ 4.2

2. 5.3 ◯ 5.5

3. 5.0 ◯ 4.9

4. 5.1 ◯ 5.7

5. 4.1 ◯ 4.1

6. 5.6 ◯ 5.0

Order each set of numbers from least to greatest.

7. 0.40, 0.26, 0.83

8. 3.43, 3.34, 33.4

9. 8.91, 8.9, 8.09

_____

_____

_____

10. 17.7, 1.77, 1.17

11. 83.47; 8,347; 834.7

12. 2,589; 2,958; 2,598

_____

_____

_____

Compare the numbers. Write >, <, or =.

13. 174,698 ◯ 274,239

14. 659,772 ◯ 348,974

15. 4,321 ◯ 4,682

16. 319.3 ◯ 317.4

17. 216.23 ◯ 223.16

18. 53.716 ◯ 53.176

Solve each problem.

19. Devon wrote his age as 14.75 years. Bella wrote her age as 14.25 years. Who is older?

_____

20. Mr. Wynn drove 36.4 miles on Monday, 34.6 miles on Tuesday, and 36.6 miles on Wednesday. How would he list the days from least to greatest distance driven? Explain how you found your answer.

_____

_____

_____

_____

21. Dixie was asked which value was greater, 8.02 or 8.004? She said that because 4 is greater than 2, 8.004 must be greater than 8.02. Do you agree with Dixie? Explain why or why not.

_____

_____

_____

_____

Directions: Read each question. Then circle the letter for the best answer.

1. Which of the following is **greater than** 496,784?

   A 456,784

   B 456,984

   C 496,782

   D 496,946

2. Which of the following numbers has the **greatest** value?

   A 3,914.32

   B 3,914.3

   C 3,292.9

   D   372.7

3. Which of the following numbers has the **least** value?

   A   68.05

   B   8.5065

   C 680.5

   D   85.6

4. Which of the following numbers has the **greatest** value?

   A 1.225

   B 1.256

   C 1.235

   D 1.267

5. Paula measured the amount of rainfall each week for one month. She recorded her data in the table below.

Week	Rainfall (in inches)
1	3.4
2	2.8
3	2.5
4	3.1

   How would she list the weeks from **least** to **greatest** rainfall?

   A 2, 3, 1, 4

   B 3, 2, 4, 1

   C 2, 1, 3, 4

   D 1, 4, 2, 3

6. Which of the following numbers is **less than** 2,764.2?

   A 2,764.1

   B 2,765.12

   C 2,764.3

   D 2,765.13

Focus on the Pennsylvania Academic Standards

Lesson 2 — Add and Subtract Whole Numbers and Decimals

Assessment Anchors/Eligible Content: M7.A.3.2.1 Solve problems involving operations (+, −, ×, ÷) of whole numbers, decimals, fractions, or mixed numbers (straight computation or word problems).

Academic Standards: 2.2.8.B, 2.4.8.D

You can add or subtract whole numbers and decimals to solve problems. When you are adding or subtracting decimals, first line up the decimal points. Then add or subtract as you would whole numbers. Remember to write the decimal point in the answer.

Guided Instruction

Problem 1

The distance from Jacksonville to Orlando is 141.31 miles. The distance from Jacksonville to Miami is 209.96 miles farther than the distance from Jacksonville to Orlando. If Mr. Diaz drove from Jacksonville to Miami, how far did he drive?

Add to find the total distance.

Step 1 Line up the decimal points.

$$\begin{array}{r} 141.31 \\ + 209.96 \\ \hline \end{array}$$

Step 2 Add as you would with whole numbers. Bring down the decimal point so it is in the same location in the sum as in the addends.

$$\begin{array}{r} 141.31 \\ + 209.96 \\ \hline \end{array}$$

Solution How far did Mr. Diaz drive? _____

Problem 2

Rosalie drove 128 miles on Monday. On Tuesday, she drove another 68.7 miles. How much farther did Rosalie drive on Monday than on Tuesday?

Subtract to find the difference.

Step 1 Place a decimal point and a zero at the end of the whole number. Then line up the decimal points.

$$\begin{array}{r} 128.0 \\ - 68.7 \\ \hline \end{array}$$

Step 2 Subtract as you would with whole numbers. Remember to bring the decimal point down into your answer.

$$\begin{array}{r} 128.0 \\ - 68.7 \\ \hline \end{array}$$

Solution How much farther did Rosalie drive on Monday than on Tuesday? _____

Measuring Up® to the Pennsylvania Academic Standards

Apply the
Pennsylvania
Academic
Standards

Without using a calculator, add to find each total.

1. 715.6 + 21.031

_____

2. 3.01 + 124

_____

3. 27,458 + 1,345

_____

4. 317 + 54.29

_____

5. 65.398 + 2,802.6

_____

6. 450,764 + 974.26

_____

Without using a calculator, subtract to find each difference.

7. 61 − 11.12

_____

8. 36.042 − 17

_____

9. 1,782 − 985

_____

10. 112.09 − 75.334

_____

11. 5,376 − 284.64

_____

12. 89.3 − 24.671

_____

Use a calculator to solve problem 13.

13. Kimberly, Dana, and Steven are working on their seventh-grade science project. They need to find the difference between the diameter of the Sun and the diameter of Earth. The diameter of the Sun is 1,390,000.1 kilometers, and the diameter of Earth is 12,756.3 kilometers. What is the difference between the two diameters?

_____

Use the information below to solve problems 14–16.

Suppose Dale, Adam, and Jon are vacationing in Florida. Each recorded the number of miles traveled in the table.

14. Dale drove from Daytona Beach to Fort Lauderdale and then to Stuart. Altogether, how far did he drive?

_____

15. Adam met Jon in Tampa. Adam drove from Destin. Jon drove from Tallahassee. Who drove the longer distance? How much farther did he drive?

_____

Driving Distances Between Cities in Florida

From	To	Distance (in miles)
Daytona Beach	Fort Lauderdale	242.22
Fort Lauderdale	Stuart	81.55
Tallahassee	Tampa	277.55
Tampa	Destin	435.19

16. What is the difference between the least and the greatest distances listed in the table? Explain how you found your answer.

_____

_____

PSSA Practice Directions: Read each question. Then circle the letter for the best answer.

1. Jack drove 429.91 miles from his home in Clearwater to a friend's house in Key West. Then he drove back home. Altogether how long was Jack's trip?

   A 859.82 miles

   B 848.82 miles

   C 839.22 miles

   D 828.42 miles

2. Donna removed 14.25 grams of soil from a container holding 68 grams of soil. How much soil does the container now hold?

   A 14.43 grams

   B 54.25 grams

   C 53.75 grams

   D 82.25 grams

3. Tess rode her bike 3.6 kilometers in the morning. In the afternoon, she rode twice as far as she had in the morning. How far did Tess ride her bike in all?

   A 5.6 kilometers

   B 7.2 kilometers

   C 10.8 kilometers

   D 14.4 kilometers

4. What is the sum of the expression 695,482 + 4,962 + 212.87 + 0.32?

   A 700,658.32   B 700,657.19

   C 701,657.48   D 800,659.19

Use the diagram below to answer questions 5–6.

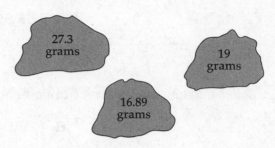

5. Zack collected the three rock samples shown above. What is the total mass of his samples?

   A 35.89 grams

   B 44.19 grams

   C 46.3 grams

   D 63.19 grams

6. What is the difference in grams between the rock with the **least** mass and the rock with the **greatest** mass?

   A 2.11 grams

   B 8.3 grams

   C 10.41 grams

   D 11.3 grams

Focus on the Pennsylvania Academic Standards

Lesson 3   Estimate Sums and Differences

Assessment Anchors/Eligible Content: M7.A.3.1.1 Estimate answers to problems involving whole numbers, decimals, fractions or mixed numbers.
Academic Standards: 2.2.8.E, 2.2.8.F, 2.4.8.D

Estimation can help you determine whether an answer to a problem is reasonable. Sometimes an estimate is all you need. The best estimate is usually one that is close to the exact answer. One way to estimate sums and differences is to use rounding.

Guided Instruction

Problem 1

José is taking his 10-year old daughter to the movies. If a child ticket costs $4.25, and an adult ticket costs $9.50, and José has $20.00 in his pocket, about how much will José have left to buy popcorn?

Round numbers to estimate the solution.

Step 1   Round each number to the nearest dollar.

9.50 rounds to _____
4.25 rounds to _____

Step 2   Find the sum of the rounded numbers.

10 + _____ = _____

Step 3   Subtract the sum from the amount of money José has in his pocket.

20 − _____ = _____

Solution

About how much will José have left to buy popcorn?

_____

Problem 2

The service elevator in a hospital has a weight limit of 1,200 pounds. Can two hospital employees who weigh 185 pounds and 110 pounds safely get on the elevator with 768 pounds of X-ray equipment?

Round the numbers to estimate the sum.

Step 1   Round each number to the nearest hundred.

185 rounds to _____
110 rounds to _____
768 rounds to _____

Step 2   Find the sum of the rounded numbers.

200 + 100 + 800 = _____

Step 3   Compare the sum with the 1,200-pound weight limit.

1,100 ◯ 1,200
So the people and the equipment _____ safely get on the elevator.

Solution

Can two hospital employees who weigh 185 pounds and 110 pounds safely get on the elevator with 768 pounds of X-ray equipment? _____

Apply the Pennsylvania Academic Standards

Estimate each sum by rounding to the specified place. Show the numbers you use.

1. 0.783 + 0.62 (nearest tenth)

_____ + _____ = _____

2. 98,671 + 247,157 (nearest hundred thousand)

_____ + _____ = _____

3. $7.04 + $83 (nearest dollar)

_____ + _____ = _____

4. 28.54 + 47.291 (nearest ten)

_____ + _____ = _____

5. 3.5 + 17.089 (nearest hundredth)

_____ + _____ = _____

6. 4.9284 + 0.67 (nearest tenth)

_____ + _____ = _____

Estimate each difference by rounding to the specified place. Show the numbers you use.

7. 91 − 26.2 (nearest ten)

_____ − _____ = _____

8. 278.09 − 94 (nearest hundred)

_____ − _____ = _____

9. 331.3 − 45.709 (nearest tenth)

_____ − _____ = _____

10. 3,287.4 − 2,200.56 (nearest thousand)

_____ − _____ = _____

11. 549 − 57.98 (nearest hundred)

_____ − _____ = _____

12. $7.30 − $2.59 (nearest dollar)

_____ − _____ = _____

Solve each problem.

13. For a fundraiser, Clara needs to ride her bicycle 25 kilometers in 2 days. She rode 2.75 kilometers this morning and 9.5 kilometers this afternoon. Does she need to ride more than 10 kilometers to meet her goal? Explain your answer.

_____

_____

14. Mrs. Jordan bought 2.5 pounds of apples, 4.75 pounds of oranges, and 1.75 pounds of bananas. She estimated that she had about 10 pounds of fruit. Is her estimate less than or greater than the exact total? Explain your answer.

_____

_____

 Measuring Up® to the Pennsylvania Academic Standards

PSSA Practice

Directions: Read each question. Then circle the letter for the best answer.

1. Mary Lou was at a sale. She bought a T-shirt for $6.95, a dress for $27.12, and a pair of shoes for $59.95. To the nearest dollar, about how much money did she spend?

   A   about $94.00
   B   about $100.00
   C   about $130.00
   D   about $160.00

2. Maria went to the mall with $56.60. She spent $18.95 on a shirt. To the nearest ten dollars, about how much money does she have left?

   A   about $10.00
   B   about $20.00
   C   about $40.00
   D   about $60.00

3. Evan worked 32.75 hours last week and 28.5 hours this week. Which of the following equations gives the closest estimate of the total number of hours he worked during the past two weeks?

   A $40 + 30 = 70$
   B $30 + 30 = 60$
   C $30 + 20 = 50$
   D $20 + 20 = 40$

Use the table below to answer questions 4–5.

Cans Collected (lbs)	
Grade 5	187.5
Grade 6	326.8
Grade 7	287.75
Grade 8	362.25

4. About how many pounds of cans were collected in all?

   A   about 1,100
   B   about 1,150
   C   about 1,200
   D   about 1,250

5. Which equation could be used to estimate the difference between the **least** and **greatest** amount of cans collected by students in different grade levels?

   A $400 - 200 = 200$
   B $400 - 100 = 300$
   C $500 - 100 = 400$
   D $400 + 200 = 600$

6. The mass of Rock A is 34.782 grams and the mass of Rock B is 78.6 grams. About how many grams is the difference in mass?

   A   30 grams
   B   33 grams
   C   40 grams
   D   45 grams

Assessment Anchors/Eligible Content: M7.A.3.2.1 Solve problems involving operations (+, −, ×, ÷) of whole numbers, decimals, fractions, or mixed numbers (straight computation or word problems).

Academic Standards: 2.2.8.B, 2.4.8.D

When you add or subtract decimals, you must line up the decimal points. You do not line up decimal points when you multiply decimals. You multiply as if they were whole numbers. Then you count the number of decimal places in both factors and put a decimal point in the product so that it has the same number of decimal places as the total in both factors.

Guided Instruction

Problem

During an experiment, a scientist poured a 0.256-liter solution into a beaker. Four-hundredths of the solution was alcohol. How much of the solution was alcohol, in liters?

Multiply as you would with whole numbers. Remember to write the decimal point in the product. You may need to write one or more zeros in the product to place the decimal point.

Step 1 Write the multiplication problem. What are the factors that you need to multiply?

$$0.256 \\ \times \ 0.04$$

_____

Step 2 Multiply as you would with whole numbers.

$$0.256 \\ \times \ 0.04$$

Step 3 Count the number of decimal places in each factor. The number of decimal places in the product is equal to the sum of the number of decimal places of each factor.
The product will have ____ decimal places.

0.256 ← ____ decimal places
$\times \ 0.04$ ← ____ decimal places
← ? decimal places

Step 4 Write the decimal point in the product.
You will need to write ____ zero(s) after the decimal point to have 5 decimal places.

$$0.256 \\ \times \ 0.04 \\ \overline{0.01024}$$

Solution How much of the solution was alcohol, in liters? _____

Another Example
Multiply 0.7 • 0.6.
Use a hundredths grid. Shade 7 columns for 7 tenths. Shade 6 rows for 6 tenths. The area where the shading overlaps shows the product, 0.42.

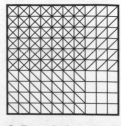

0.7 • 0.6 = 0.42

Apply the Pennsylvania Academic Standards

Write the multiplication sentence modeled by each grid. Then use the grid to find the product.

1.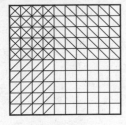

_____

2.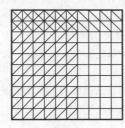

_____

Without using a calculator, find each product.

3.   784
   $\times$ 5.4

4.   66.3
   $\times$ 17.1

5.   3.34
   $\times$ 9

6.   956
   $\times$ 471

7.   1.08
   $\times$ 6.7

8.   17.22
   $\times$ 47

9. 65.632 $\times$ 12

_____

10. 1,001 $\times$ 83

_____

11. 28.4 $\times$ 0.515

_____

12. 79 $\times$ 21.3

_____

13. 15.66 $\times$ 54

_____

14. 0.329 $\times$ 0.06

_____

Solve each problem.

15. A sporting goods store just received 18 cartons of baseball bats. Each carton weighs 12.25 pounds. What is the total weight of the cartons?

_____

16. On a test, Ron wrote the product of 4.56 and 3.78 as 1,723.68. His teacher said his answer was incorrect. What mistake did Ron make? Explain your answer.

_____

_____

_____

PSSA Practice Directions: Read each question. Then circle the letter for the best answer.

1. Ryan has a rectangular patio in his backyard. He measured the patio and found that it was 3.25 yards long and 4.75 yards wide. To find the total area of the patio, he multiplied the length times the width. What is the area of the patio?

A   1.54375 square yards

B   15.4375 square yards

C   154.375 square yards

D   1,543.75 square yards

2. A florist uses 14.75 pounds of fruit in each fruit basket she makes. How much fruit does she need to make 6 fruit baskets?

A   0.885 pound

B   8.85 pound

C   88.5 pounds

D   885 pounds

3. A jug holds 3.25 gallons of liquid. The Hawks soccer team drank 6.5 jugs during a game. How many gallons of liquid did the team drink?

A   2,112.5 gallons

B   211.25 gallons

C   21.125 gallons

D   2.1125 gallons

4. What is the product of 9 tenths and 27 thousandths?

A   2.43

B   0.243

C   0.0243

D   0.00243

5. A factory makes 32,764 buttons every hour. How many buttons does the factory produce during an 8-hour workday?

A   256,082

B   262,112

C   266,182

D   268,102

6. A chef filled 18 containers with soup. Each container holds 2.25 quarts. How much soup did the chef make?

A   20.25 quarts

B   40.5 quarts

C   42.5 quarts

D   405 quarts

Lesson 5 Divide Whole Numbers and Decimals

Assessment Anchors/Eligible Content: M7.A.3.2.1 Solve problems involving operations (+, −, ×, ÷) of whole numbers, decimals, fractions, or mixed numbers (straight computation or word problems).

Academic Standards: 2.2.8.B, 2.4.8.D

You can divide whole numbers and decimals. If a problem has a decimal divisor, move the decimal point to make it a whole number. Then move the decimal point the same number of places in the dividend. Put a decimal point in the same location of the quotient. Then divide as you would with whole numbers.

$$\text{divisor} \rightarrow 8\overline{)24} \begin{array}{l} 3 \leftarrow \text{quotient} \\ \leftarrow \text{dividend} \end{array}$$

Guided Instruction

Problem Jon cycled 42.8 miles in 2.75 hours. What was his average rate of speed in miles per hour? Round your answer to the nearest tenth.

When the divisor is a decimal, multiply the divisor and the dividend by the same power of ten so the divisor becomes a whole number. Then divide as you would whole numbers.

Step 1 Write the division problem.

$$\underline{}\overline{)}$$

Step 2 Rewrite the division problem so the new divisor is a whole number. How many decimal places does the divisor have? ____

$$100 \cdot 2.75 = \underline{}$$

What power of ten do you need to multiply the divisor by to make it a whole number?

$$100 \cdot 42.8 = \underline{}$$

_____

Rewrite the division problem.

$$\underline{}\overline{)}$$

Step 3 Place the decimal point in the quotient. Then divide as with whole numbers. Continue to divide by writing zeros in the dividend until the quotient is expressed through the hundredths place.

$$\begin{array}{r} 275\overline{)4{,}280.} \\ -275 \\ \hline 1{,}530 \\ -1{,}375 \\ \hline 1{,}550 \\ -1{,}375 \\ \hline 1{,}750 \\ -1{,}650 \\ \hline 100 \end{array}$$

Step 4 Round the quotient to the nearest tenth.

15.56 rounds to _____.

What was Jon's average rate of speed in miles per hour?

Solution _____

Another Example

Divide 1.2 ÷ 0.3

Count the decimal places in the divisor. Because there is 1 decimal place, multiply the divisor and dividend by 10. Then rewrite the division problem and divide.

So 1.2 ÷ 0.3 = 4.

$$1.2 \cdot 10 = 12$$
$$0.3 \cdot 10 = 3$$
$$\begin{array}{r} 4 \\ 3\overline{)12} \\ -12 \\ \hline 0 \end{array}$$

Without using a calculator, find each quotient.

1. $100.98 \div 66$

2. $35.99 \div 12.2$

3. $0.186 \div 0.2$

4. $3,901 \div 83$

5. $125 \div 0.5$

6. $6.39 \div 0.9$

7. $38.52 \div 12$

8. $840 \div 3.2$

9. $6.36 \div 6$

10. $42.363 \div 8.1$

11. $53.94 \div 9.3$

12. $0.08 \div 0.04$

13. $10.26 \div 3.42$

14. $34.8 \div 12$

15. $809.38 \div 2.6$

Solve each problem.

16. Evan rides her bike 50.7 miles every day. If it takes her 3 hours to ride this distance, how many miles does she ride per hour?

17. Jada earned $29.75 in 3.5 hours. How much did she earn per hour?

18. The Snack Stop received 252 pounds of dried fruit. The fruit was packed in cartons containing 24 bags each. If each bag weighs 1.75 pounds, how many cartons were delivered to the shop? Explain your answer.

19. On a test, Ron said that 16.8 divided by 0.02 is 84. His teacher said his answer was incorrect. What mistake did Ron make? Explain your answer.

PSSA Practice Directions: Read each question. Then circle the letter for the best answer.

1. Stacey earned $201.25 this week. If she worked 23 hours, what is her hourly wage?

   A $9.25

   B $8.75

   C $7.25

   D $6.45

 2. During the month of July, 2,976 water ices were bought from the Sweet Ice Shoppe. What was the average number of water ices sold each day?

   A 88

   B 92

   C 96

   D 99

3. Rico uses 3.65 meters of wire in every birdhouse he makes. How many birdhouses can he make from 62.05 meters of wire?

   A 17

   B 15

   C 14

   D 11

4. Kellie rode her bicycle 35.75 miles in 5.5 hours. What was her average speed in miles per hour?

   A 3.5 miles per hour

   B 6.5 miles per hour

   C 15 miles per hour

   D 65 miles per hour

5. Dan's car used 19.2 gallons of gasoline to travel 491.52 miles. How many miles per gallon did the car get?

   A 28.3

   B 27.5

   C 26.6

   D 25.6

 6. A chef made 19.125 gallons of soup. He wants to package the soup in 2.25-gallon containers. How many containers will he need to hold all the soup?

   A 8

   B 9

   C 10

   D 12

Focus on the Pennsylvania Academic Standards

Lesson 6 Estimate Products and Quotients

Assessment Anchors/Eligible Content: M7.A.3.1.1 Estimate answers to problems involving whole numbers, decimals, fractions or mixed numbers.

Academic Standards: 2.2.8.B, 2.4.8.D

When you **estimate,** you find an answer that is close to the exact answer. One way to estimate a product is to **round** each factor to its greatest place. Then multiply the rounded factors.

One way to estimate a quotient is to use compatible numbers. **Compatible numbers** are numbers that are close to the actual numbers but are easier to divide.

Guided Instruction

Problem 1 Wesley works 7.5 hours a day. About how many hours does he work in a month with 22 workdays?

Round the factors. Find the product of the rounded factors.

Step 1 Round each factor to its greatest place.

7.5 rounds to _____

22 rounds to _____

Step 2 Find the product of the rounded factors.

$8 \times 20 =$ _____

Solution About how many hours does he work in a month with 22 workdays

_____

Problem 2 Gail's car used 16.2 gallons of gas to go 443.7 miles. About how many miles did the car travel per gallon of gas?

Use compatible numbers to estimate the quotient.

Step 1 Think: 16.2 is close to 15.

What number is close to 443.7 and divisible by 15? _____

Step 2 Find the quotient of the compatible numbers. $450 \div$ _____ $=$ _____

Solution About how many miles did the car travel per gallon of gas?

_____

Apply the Pennsylvania Academic Standards

Round each factor to its greatest place to estimate each product. Show the numbers you used.

1. 86.4 × 32

_____

2. 673 × 215

_____

3. 55.33 × 29.54

_____

4. 826 × 14.2

_____

5. 7,653 × 24

_____

6. 1,186 × 94.2

_____

7. 43.081 × 556

_____

8. 63.31 × 9.09

_____

9. 2,845 × 7,142

_____

Change the divisor and the dividend to compatible numbers. Then use the compatible numbers to estimate the quotient.

10. 1,741 ÷ 57.2

_____

11. 23.78 ÷ 3.9

_____

12. 81.4 ÷ 19.36

_____

13. 5,789 ÷ 105.3

_____

14. 35.26 ÷ 8.3

_____

15. 467.6 ÷ 38

_____

16. 2,792 ÷ 74.1

_____

17. 937.2 ÷ 17.8

_____

18. 64,975 ÷ 77.8

_____

Solve each problem.

19. Maury worked 24 days during the month of April. He drove 73.5 miles to work and back each workday. Maury estimated that he commuted about 1,400 miles during the month. Is his estimate less than or greater than his exact commute? Explain your answer.

_____

_____

_____

20. Zack and Deb were asked to estimate the quotient of 4,328 ÷ 76. Zack used the compatible numbers 4,000 ÷ 80 to estimate a quotient of 50. Deb used the compatible numbers 4,200 ÷ 70 to estimate a quotient of 60. Are both estimates reasonable? Explain your answer.

_____

_____

PSSA
Practice

Directions: Read each question. Then circle the letter for the best answer.

1. A total of 28 buses transport students to Center City High School each day. If a bus holds a maximum of 52 students, about how many students ride buses to the school each day?

   A about 80 students

   B about 150 students

   C about 1,000 students

   D about 1,500 students

2. Leo used these compatible numbers to estimate a quotient.

   $$600 \div 30 = 20$$

   For which division problem could Leo have been estimating a solution?

   A 515 ÷ 11

   B 586 ÷ 29

   C 668 ÷ 47

   D 690 ÷ 73

3. Ella wrote 68.4 × 19.37 = 1,324.908. Which multiplication sentence could she use to check the reasonableness of her answer?

   A 70 × 30 = 2,100

   B 70 × 20 = 1,400

   C 40 × 30 = 1,200

   D 50 × 20 = 1,000

4. During the first three months of this year, a gift shop sold 7,831 cards. If the shop is open seven days a week, about how many cards did the shop sell each day?

   A about 3,000

   B about 2,500

   C about 300

   D about 90

5. This week, Macoun apples cost $2.69 per pound. If Bud buys 2.12 pounds of Macouns, about how much will the apples cost?

   A about $6.00

   B about $7.00

   C about $8.00

   D about $9.00

6. The machines in a bakery produce 8 dozen donuts a minute. About how many donuts do the machines produce every hour?

   A about 4,000

   B about 6,000

   C about 10,000

   D about 60,000

Measuring Up® to the Pennsylvania Academic Standards

Focus on the Pennsylvania Academic Standards

Lesson 7   Write a Response to an Open-Ended Item

Assessment Anchors/Eligible Content: M7.A.3.2.1 Solve problems involving operations ($+$, $-$, $\times$, $\div$) of whole numbers, decimals, fractions, or mixed numbers (straight computation or word problems).

Academic Standards: 2.1.8.A, 2.5.8.A

Some problems will ask you to explain how you reached a conclusion or how you can verify your solutions. These problems are called open-ended items. You can write responses to open-ended items by explaining the steps you take to solve each problem.

Guided Instruction

Problem

Rebecca ran 2.25 times around the local community track. The distance around the track is about 213.34 meters. Rebecca said that she had run 4,800.15 meters. Is Rebecca correct?

Step 1   Understand the problem.

What is the problem asking you to find?

_____

Step 2   Make a plan.

Find the product of the two decimals, using the rules for multiplication.

Step 3   Solve the problem.

$$
\begin{array}{r}
213.34 \\
\times\ 2.25 \\
\hline
\end{array}
$$

Step 4   Explain how you found your answer. If it is different than Rebecca's, explain why.

_____

_____

_____

_____

_____

Solution

Is Rebecca correct?

_____

_____

Apply the Pennsylvania Academic Standards

Solve each problem.
Show your work and explain your answer.

1. The Jones family went bowling on several nights during their family reunion. Each night of bowling cost $17.65. They spent a total of $70.60 for bowling during their reunion. How many nights did the Jones family go bowling? Explain your answer.

Work Space

_____

_____

_____

_____

2. Andrew worked 17.5 hours and earned $140. Ruben worked 8.5 hours and earned $102. How much greater was the amount Ruben was paid per hour than the amount Andrew was paid per hour? Explain your answer.

_____

_____

_____

_____

3. Ray measures his rectangular patio. The length is 5.2 meters and the width is 3.4 meters. He wants to make the patio 25 square meters larger. What will be the new area of the patio? Explain how you got your answer. (Hint: The formula for the area of a rectangle is $A = l \times w$, where l is the length and w is the width of the rectangle.)

_____

_____

_____

_____

   Measuring Up® to the Pennsylvania Academic Standards

Open-Ended Items

4. Morgan received $250 for her 14th birthday. She went to the mall on Tuesday and bought a shirt for $15.27. On Wednesday, she returned to the mall and bought a pair of pants for $26.75 and three shirts for $17.87 each.

A. How much money did Morgan have on Wednesday before she went to the mall? Explain how you got your answer.

B. How much money did Morgan spend on shirts on Wednesday? Explain how you got your answer.

C. How much money did Morgan have left after she went to the mall on Wednesday? Explain how you got your answer.

Directions: Read each question. Then circle the letter for the best answer.

1. Which of the following is **not** a true statement?

A   2.44 > 2.044 > 2.0044

B   2.33 < 2.32 < 2.31

C   214,980 > 214,975 > 213,999

D   105,472 > 105,427 > 105,274

2. Sophie worked one 4.5-hour shift, two 7.75-hour shifts and a 6-hour shift last week. If she earns $11 an hour, how much did Sophie earn last week?

A $200.75   B $286.00

C $335.50   D $401.50

3. Wilson had $67.32 when he returned from the mall. He bought a pair of pants for $23.25 and a T-shirt for $12.45. To the nearest ten, **about** how much money did he have before he went to the mall?

A $30   B $90

C $100   D $120

4. Students in a science class are comparing the mass of two different rocks. The mass of Rock A is 34.782 grams and the mass of Rock B is 78.6 grams. How much **greater** is the mass of Rock B than the mass of Rock A?

A   43.818 grams

B   40 grams

C   33.996 grams

D   30 grams

5. Which of the following expressions has a quotient **greater** than 1?

A   0.08 ÷ 0.2

B   0.5 ÷ 0.25

C   2.4 ÷ 3.2

D   40 ÷ 50

6. In 2000, there were 69,297,290 U.S. households with cable television. In 1990, there were 54,871,330 U.S. households with cable television. Which is the **best** estimate for the increase in U.S. households with cable television from 1990 to 2000?

A   10 million

B   11 million

C   15 million

D   20 million

7. What is the sum of the expression shown below?

$$695,114 + 6,951 + 695.1 + 69.5 + 6.9$$

A   906,745.2

B   802,951.2

C   702,836.5

D   702,776.5

8. Linda earns $12.50 per hour at her job. If she works 17.50 hours this week, how much money will she earn?

A $289.90   B $250.22

C $232.43   D $218.75

9. Which of the following is a true statement?

A $(2.3 + 0.04) > (2.3 + 0.4) > (2.3 + 4)$

B $(4.02 - 0.1) > (4.02 - 0.01) > (4.2 - 1)$

C $(3.45 + 1) < (2.45 + 3) < (1.45 + 5)$

D $(5.1 - 1) < (5.1 - 2) < (5.1 - 3)$

10. The table shows the fuel efficiency of four cars.

Car	Gas Used	Miles Traveled
A	12.5 gal	255.0
B	13.8 gal	269.1
C	10.6 gal	233.2
D	21.5 gal	395.6

Which car averages the **most** miles per gallon?

A Car A   B Car B

C Car C   D Car D

11. A kayak rental company charged $81.00 for a 4.5-hour rental. What is the charge for one hour?

A $16.25

B $18.00

C $19.25

D $21.75

12. The Philadelphia 76ers play in an arena that seats 21,600 people. The team plays 41 home games each season. If the team sells all of its seats for each game, which is the best estimate for the season's attendance?

A   400,000

B   500,000

C   800,000

D   1,000,000

13. A cyclist biked 23.25 miles, riding the same loop. If she completed 15.5 laps before getting a flat tire, how many miles long is a loop?

A   38.75 miles   B   7.75 miles

C   1.5 miles   D   0.67 miles

14. Sam was playing a game with his friend Carol. She told him to think of a number. She then told him to multiply that number by 0.3, add 4.2, and then subtract 1.75. Sam then told Carol that the resulting number was 5.15, and she correctly guessed Sam's original number. What number did Carol guess as Sam's original number? (Hint: Work backwards.)

A   5   B   6.9

C   7   D   9

15. Which of the following statements is **not** true?

A $444,094 > 445,940 > 446,490$

B $103,126 < 204,162 < 204,216$

C $214,980 > 214,975 > 213,999$

D $105,472 > 105,427 > 105,274$

Open-Ended Items

16. The yearly sales for a certain company are shown in the table below.

Year	Total Sales
1990	$560,025.86
2000	$1,120,051.72

A. What is the difference between total sales in the year 2000 and the total sales for the year 1990? Explain your answer.

B. If the increase between 2000 and 2010 is the same as the increase between 1990 and 2000, **about** how much will the total sales for the year 2010 be? Explain your answer.

17. The students at a local middle school had a walk-a-thon to raise money for their school.

A. Kate was one of the participants in the walk-a-thon and was able to get 10 sponsors. If she raised $25.60 in total, and each sponsor paid an equal amount, how much money did she earn per sponsor? Explain your answer.

17. *Continued*

B. Complete the table below to show the amount of money earned by three other participants of the walk-a-thon, if the amount earned per sponsor is the same for every participant. Explain your answers.

Money Earned per Participant

Participant	Number of Sponsors	Money Earned
Kate	10	$25.60
Gloria	20	
Shuyun	15	
Miguel	25	

C. Suppose the goal for each walk-a-thon participant is to contribute a minimum of $50.00. Which participants will need more sponsors to meet their goal, and how many? Show your work.

Focus on the Pennsylvania Academic Standards

Chapter 2
Lesson 8   Equivalent Fractions

Assessment Anchors/Eligible Content: M7.A.1.1.1 Convert between fractions, decimals and/or percents (e.g., 20% = 0.2 = $\frac{1}{5}$) (terminating decimals only).

Academic Standards: 2.1.8.A

You can use multiplication and division to find equivalent fractions.

Equivalent fractions are fractions that name the same number. A fraction is in **simplest form** when the numerator and the denominator have no common factors other than 1. You can use the **greatest common factor** (GCF) to determine if a fraction is in simplest form.

Guided Instruction

Problem

Nikki and Sam make sandwiches for a party. They make $\frac{1}{4}$ of the sandwiches on wheat bread, $\frac{4}{8}$ on white bread, and $\frac{3}{12}$ on oat bread. On which kinds of bread do they make the same number of sandwiches?

Find equivalent fractions to solve the problem.

Step 1   To determine if $\frac{1}{4}$ and $\frac{4}{8}$ are equivalent fractions, you can write $\frac{4}{8}$ in simplest form and compare.

Use the GCF of 4 and 8 to find simplest form. Circle the greatest common factor.

Factors of 4: 1, 2, 4
Factors of 8: 1, 2, 4, 8

Divide the numerator and denominator of $\frac{4}{8}$ by the GCF.
Are $\frac{1}{4}$ and $\frac{4}{8}$ equivalent? _____

$$\frac{4 \div 4}{8 \div 4} = \underline{\hspace{1cm}}$$

Step 2   You can use multiplication to show that $\frac{1}{4}$ is equivalent to $\frac{3}{12}$.

Multiply the numerator and denominator by the same number to get the product $\frac{3}{12}$.

$$\frac{1 \times}{4 \times 3} = \frac{3}{12}$$

Think: Multiplying by $\frac{3}{3}$ is the same as multiplying by 1.

So the fractions $\frac{1}{4}$ and $\frac{3}{12}$ are _____.

Solution

On which kinds of bread did they make the same number of sandwiches?

_____

Tell whether each pair of fractions is equivalent. Write yes or no.

1. $\frac{5}{6}$ and $\frac{7}{8}$ _____

2. $\frac{4}{8}$ and $\frac{3}{6}$ _____

3. $\frac{4}{5}$ and $\frac{5}{6}$ _____

4. $\frac{1}{3}$ and $\frac{3}{8}$ _____

5. $\frac{12}{24}$ and $\frac{9}{18}$ _____

6. $\frac{22}{40}$ and $\frac{11}{20}$ _____

7. $\frac{3}{17}$ and $\frac{7}{13}$ _____

8. $\frac{5}{7}$ and $\frac{25}{35}$ _____

Write each fraction in simplest form.

9. $\frac{4}{8} =$ _____

10. $\frac{6}{16} =$ _____

11. $\frac{15}{25} =$ _____

12. $\frac{9}{27} =$ _____

Write three equivalent fractions for each.

13. $\frac{2}{3} =$ _____

14. $\frac{14}{16} =$ _____

15. $\frac{44}{55} =$ _____

16. $\frac{4}{9} =$ _____

17. $\frac{15}{27} =$ _____

18. $\frac{48}{54} =$ _____

Solve each problem.

19. Jessica made 16 goals out of 20 shots at soccer practice. Samantha made 14 goals out of 18 shots. Carmen made $\frac{4}{5}$ of her shots. Which girls made goals for the same fraction of shots?

_____

20. Out of 16 birthday cards that Fred received, 12 were from family. Evan says $\frac{1}{4}$ of Fred's cards were not from family, and Fred says $\frac{2}{8}$ of his cards were not from family. Who is correct?

_____

21. Emily finished reading $\frac{3}{5}$ of a book. Wesley finished reading $\frac{15}{20}$ of the same book. Did they read the same number of pages? Explain how you used equivalent fractions to solve the problem.

_____

_____

_____

PSSA Practice

Directions: Read each question. Then circle the letter for the best answer.

1. Which number is **not** equivalent to $\frac{7}{8}$?

   A $\frac{14}{16}$

   B $\frac{17}{18}$

   C $\frac{21}{24}$

   D $\frac{42}{48}$

2. The table below shows the number of boys and girls in three school clubs.

   Club Membership

Club	Hiking	Drama	Photography
Girls	15	8	18
Boys	5	12	6

   Compare the number of girls in each group to the total number of students in each group. For which clubs does the comparison result in equivalent fractions?

   A Hiking and Drama

   B Hiking and Photography

   C Drama and Photography

   D Hiking, Drama, and Photography

3. Which list shows only equivalent fractions?

   A $\frac{6}{8}, \frac{3}{4}, \frac{8}{16}$

   B $\frac{80}{100}, \frac{40}{50}, \frac{2}{5}$

   C $\frac{1}{3}, \frac{11}{36}, \frac{33}{99}$

   D $\frac{14}{49}, \frac{2}{7}, \frac{6}{21}$

4. A movie theater has 200 of its 250 seats occupied. Which fraction shows the number of **empty** seats?

   A $\frac{1}{5}$

   B $\frac{4}{10}$

   C $\frac{5}{9}$

   D $\frac{4}{5}$

5. Ellen read 40 pages of a 200-page book. Ken read 60 pages of a 220-page book, and Hallie read 70 pages of a 350-page book. Which students read the same fraction of their books?

   A Ellen and Ken

   B Ken and Hallie

   C Ellen and Hallie

   D Ellen, Ken, and Hallie

Assessment Anchors/Eligible Content: M7.A.1.1.1 Convert between fractions, decimals and/or percents (e.g., 20% = 0.2 = $\frac{1}{5}$) (terminating decimals only).

M7.A.1.2.1 Compare and/or order integers, mixed numbers, fractions and decimals (fractions and decimals may be mixed – no more than 5 numbers in a set to be ordered).

Academic Standards: 2.1.8.A

You can compare fractions and mixed numbers by writing equivalent fractions. To compare fractions with *unlike* denominators, use the LCD (least common denominator) to find equivalent fractions with *like* denominators. The **least common denominator** is the least common multiple of the denominators.

Mixed numbers are fractions that have a whole number part and a fraction part. A mixed number can be written as an improper fraction. An **improper fraction** has a numerator that is greater than or equal to its denominator.

Guided Instruction

Problem

Vanessa planted flowers in $\frac{3}{16}$ of the garden on Friday, $\frac{3}{8}$ of the garden on Saturday, and $\frac{1}{8}$ of the garden on Sunday. On which day did Vanessa plant the greatest part of the garden?

To compare, first write equivalent fractions by finding the least common denominator. Then compare the numerators.

Step 1 To compare $\frac{3}{16}$, $\frac{3}{8}$, and $\frac{1}{8}$, find their least common denominator.
Circle the LCM of 8 and 16.

Multiples of 8: 8, 16, 24, 32, 40, …

Multiples of 16: 16, 32, 48, 64, …

Step 2 Write equivalent fractions, using 16 as the denominator.

$$\frac{1 \times}{8 \times 2} = \frac{}{16} \qquad \frac{3 \times 2}{8 \times} = \frac{}{16}$$

Step 3 Order the fractions by comparing the numerators. Then write your results using the original fractions.

$$\frac{2}{16} < \frac{3}{16} < \frac{6}{16}$$

$$\underline{\quad} < \frac{3}{16} < \underline{\quad}$$

Solution

On which day did Vanessa plant the greatest part of the garden?

_____

Another Example

Write $\frac{2}{3}$, $1\frac{1}{2}$, and $1\frac{1}{3}$ in order from least to greatest.

The fraction $\frac{2}{3}$ is the least number because it is less than 1.

Because the mixed numbers $1\frac{1}{2}$ and $1\frac{1}{3}$ have the same whole number, compare their fractions.

$$\frac{1}{2} = \frac{3}{6} \qquad \frac{1}{3} = \frac{2}{6}$$

$$\frac{3}{6} > \frac{2}{6}, \text{ so } \frac{1}{2} > \frac{1}{3}$$

So $1\frac{1}{3}$ is less than $1\frac{1}{2}$.

Written in order from least to greatest, the fractions are $\frac{2}{3}$, $1\frac{1}{3}$, $1\frac{1}{2}$.

Measuring Up® to the Pennsylvania Academic Standards

Apply the Pennsylvania Academic Standards

Use >, < or = to compare each pair. If necessary, find a common denominator.

1. $\frac{7}{16}$ ◯ $\frac{3}{16}$

2. $\frac{8}{10}$ ◯ $\frac{4}{5}$

3. $\frac{11}{12}$ ◯ $1\frac{1}{2}$

4. $\frac{5}{6}$ ◯ $\frac{4}{5}$

5. $\frac{1}{3}$ ◯ $\frac{5}{15}$

6. $\frac{7}{9}$ ◯ $\frac{5}{8}$

7. $4\frac{2}{3}$ ◯ $4\frac{6}{9}$

8. $1\frac{17}{24}$ ◯ $1\frac{3}{4}$

9. $3\frac{7}{8}$ ◯ $4\frac{5}{16}$

Write each set of numbers in order from *least* to *greatest*.

10. $\frac{2}{9}, \frac{7}{9}, \frac{1}{2}$ _____

11. $\frac{11}{20}, \frac{4}{5}, \frac{3}{10}$ _____

12. $\frac{7}{26}, \frac{1}{2}, \frac{4}{13}$ _____

Write each set of numbers in order from *greatest* to *least*.

13. $\frac{7}{8}, 1\frac{1}{4}, \frac{3}{4}$ _____

14. $2\frac{7}{15}, 3\frac{1}{5}, 2\frac{2}{3}$ _____

15. $5\frac{3}{4}, 5\frac{5}{6}, 5\frac{3}{8}$ _____

Use the data in the table below for problems 16–19.

16. Which day had the least rain? _____

17. Was there more rain on Tuesday or on Thursday? _____

18. Was there more rain on Monday or Friday? _____

19. Write the days in order of the rainfall from least to greatest. Explain how you find your answer.

_____

_____

_____

_____

_____

Daily Rainfall in Middletown

Day	Inches of Rain
Monday	$\frac{1}{2}$
Tuesday	$\frac{5}{8}$
Wednesday	$1\frac{1}{4}$
Thursday	$\frac{3}{4}$
Friday	$\frac{3}{10}$

PSSA Practice Directions: Read each question. Then circle the letter for the best answer.

1. Ashley's recipe needs $\frac{2}{3}$ cup of flour. Nadia's recipe needs $\frac{3}{4}$ cup of flour. Which statement about the amount of flour needed for the recipes is true?

   A   Ashley's recipe needs less than $\frac{1}{2}$ cup of flour.

   B   Nadia's recipe needs more flour than Ashley's.

   C   Nadia's recipe needs less than $\frac{2}{3}$ cup of flour.

   D   Ashley's recipe needs more flour than Nadia's.

2. Miguel hikes the Yellow Trail $4\frac{1}{8}$ miles to a lake. He can return by the same route or by one of three other trails. The Red Trail is $4\frac{1}{6}$ miles long, the Green Trail is $4\frac{1}{3}$ miles long, and the Blue Trail is $4\frac{1}{2}$ miles long. He wants to take the shortest route. Which trail should he take?

   A   Red Trail

   B   Green Trail

   C   Blue Trail

   D   Yellow Trail

3. Which one of the following fractions is **greater** than $\frac{18}{54}$?

   A $\frac{1}{4}$

   B $\frac{3}{27}$

   C $\frac{5}{18}$

   D $\frac{32}{60}$

4. Which set of fractions is in order from **least** to **greatest**?

   A $\frac{27}{100}, \frac{3}{50}, \frac{7}{10}, \frac{4}{5}$

   B $\frac{3}{50}, \frac{27}{100}, \frac{7}{10}, \frac{4}{5}$

   C $\frac{3}{50}, \frac{7}{10}, \frac{27}{100}, \frac{4}{5}$

   D $\frac{3}{50}, \frac{7}{10}, \frac{4}{5}, \frac{27}{100}$

5. A box is $3\frac{5}{8}$ feet wide, $3\frac{11}{16}$ feet long, and $3\frac{3}{4}$ feet high. Which of the following statements is true?

   A   The box's height is less than its width.

   B   The box's height is greater than its length.

   C   The box's length is greater than its height.

   D   The box's width is equal to its height.

Assessment Anchors/Eligible Content: M7.A.1.1.1 Convert between fractions, decimals and/or percents (e.g., 20% = 0.2 = $\frac{1}{5}$) (terminating decimals only).

M7.A.1.2.1 Compare and/or order integers, mixed numbers, fractions and decimals (fractions and decimals may be mixed — no more than 5 numbers in a set to be ordered).

M7.A.1.2.2 Locate/identify decimals, fractions, mixed numbers and/or integers on a number line (a mix of these number forms may be on the same number line).

Academic Standards: 2.1.8.A, 2.2.8.B, 2.4.8.B

Equivalent numbers have the same value.

In order to compare fractions and decimals, you may need to write one or more of the numbers into an equivalent form.

To write a decimal as an equivalent fraction, use place value. Write the digits after the decimal point as the numerator and write the denominator as a power of 10.

$$1.3 = 1\frac{3}{10} \qquad\qquad 0.75 = \frac{75}{100} \qquad\qquad 0.108 = \frac{108}{1,000}$$

To write a fraction as an equivalent decimal, divide the numerator by the denominator.

$$\frac{1}{5} = 1 \div 5 = 0.2 \qquad\qquad\qquad \frac{66}{100} = 66 \div 100 = 0.66$$

Guided Instruction

Problem

Mary and Dorian live in the same apartment building. Mary has walked $\frac{7}{8}$ of the distance to school, and Dorian has walked 0.85 of the distance to school. Who is closer to the school?

Write equivalent numbers to compare.

Step 1 Write $\frac{7}{8}$ as a decimal.

What is 7 ÷ 8? _____

Step 2 Compare the decimal numbers. Use a number line.

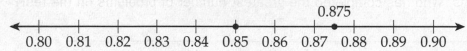

0.875

0.80 0.81 0.82 0.83 0.84 0.85 0.86 0.87 0.88 0.89 0.90

Step 3 Write the comparison. 0.875 ◯ 0.85

Solution Who is closer to the school? _____

Other Examples

A. Write 0.2 as a fraction in simplest form.

0.2 is read as "two tenths."

$$0.2 = \frac{2}{10} = \frac{1}{5}$$

So 0.2 is $\frac{1}{5}$, in simplest form.

B. Compare 0.75, $\frac{7}{10}$, and $\frac{7}{8}$.

$$\frac{7}{10} = 0.7$$

$$\frac{7}{8} = 7 \div 8 = 0.875$$

Use place value to compare.

0.7 < 0.75 < 0.875

So $\frac{7}{10}$ < 0.75 < $\frac{7}{8}$.

Convert each fraction to a decimal or each decimal to a fraction. Write each fraction in simplest form.

1. $\frac{9}{10}$

_____

2. $\frac{4}{5}$

_____

3. $\frac{3}{20}$

_____

4. 0.6

_____

5. 0.25

_____

6. 0.44

_____

Compare by converting each fraction to a decimal. Write >, <, or =.

7. $\frac{1}{4}$ and 0.2

_____

8. $\frac{3}{5}$ and 0.5

_____

9. $\frac{4}{5}$ and 0.8

_____

Order these numbers from _least_ to _greatest_.

10. $\frac{5}{8}$, 0.55, $\frac{3}{4}$, $\frac{1}{2}$, 0.77

_____

11. $\frac{5}{8}$, 0.72, 0.68, $\frac{3}{4}$, $\frac{1}{3}$

_____

12. $\frac{7}{10}$, $\frac{21}{25}$, 0.79, $\frac{12}{24}$, 0.44

_____

Solve each problem.

13. Manny has completed $\frac{3}{5}$ of the math problems on a test. Sharon has completed 0.4 of the math problems. Mei has completed $\frac{22}{25}$ of the math problems. Who has completed the greatest number of problems on the test?

_____

14. Christopher finds two identical containers holding water. The first is labeled "$\frac{3}{4}$ full" and the second is labeled "0.28 empty." Which container has more water in it? Explain your thinking.

_____

_____

_____

PSSA Practice Directions: Read each question. Then circle the letter for the best answer.

1. Marisa used 0.8 gallon of paint to cover three walls. Which fraction is equal to the part of the gallon that is left?

    A $\frac{4}{5}$ B $\frac{2}{5}$

    C $\frac{8}{10}$ D $\frac{1}{5}$

2. Harry uses 0.75 of the space in his locker. Beverly uses $\frac{5}{6}$ of her locker. Jason uses $\frac{2}{3}$ of his locker. Which of the following lists space used in order from **least** to **greatest**?

    A Harry, Beverly, Jason

    B Jason, Beverly, Harry

    C Jason, Harry, Beverly

    D Beverly, Jason, Harry

3. Isaac uses 0.6 of the orange juice in a container to make a smoothie. Which fraction shows how much orange juice is left?

    A $\frac{3}{5}$ B $\frac{29}{50}$

    C $\frac{57}{100}$ D $\frac{2}{5}$

4. Georgia buys a water bottle that contains $\frac{5}{8}$ liter of water. The label also shows the amount as a decimal. Which decimal is on the label?

    A 0.58 liter

    B 0.625 liter

    C 0.7 liter

    D 0.85 liter

5. Lonnie has completed $\frac{1}{8}$ of a race. Steven has completed 0.20 of the race. Margaret has completed $\frac{3}{25}$ of the race. In terms of how much of the race they have completed, which of the following lists the students in order from **greatest** to **least**?

    A Steven, Lonnie, Margaret

    B Margaret, Steven, Lonnie

    C Margaret, Lonnie, Steven

    D Steven, Margaret, Lonnie

6. Vicky uses $\frac{1}{4}$ bag of potting soil to pot a plant. Which decimal shows how much potting soil is left?

    A 0.14

    B 0.25

    C 0.75

    D 0.95

7. Octavio has completed $\frac{3}{4}$ of the reading assignment. Wei has completed 0.7 of the reading. Joanne has completed $\frac{4}{5}$ of the assignment, and Mike has completed 0.81. Who has completed the **most** reading?

    A Octavio

    B Wei

    C Joanne

    D Mike

Focus on the Pennsylvania Academic Standards

Lesson 11 — Add and Subtract Fractions and Mixed Numbers

Assessment Anchors/Eligible Content: M7.A.3.2.1 Solve problems involving operations (+, −, ×, ÷) of whole numbers, decimals, fractions, or mixed numbers (straight computation or word problems).

Academic Standards: 2.2.8.B, 2.4.8.D

You can add or subtract fractions and mixed numbers by using the least common denominator. The **least common denominator (LCD)** is the least common multiple of the denominators. When two fractions have the same denominators, you can add or subtract the numerators. To add mixed numbers, add the fractions and whole numbers separately, and then combine the results.

Guided Instruction

Problem 1

Owen and Patrick each ordered a small pizza for lunch. Owen ate $\frac{3}{4}$ of his pizza. Patrick ate $\frac{2}{3}$ of his pizza. What fraction of the pizzas did they eat?

Convert each fraction to an equivalent fraction with a common denominator.

Step 1   Find the least common multiple for both denominators.

What is the least common multiple of 4 and 3? _____

Step 2   Convert the fractions to equivalent fractions, using the least common denominator.

$\frac{3}{4} =$ _____

$\frac{2}{3} =$ _____

Step 3   Add the numerators and place the sum over the denominator.

$\frac{9}{12} + \frac{8}{12} =$ _____

Step 4   Simplify. Divide the numerator by the denominator. Write the remainder over the denominator.

$\frac{17}{12} =$ _____

Solution   What fraction of the pizzas did they eat? _____

Problem 2 Sophia has $5\frac{5}{8}$ pounds of cookie dough. She gives $2\frac{4}{5}$ pounds to Luis. How many pounds of cookie dough will she have left?

Step 1 Find the difference. First find the least common denominator.

What is the least common multiple of 8 and 5? ____

Step 2 Write each fraction as an equivalent fraction with a denominator of 40.

$\frac{5}{8} = \frac{5}{8} \times \frac{5}{5} =$ _____, so $5\frac{5}{8} =$ _____

$\frac{4}{5} = \frac{4}{5} \times \frac{8}{8} =$ _____, so $2\frac{4}{5} =$ _____

Step 3 Rename before you subtract because $\frac{25}{40} < \frac{32}{40}$.

Rename 1 whole as $\frac{40}{40}$.

$5\frac{25}{40} = 4 + \frac{40}{40} + \frac{25}{40} =$ _____

Step 4 Subtract.

$4\frac{65}{40} - 2\frac{32}{40} =$ _____

Solution How many pounds of cookie dough will she have left? _____

Another Example

Find the difference. $1\frac{9}{10} - \frac{4}{5}$

Use the least common denominator to write equivalent fractions.

The LCD for $\frac{9}{10}$ and $\frac{4}{5}$ is 10.

So write $\frac{4}{5}$ as $\frac{8}{10}$.

Subtract the fractions.

$\frac{9}{10} - \frac{8}{10} = \frac{1}{10}$

Subtract whole numbers.

$1 - 0 = 1$

Combine the differences.

$1\frac{9}{10} - \frac{4}{5} = 1\frac{1}{10}$

Apply the Pennsylvania Academic Standards

Find each sum or difference. Simplify if possible.

1. $\frac{3}{10} + \frac{4}{6}$

_____

2. $\frac{5}{6} - \frac{2}{3}$

_____

3. $\frac{2}{5} + \frac{1}{4}$

_____

4. $\frac{7}{8} - \frac{4}{5}$

_____

5. $\frac{1}{9} + \frac{5}{12}$

_____

6. $\frac{9}{10} - \frac{3}{4}$

_____

7. $1\frac{2}{5} + 2\frac{3}{10}$

_____

8. $3\frac{2}{3} - 1\frac{5}{8}$

_____

9. $1\frac{1}{2} + 2\frac{5}{6}$

_____

10. $2\frac{1}{2} + 1\frac{4}{5}$

_____

11. $3\frac{5}{8} + 6\frac{3}{10}$

_____

12. $7\frac{3}{5} - 4\frac{11}{15}$

_____

13. $9\frac{1}{3} + 5\frac{7}{9}$

_____

14. $8\frac{9}{10} - 3\frac{5}{6}$

_____

15. $3\frac{7}{12} + \frac{8}{15}$

_____

Solve each problem.

16. Danielle finds two orange juice bottles. The first bottle is labeled $\frac{5}{8}$ liter and the second bottle is labeled $\frac{7}{12}$ liter. If she were to pour all the juice from both bottles into one pitcher, how much orange juice would the pitcher contain? Explain your answer.

_____

_____

17. Jody bought two pineapples. The first pineapple weighed $4\frac{5}{8}$ pounds. The second pineapple weighed $3\frac{7}{16}$ pounds. If she put both pineapples on a scale, how many pounds would they weigh altogether? Explain your answer.

_____

_____

PSSA Practice Directions: Read each question. Then circle the letter for the best answer.

1. The shaded part of the first circle represents the fraction of Amy's soccer practice that she spent doing drills. The shaded part of the second circle represents the fraction of Amy's soccer practice that she spent playing mock games. What fraction of the soccer practice does she spend running drills **and** playing mock games?

A $\frac{3}{5}$

B $\frac{10}{13}$

C $\frac{31}{40}$

D $\frac{21}{8}$

2. Hillary mixes $\frac{11}{15}$ cup of flour with $\frac{3}{5}$ cup of sugar. How many cups is the mixture?

A $\frac{14}{20}$ B $1\frac{2}{15}$

C $1\frac{1}{3}$ D $1\frac{20}{15}$

3. There are two hiking trails in the forest. The Lake Trail is $13\frac{5}{8}$ miles long. The Falls Trail is $9\frac{3}{4}$ miles long. How much longer is the Lake Trail than the Falls Trail?

A $3\frac{1}{2}$ miles   B $3\frac{7}{8}$ miles

C $4\frac{1}{2}$ miles   D $4\frac{7}{8}$ miles

4. The shaded part of the circle on the left represents how much of a book John had left to read yesterday. The shaded part of the circle on the right represents how much of the book John has left to read today. According to the circles, what fraction of the book did he read between yesterday and today?

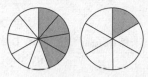

A $\frac{5}{18}$ B $\frac{5}{9}$

C $\frac{11}{18}$ D $\frac{3}{3}$

5. Jason is carving a sculpture from a block of marble that weighs $1\frac{7}{8}$ tons. After he is finished, he measures the debris and finds that he has chiseled $\frac{23}{24}$ ton of marble off the block. How much does the finished sculpture weigh?

A $\frac{11}{12}$ ton   B $\frac{23}{24}$ ton

C $\frac{45}{24}$ tons   D $2\frac{4}{5}$ tons

6. Jamie's cat is two years old and weighs $8\frac{1}{4}$ pounds. Six months ago the cat weighed $7\frac{5}{8}$ pounds. How many pounds has the cat gained in six months?

A $\frac{1}{2}$ pound   B $\frac{5}{8}$ pound

C $1\frac{1}{2}$ pounds   D $1\frac{5}{8}$ pounds

Focus on the Pennsylvania Academic Standards **Lesson 12** **Multiply Fractions and Mixed Numbers**

Assessment Anchors/Eligible Content: M7.A.3.2.1 Solve problems involving operations (+, −, ×, ÷) of whole numbers, decimals, fractions, or mixed numbers (straight computation or word problems).
Academic Standards: 2.2.8.B, 2.4.8.D

To multiply fractions, first multiply the numerators, and then multiply the denominators.

To multiply mixed numbers, first write the mixed numbers as improper fractions. Then multiply the numerators and then the denominators.

Sometimes you can simplify before you multiply by dividing a numerator and a denominator by a common factor.

Guided Instruction

Problem 1

Trudy belongs to a quilting club. Each member works on one piece of the quilt. The piece of quilt that Trudy is working on is $\frac{4}{15}$ of the whole quilt. She has finished $\frac{5}{12}$ of this piece. What fraction of the whole quilt has she finished?

Multiply to solve the problem. Simplify if you can before you multiply.

Step 1   Write the multiplication expression. Look for common factors in the numerators and denominators.

$$\frac{4}{15} \times \frac{5}{12}$$

Is 12 divisible by 4? _____

$$\frac{\overset{1}{4}}{15} \times \frac{5}{\underset{3}{12}} = \frac{1}{15} \times \frac{5}{3}$$

Is 15 divisible by 5? _____

$$\frac{1}{\underset{3}{15}} \times \frac{\overset{1}{5}}{3} = \frac{1}{3} \times \frac{1}{3}$$

Step 2   Multiply the numerators and the denominators to find the product.

$$\frac{1}{3} \times \frac{1}{3} = \underline{\hspace{2cm}}$$

Solution   What fraction of the whole quilt has Trudy finished? _____

Problem 2 Cara's garden is $8\frac{1}{2}$ square feet. Alejandro's garden is $2\frac{4}{5}$ times as large as Cara's garden. How large is Alejandro's garden?

Step 1 Convert the mixed numbers to improper fractions.

$$2\frac{4}{5} \times 8\frac{1}{2} = \underline{\hspace{1.5cm}} \times \underline{\hspace{1.5cm}}$$

Step 2 Simplify, if possible, before multiplying.

$$\overset{7}{\cancel{\frac{14}{5}}} \times \frac{17}{\underset{1}{\cancel{2}}} = \underline{\hspace{1.5cm}} \times \underline{\hspace{1.5cm}}$$

Step 3 Multiply.

$$\frac{7}{5} \times \frac{17}{1} = \frac{119}{5} = \underline{\hspace{1.5cm}}$$

Solution How large is Alejandro's garden? $\underline{\hspace{5cm}}$

Problem 3 Danny has $32\frac{1}{2}$ pounds of flour. He uses $\frac{1}{3}$ of that amount to make cakes for a party. How many pounds of flour did he use?

Step 1 Convert the mixed number to an improper fraction.

$$32\frac{1}{2} \cdot \frac{1}{3} = \underline{\hspace{2.5cm}}$$

Step 2 Multiply and simplify.

$$\frac{65}{2} \cdot \frac{1}{3} = \frac{65}{6} = \underline{\hspace{2.5cm}}$$

Solution How many pounds of flour did he use? $\underline{\hspace{5cm}}$

Apply the Pennsylvania Academic Standards

Find each product. Simplify, if possible, before multiplying.

1. $\frac{1}{2} \times \frac{3}{4}$

2. $\frac{2}{7} \times \frac{3}{10}$

3. $\frac{2}{5} \times \frac{7}{8}$

4. $\frac{3}{8} \times \frac{2}{3}$

5. $\frac{5}{8} \times \frac{4}{15}$

6. $\frac{8}{15} \times \frac{5}{24}$

7. $\frac{7}{9} \times \frac{27}{49}$

8. $\frac{4}{9} \times \frac{3}{16}$

9. $\frac{25}{48} \times \frac{12}{100}$

Multiply.

10. $2\frac{4}{5} \times \frac{15}{16}$

11. $3\frac{3}{4} \times \frac{2}{9}$

12. $6\frac{1}{2} \times \frac{2}{3}$

13. $1\frac{5}{9} \times 6$

14. $2\frac{1}{6} \times 3$

15. $2\frac{3}{5} \times 20$

16. $1\frac{5}{6} \times \frac{9}{16}$

17. $\frac{5}{8} \times 3\frac{7}{8}$

18. $3\frac{9}{20} \times 4\frac{5}{9}$

Solve each problem.

19. Missy owns 50 shares of stock. Today, the stock price went up $2\frac{3}{5}$ points. If each point is worth $1, how much more is Missy's stock worth today? Explain your answer.

_____

_____

_____

20. Steve knows that a person cross-country skiing burns 610 calories per hour. If he skis for $4\frac{1}{2}$ hours before lunch and $1\frac{1}{4}$ hours afterward, how many calories does he burn? Explain your answer.

_____

Measuring Up® to the Pennsylvania Academic Standards

1. Barbara is working on a math puzzle. She has to multiply the two fractions represented by the rows and columns in the diagram. What is her solution, in simplest form?

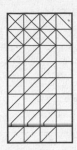

A $\frac{3}{32}$ B $\frac{3}{16}$

C $\frac{1}{2}$ D 1

2. Chris buys 3 containers of juice mix. Each container can make $2\frac{1}{12}$ quarts of juice. How many glasses of juice can he make, if each quart can fill 16 glasses?

A $\frac{25}{12}$

B $6\frac{1}{4}$

C $33\frac{1}{3}$

D 100

3. Cathy runs one mile in $8\frac{1}{4}$ minutes. At that rate, how long does it take her to run 4 miles?

A   20 minutes

B   33 minutes

C   37 minutes

D   132 minutes

4. The beaker below holds 16 ounces. How many ounces did Paul put into it?

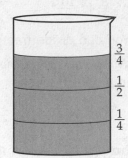

$\frac{3}{4}$

$\frac{1}{2}$

$\frac{1}{4}$

A $\frac{1}{12}$

B $1\frac{1}{3}$

C 4

D 12

5. Bob sold $\frac{1}{2}$ of a 32-acre plot. He then sold $\frac{2}{3}$ of the remaining piece. How much of the 32 acres remained unsold?

A $2\frac{4}{5}$ acres   B $5\frac{1}{3}$ acres

C $5\frac{2}{3}$ acres   D $10\frac{4}{5}$ acres

6. A developer can build on only $\frac{2}{3}$ of a $\frac{3}{4}$-acre lot. How much of an acre can be used for building?

A $\frac{5}{12}$ acre

B $\frac{1}{2}$ acre

C $\frac{6}{7}$ acre

D $\frac{8}{9}$ acre

Lesson 13 Divide Fractions and Mixed Numbers

Assessment Anchors/Eligible Content: M7.A.3.2.1 Solve problems involving operations ($+$, $-$, $\times$, $\div$) of whole numbers, decimals, fractions, or mixed numbers (straight computation or word problems).

Academic Standards: 2.2.8.B, 2.4.8.D

The **reciprocal** of any fraction $\frac{a}{b}$ is $\frac{b}{a}$. For example, the reciprocal of $\frac{4}{5}$ is $\frac{5}{4}$, and the reciprocal of $\frac{3}{10}$ is $\frac{10}{3}$.

You can divide fractions by multiplying by the reciprocal of the divisor.

When you divide mixed numbers, first convert the mixed numbers to improper fractions.

Guided Instruction

Problem 1 Felicia needs to divide $\frac{5}{8}$ by $\frac{15}{16}$. What is the quotient?

Multiply by the reciprocal to divide the fractions.

Step 1 Write the division expression and find the reciprocal of the divisor.

$$\frac{5}{8} \div \frac{15}{16}$$

Remember: The product of a number and its reciprocal is 1.

Think: $\frac{15}{16} \times \underline{\hspace{2cm}} = 1$

What is the reciprocal of $\frac{15}{16}$? $\underline{\hspace{1.5cm}}$

Step 2 Rewrite the problem to multiply by the reciprocal.

$$\frac{5}{8} \div \frac{15}{16} = \frac{5}{8} \times \underline{\hspace{1.5cm}}$$

Step 3 Simplify before multiplying.

$15 \div 5 = \underline{\hspace{1.5cm}}$

$16 \div 8 = \underline{\hspace{1.5cm}}$

$$\frac{5}{8} \times \frac{16}{15} = \frac{\overset{1}{\cancel{5}}}{\underset{1}{\cancel{8}}} \times \frac{\overset{2}{\cancel{16}}}{\underset{3}{\cancel{15}}}$$

Step 4 Multiply the numerators and the denominators.

$$\frac{1}{1} \times \frac{2}{3} = \underline{\hspace{1.5cm}}$$

Solution What is the quotient of $\frac{5}{8} \div \frac{15}{16}$? $\underline{\hspace{1.5cm}}$

Problem 2

George's school is having a bake sale. The cookie table is $9\frac{3}{4}$ feet long. Each type of cookie being sold is given $1\frac{5}{8}$ feet of the table. If the entire table is used, how many different kinds of cookies are for sale?

Step 1 Write the division problem.

$$9\frac{3}{4} \div 1\frac{5}{8}$$

Step 2 Rewrite each mixed number as an improper fraction.

$$9\frac{3}{4} = \frac{9 \times 4 + 3}{4} = \underline{\hspace{1.5cm}}$$

$$1\frac{5}{8} = \frac{1 \times 8 + 5}{8} = \underline{\hspace{1.5cm}}$$

So $9\frac{3}{4} \div 1\frac{5}{8} = \underline{\hspace{1.5cm}}$

Step 3 Rewrite the problem as a multiplication problem using a reciprocal.

$$\frac{39}{4} \div \frac{13}{8} = \frac{39}{4} \times \underline{\hspace{1.5cm}}$$

Step 4 Multiply. Simplify first if possible.

$$\overset{3}{\underset{1}{\cancel{\frac{39}{4}}}} \times \overset{2}{\underset{1}{\cancel{\frac{8}{13}}}} = \underline{\hspace{1.5cm}}$$

Solution How many different kinds of cookies are for sale? \underline{\hspace{1.5cm}}

Other Examples

A. Find the product of $1\frac{1}{3} \cdot \frac{9}{16}$.

Write the mixed number as an improper fraction. $\frac{4}{3} \cdot \frac{9}{16}$

Multiply. Simplify first if possible. $\overset{1}{\underset{1}{\cancel{\frac{4}{3}}}} \cdot \overset{3}{\underset{4}{\cancel{\frac{9}{16}}}} = \frac{3}{4}$

B. Find the quotient of 3 divided by $\frac{9}{11}$.

Write the 3 as an improper fraction. $\frac{3}{1} \div \frac{9}{11}$

Rewrite the division as a multiplication problem using the reciprocal. $\frac{3}{1} \cdot \frac{11}{9}$

Multiply. Simplify first if possible. $\overset{1}{\underset{1}{\cancel{\frac{3}{1}}}} \cdot \underset{3}{\frac{11}{\cancel{9}}} = \frac{11}{3}$

Write the product as a mixed number.

Find each quotient. Simplify, if possible, before dividing.

1. $\dfrac{2}{3} \div \dfrac{5}{6}$

_____

2. $\dfrac{7}{8} \div \dfrac{5}{24}$

_____

3. $\dfrac{3}{5} \div \dfrac{9}{10}$

_____

4. $\dfrac{3}{4} \div \dfrac{5}{12}$

_____

5. $\dfrac{9}{10} \div \dfrac{3}{20}$

_____

6. $\dfrac{3}{7} \div \dfrac{15}{28}$

_____

7. $\dfrac{9}{16} \div \dfrac{3}{32}$

_____

8. $\dfrac{9}{50} \div \dfrac{18}{25}$

_____

9. $\dfrac{13}{20} \div \dfrac{39}{40}$

_____

Divide.

10. $1\dfrac{2}{3} \div \dfrac{8}{9}$ _____

11. $2\dfrac{5}{6} \div \dfrac{3}{8}$

_____

12. $5\dfrac{1}{2} \div \dfrac{11}{12}$

_____

13. $3\dfrac{4}{5} \div 2$

_____

14. $4\dfrac{8}{9} \div 4$

_____

15. $6\dfrac{5}{12} \div 7$

_____

16. $19\dfrac{4}{5} \div \dfrac{12}{15}$

_____

17. $6\dfrac{2}{3} \div \dfrac{5}{4}$

_____

18. $12\dfrac{3}{5} \div \dfrac{7}{10}$

_____

Solve each problem.

19. Greg has a container that holds $3\dfrac{3}{4}$ pounds of flour and a scoop that holds $\dfrac{1}{8}$ pound of flour. How many $\dfrac{1}{8}$-pound scoops of flour are in the full container? Explain your answer.

_____

_____

20. A surveying team surveys 20 city blocks in $2\dfrac{1}{2}$ hours. How many blocks does the team survey per hour? Explain your answer.

_____

_____

PSSA Practice   Directions: Read each question. Then circle the letter for the best answer.

1. Allisa is cutting a ribbon that is $\frac{5}{6}$ yard long into pieces that are $\frac{1}{12}$ yard long. How many pieces does Allisa have?

   A   10

   B $\frac{60}{10}$

   C   6

   D $\frac{1}{10}$

2. Bill has a container filled with 7 liters of water. He has smaller containers that hold $2\frac{5}{8}$ liters of water. How many smaller containers can he fill from the larger container?

   A $2\frac{2}{3}$

   B $8\frac{1}{2}$

   C $18\frac{3}{8}$

   D $56\frac{1}{2}$

3. Marcus is making chocolate-chip muffins. If the recipe calls for $2\frac{1}{3}$ cups of flour, how much flour will he need to make half the recipe?

   A $\frac{3}{14}$ cup

   B $\frac{6}{7}$ cup

   C $1\frac{1}{6}$ cups

   D $4\frac{2}{3}$ cups

4. Sofia is planning a hike at a national park. The trail is $8\frac{1}{3}$ miles long. She wants to stop twice during her hike so that each time she will have covered $\frac{1}{3}$ of the trail. After how many miles will she make her first stop?

   A $\frac{3}{25}$

   B $\frac{9}{25}$

   C $2\frac{2}{3}$

   D $2\frac{7}{9}$

5. Joe used $\frac{1}{3}$ cup of olive oil, which was $\frac{3}{4}$ of the amount that he had. How much olive oil did he have?

   A $\frac{3}{4}$ cup

   B $\frac{4}{9}$ cup

   C $\frac{3}{8}$ cup

   D $\frac{1}{4}$ cup

6. Pam's fundraising letter is on a paper that is $8\frac{1}{4}$ inches wide with an area of 88 square inches. How many inches long is the paper?

   A $\frac{3}{32}$ inch

   B $10\frac{2}{3}$ inches

   C   11 inches

   D   22 inches

Assessment Anchors/Eligible Content: M7.A.3.1.1 Estimate answers to problems involving whole numbers, decimals, fractions or mixed numbers.

M7.A.3.2.1 Solve problems involving operations ($+, -, \times, \div$) of whole numbers, decimals, fractions, or mixed numbers (straight computation or word problems).

Standards: 2.2.8.E, 2.2.8.F, 2.4.8.D

You can round numbers to get an estimate, or an approximation. Use the symbol ≈, which means *is approximately equal to*.

Guided Instruction

Problem 1

Mildred walked $\frac{7}{8}$ of a mile on Monday, $1\frac{2}{5}$ miles on Tuesday, and $1\frac{1}{2}$ miles on Wednesday. About how many miles altogether did Mildred walk?

Step 1   Round the miles walked each day to the nearest mile.

If a fraction is equal to or greater than $\frac{1}{2}$, round up to the next whole number.

If a fraction is less than $\frac{1}{2}$, round down to the previous whole number.

$\frac{7}{8}$ rounds up to _____.

$1\frac{2}{5}$ rounds down to _____.

$1\frac{1}{2}$ rounds up to _____.

Step 2   Add the rounded numbers to get an estimated sum.

$1 + 1 + 2 =$ _____

So $\frac{7}{8} + 1\frac{2}{5} + 1\frac{1}{2} \approx$ _____.

Solution

About how many miles did Mildred walk during those days? _____

Another Example

Estimate the product of $2\frac{9}{11}$ and $1\frac{2}{3}$.

Round each mixed number to the nearest whole number.

$$2\frac{9}{11} \approx 3$$

$$1\frac{2}{3} \approx 2$$

Find the estimated product.

$$3 \cdot 2 = 6$$

So $2\frac{9}{11} \cdot 1\frac{2}{3} \approx 6$.

Apply the Pennsylvania Academic Standards

Estimate each sum or difference.

1. $\frac{3}{5} + \frac{1}{2}$

2. $1\frac{1}{8} - \frac{3}{4}$

3. $1\frac{2}{9} - \frac{2}{5}$

_____

_____

_____

Estimate each product or quotient.

4. $2\frac{2}{3} \cdot \frac{7}{12}$

5. $3\frac{2}{5} \cdot 2\frac{7}{9}$

6. $\frac{4}{7} \div \frac{2}{3}$

_____

_____

_____

Solve each problem.

7. Phyllis is running some errands. She bikes $7\frac{2}{3}$ miles from home to school. She then bikes $1\frac{1}{5}$ miles to the library, and another $6\frac{3}{5}$ miles from the library to her home. About how many miles did she travel? Show your work.

_____

_____

8. Vera needs to divide a plank of wood $5\frac{4}{9}$ meters long into equal pieces, each measuring $1\frac{2}{11}$ meters. About how many pieces will Vera have? Show your work.

_____

_____

9. *Compatible numbers* are numbers that make it easy to estimate a product or quotient. The expression $52 \div 5$ is approximately equal to 10 because $52 \approx 50$ and $50 \div 5 = 10$. Explain how you would use compatible numbers to estimate the product $\frac{2}{7} \cdot 34$.

_____

_____

10. Using compatible numbers, what is the estimate of $\frac{4}{9} \div \frac{15}{34}$?

_____

_____

PSSA Practice Directions: Read each question. Then circle the letter for the best answer.

1. Allan uses different types of flour for the recipe he is making. The recipe uses $\frac{1}{2}$ cup of wheat flour, $2\frac{6}{11}$ cups of all-purpose flour, and $1\frac{1}{4}$ cups of corn flour. About how many cups of flour will he use altogether?

   A   3 cups

   B   4 cups

   C   5 cups

   D   6 cups

2. An art class is completing an embroidery project. The project uses $3\frac{1}{8}$ yards of yellow thread, and $\frac{2}{3}$ of that thread is the darkest shade of yellow. About how many yards of the darkest shade of yellow are used?

   A   0 yards

   B   1 yard

   C   2 yards

   D   4 yards

3. Mark has three bottles of juice. One bottle contains $3\frac{1}{2}$ liters of juice, the second bottle contains $\frac{7}{8}$ liter of juice, and the third bottle contains $1\frac{1}{5}$ liters of juice. About how many liters of juice does Mark have in total?

   A   3 liters

   B   4 liters

   C   5 liters

   D   6 liters

4. Eva's class is displaying their art projects on a table that is $11\frac{3}{4}$ feet long. Each project being displayed uses $2\frac{5}{8}$ feet of the table. About how many different projects can be displayed on the table?

   A   3 projects

   B   4 projects

   C   5 projects

   D   6 projects

5. Pablo runs one mile in $8\frac{3}{4}$ minutes. At that rate, about how long does it take him to run $3\frac{1}{5}$ miles?

   A   18 minutes

   B   24 minutes

   C   27 minutes

   D   32 minutes

6. Paula's puppy weighs $3\frac{7}{10}$ pounds. Johnny's puppy weighs $5\frac{1}{2}$ pounds. About how many **more** pounds does Johnny's puppy weigh?

   A   2 pounds

   B   4 pounds

   C   6 pounds

   D   8 pounds

Directions: Read each question. Then circle the letter for the best answer.

1. Brad is making bread. The recipe calls for $\frac{6}{8}$ teaspoon of baking powder. His measuring spoon only measures in fourths. Which of the following fractions would be equivalent to $\frac{6}{8}$?

   A $\frac{1}{4}$

   B $\frac{2}{3}$

   C $\frac{3}{4}$

   D $1\frac{1}{4}$

2. Which list shows only equivalent fractions?

   A $\frac{9}{12}, \frac{6}{8}, \frac{3}{4}$

   B $\frac{4}{11}, \frac{2}{5}, \frac{1}{2}$

   C $\frac{24}{50}, \frac{15}{25}, \frac{3}{15}$

   D $\frac{4}{13}, \frac{6}{18}, \frac{7}{25}$

3. Which fraction is **not** equivalent to $\frac{5}{6}$?

   A $\frac{25}{30}$ B $\frac{15}{18}$

   C $\frac{20}{24}$ D $\frac{18}{25}$

4. Which fraction is **greater** than $\frac{17}{64}$?

   A $\frac{16}{30}$ B $\frac{18}{74}$

   C $\frac{14}{56}$ D $\frac{22}{89}$

5. Martha and Steve both made a gallon of lemonade to sell to the neighbors. Martha's recipe uses $\frac{3}{4}$ cup of sugar. Steve's recipe needs $\frac{4}{5}$ cup of sugar. Which of the following statements about the amount of sugar in the lemonade recipes is true?

   A Steve's recipe uses $\frac{2}{10}$ cup of sugar

   B Steve's recipe uses more sugar than Martha's recipe.

   C Martha's recipe uses more sugar than Steve's recipe.

   D Martha's recipe uses $\frac{5}{8}$ cup of sugar.

6. Which list of numbers is in order from **least** to **greatest**?

   A $\frac{3}{12}, 1\frac{3}{8}, \frac{3}{4}$

   B $\frac{3}{4}, 1\frac{3}{8}, \frac{9}{12}$

   C $\frac{3}{12}, \frac{3}{4}, 1\frac{3}{8}$

   D $1\frac{3}{8}, \frac{9}{12}, \frac{3}{4}$

7. Sarah used $\frac{2}{8}$ cup of water for her science project. Which of the following decimals is **equivalent** to the amount of water used?

   A 0.25   B 0.33

   C 0.45   D 0.57

8. Which of the following fractions is **less** than $\frac{19}{36}$?

   A $\frac{7}{4}$

   B $\frac{10}{12}$

   C $\frac{9}{13}$

   D $\frac{11}{24}$

9. Before Cory mowed the lawn, there was one gallon of gas in the tank of the lawn mower. After Cory mowed the lawn, there was 0.6 gallon of gas in the tank of the lawn mower. How much gas did Cory use mowing the lawn?

   A $\frac{3}{8}$ gallon

   B $\frac{2}{5}$ gallon

   C $\frac{6}{10}$ gallon

   D $\frac{4}{9}$ gallon

10. Carrie ate $1\frac{1}{3}$ apple tarts, Mark ate $2\frac{1}{4}$ apple tarts. Altogether, how many apple tarts did they eat?

    A $3\frac{3}{4}$

    B $3\frac{2}{3}$

    C $3\frac{7}{12}$

    D $3\frac{1}{2}$

11. Tony had $6\frac{7}{8}$ gallons of paint. If he and three friends each used $1\frac{3}{16}$ gallons to paint different sections of Tony's house, how much paint does Tony have left?

    A $5\frac{15}{19}$ gallons

    B $4\frac{3}{4}$ gallons

    C $4\frac{1}{2}$ gallons

    D $2\frac{1}{8}$ gallons

12. Heather drank $\frac{44}{64}$ gallon of water on Tuesday. If Heather drinks the same amount of water for six days, **about** how much water will she have consumed?

    A 2 gallons

    B 3 gallons

    C 4 gallons

    D 7 gallons

13. Which list of numbers is in order from **least** to **greatest**?

    A $0.468, \frac{3}{12}, 0.125, \frac{1}{5}$

    B $\frac{1}{5}, 0.125, 0.468, \frac{3}{12}$

    C $0.125, \frac{1}{5}, \frac{3}{12}, 0.468$

    D $\frac{3}{12}, 0.468, \frac{1}{5}, 0.125$

Open-Ended Items

14. Miguel hikes the Yellow Trail $4\frac{1}{8}$ miles to a lake. He can return by the same route or by one of three other trails. The Red Trail is $4\frac{1}{6}$ miles long, the Green Trail is $4\frac{1}{3}$ miles long, and the Blue Trail is $4\frac{1}{2}$ miles long.

A. Miguel decides to take the Red Trail back instead of the Yellow Trail. How much **shorter** is the Yellow Trail than the Red Trail? Explain your answer.

B. After walking $\frac{2}{3}$ of the Red Trail, Miguel realized that he forgot his towel at the lake. To the nearest tenth of a mile, how far is Miguel from the lake? Explain your answer.

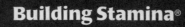
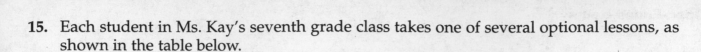

15. Each student in Ms. Kay's seventh grade class takes one of several optional lessons, as shown in the table below.

Type of Lesson	Number of Students
Piano	7
Dance	8
Percussion	5
Guitar	4
Gymnastics	6

A. What fraction of the class studies a musical instrument? Explain your answer.

15. Continued.

B. What fraction of the class studies dance or percussion? Explain your answer.

C. What fraction of the students do not take percussion lessons? Explain your answer.

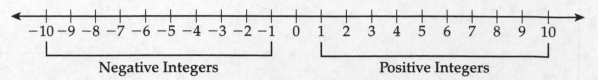

Assessment Anchors/Eligible Content: M7.A.1.2.2 Locate/identify decimals, fractions, mixed numbers and/or integers on a number line (a mix of these number forms may be on the same number line).

Academic Standards: 2.1.8.F

The **integers** are the set of positive and negative whole numbers, and zero.

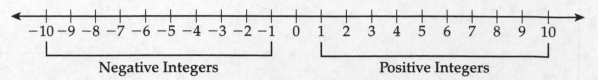

On a horizontal number line, **positive integers** lie to the right of zero. They are greater than zero, and may be written with or without the positive sign (+). Their opposites, the **negative integers**, lie to the left of zero. They are less than zero and must be written with the negative sign (−). Zero is neither positive nor negative. A number line can help you compare and order integers.

Guided Instruction

Problem   Faye has a debt of $24. What integer can represent Faye's debt in dollars?

Step 1   Determine which words in the problem can be represented by an integer.

a debt of $24

Step 2   Decide whether to write a positive or negative sign.

A debt is _____ than 0 dollars.

So a debt of $24 can be represented by _____ dollars.

Solution   What integer can represent Faye's debt in dollars? _____

Another Example

Use a number line to order the integers −4, 2, −2, 3, and 1 from least to greatest.

Use a number line.

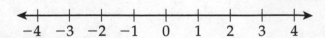

Plot each integer on the number line.

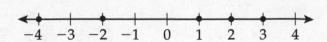

Numbers increase in value from left to right on the number line.
Write the numbers in order from least to greatest.   −4, −2, 1, 2, 3

Apply the Pennsylvania Academic Standards

Write an integer to represent each situation.

1. a profit of $7 selling T-shirts

_____

2. a temperature 11 degrees Fahrenheit below zero

_____

3. 250 feet above sea level

_____

4. a 3-foot drop

_____

Use the number line below to order the integers from least to greatest.

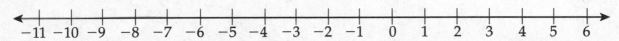

5. −10, −3, −7, −11, −9, 4

_____

6. 0, −4, 3, 2, 6, −2, −5

_____

Compare the integers. Use > or <.

7. −4 ◯ 4

8. 100 ◯ −99

9. −264 ◯ −265

10. 16 ◯ 19

11. 0 ◯ −5

12. −1 ◯ −24

13. −6 ◯ 2

14. −29 ◯ 30

Solve each problem.

15. What integer is neither negative *nor* positive? _____

16. If 5 represents 5 years from now, what does the opposite represent?

_____

17. Which of the following numbers are *not* integers? Explain.

$-5, 2.6, -\frac{3}{4}, 7, -152$

_____

_____

_____

PSSA Practice Directions: Read each question. Then circle the letter for the best answer.

1. Use the number line below to help answer the question.

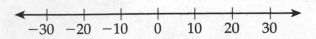

If the integers −10, −25, 10, 25, and −1 are listed in order from **greatest** to **least**, which integer will come **first** in the list?

A   −25

B   −10

C   10

D   25

2. Look at the number line below.

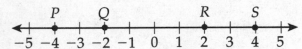

Which point on the number line could represent four feet below sea level?

A   point P

B   point Q

C   point R

D   point S

3. Use the number line below to help answer the question.

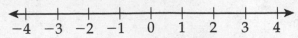

Which number is **not** an integer?

A   −20   B   −3.5

C   0   D   2

4. Which integer would come next in the pattern?

Hint: Use a number line to help you.

−7, −4, −1, 2, 5, . . .

A   12

B   10

C   8

D   6

Use the number line below to answer questions 5–6.

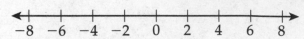

5. Which statement is **not** true?

A   −1 is less than 0.

B   −5 is less than −4.

C   −6 is greater than −5.

D   2 is greater than −2.

6. Which list of integers is ordered from **least** to **greatest**?

A   −2, −4, −7, −8

B   8, 7, 0, −5

C   2, 4, −7, −8

D   −8, −7, 0, 5

Focus on the Pennsylvania Academic Standards

Lesson 16   Absolute Value and the Number Line

Assessment Anchors/Eligible Content: M7.A.1.2.2 Locate/identify decimals, fractions, mixed numbers and/or integers on a number line (a mix of these number forms may be on the same number line).

Academic Standards: 2.1.8.F

The **absolute value** of a number is the distance from zero on the number line. So you can use a number line to find the absolute value of a number. The symbol for absolute value is | |. For example, $|-5|$ is read *the absolute value of negative five.*

Guided Instruction

Problem   What is the absolute value of 6? What is $|-6|$?

Step 1   Draw a number line.

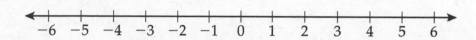

Step 2   Count the units from 0 to 6.

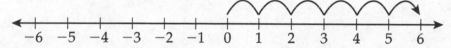

The absolute value of 6 is _____.

Step 3   Count the units from 0 to -6.

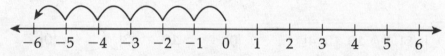

$|-6| =$ _____

Solution   What is the absolute value of 6? _____

What is $|-6|$? _____

Another Example

Add. $|-7| + |4|$

To find the sum of the absolute value of -7 and the absolute value of 4, first find the absolute value of each number.	$|-7| = 7$ $|4| = 4$
Rewrite the expression.	$7 + 4$
Add.	$7 + 4 =$ _____

Apply the Pennsylvania Academic Standards

Find the value of each expression.

1. $|-5|$

_____

2. $-|20|$

_____

3. $|-1,650|$

_____

4. $|27|$

_____

5. $-|-46|$

_____

6. $|0|$

_____

7. $|25|$

_____

8. $|-221|$

_____

Evaluate.

9. $|-15| + |-5|$

_____

10. $|12| - |3|$

_____

11. $|-21| - |10|$

_____

12. $|-16| + |-1| - |-4|$

_____

Compare. Use >, < or = to complete each statement.

13. $|-6|$ ◯ $|7|$

14. 10 ◯ $|-10|$

15. -2 ◯ $|-2|$

16. $|0|$ ◯ 0

17. $|-8|$ ◯ $|-5|$

18. $|-4|$ ◯ $|0|$

19. $-|3|$ ◯ $|0|$

20. $|-9|$ ◯ $-|-9|$

Solve each problem.

21. The absolute value of a number is never _____.

22. What is the absolute value of negative four minus the absolute value of negative one? _____

23. Debbie simplified the expression $|-3| + 13$. Her result was 10. Explain why Debbie's result was *not* correct.

_____

_____

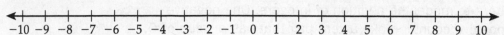

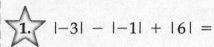

Directions: Read each question. Then circle the letter for the best answer.

Use the number line to help answer each question.

$$-10 \quad -9 \quad -8 \quad -7 \quad -6 \quad -5 \quad -4 \quad -3 \quad -2 \quad -1 \quad 0 \quad 1 \quad 2 \quad 3 \quad 4 \quad 5 \quad 6 \quad 7 \quad 8 \quad 9 \quad 10$$

1. $|-3| - |-1| + |6| =$

   A   2

   B   4

   C   8

   D   10

2. Which two numbers each have an absolute value of 12?

   A   −12 and 0

   B   0 and 12

   C   −12 and 12

   D   −144 and 144

3. $|-6| + |-10| =$

   A   16

   B   4

   C   −10

   D   −16

4. Which statement is **not** true?

   A $|-2| = |2|$

   B $|-4| > |0|$

   C $|19| < |-20|$

   D $|-3| < -|-2|$

5. Jacques's father asked him to evaluate $|-8| - |-2|$. Then he asked Jacques to evaluate $|12| + |-3|$. Finally he asked Jacques to add his two answers together. What was the final answer?

   A   −21

   B   −9

   C   9

   D   21

6. $|16| - |-12| =$

   A   28

   B   4

   C   −5

   D   −28

7. What is $-|-5|$?

   A   −5

   B   −4

   C   4

   D   5

Focus on the Pennsylvania Academic Standards

Lesson 17   Add Integers

Assessment Anchors/Eligible Content: M7.A.3.2.2 Solve problems involving addition and subtraction of integers.
Academic Standards: 2.1.8.F, 2.2.8.B, 2.4.8.B, 2.4.8.D

You can use counters to model the addition of integers. One negative counter and one positive counter make a zero pair that has a value of 0.

one negative = −1   (−)

one positive = 1 (+)

(+) (−)
$1 + (-1) = 0$
Zero Pair

Guided Instruction

Problem

Alfonso is playing a game. In each round of the game, he either loses or wins points. He is keeping track of his points using positive and negative counters. The positive counters represent the points he wins, and the negative counters represent the points he loses. What is Alfonso's score after the two rounds?

Round 1   Round 2
(+)   (−)
(+)   (−)
         (−)

Use the picture to solve the problem.

Step 1   Determine Alfonso's points in each round.

What is his score in Round 1? _____   What is his score in Round 2? _____

Step 2   Form zero pairs by circling 1 negative and 1 positive counter.

How many zero pairs are there? _____

What counter is left? _____

What is the value of that counter? _____

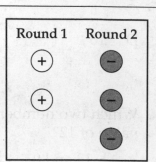

Step 3   Write an equation to represent the addition.

$2 + (-3) =$ _____

Solution   What is Alfonso's score after the two rounds? _____

Other Examples

A. Find the sum of −1 and −3.

To add two integers with the same sign, add their absolute values. Use their sign for the sign of the sum.

$|-1| = 1$ $|-3| = 3$ $1 + 3 = 4$

So $-1 + (-3) = -4$.

B. Find the sum of −3 and 2.

To add two integers with different signs, find the difference between their absolute values. Use the sign of the greater absolute value for the sign of the sum.

$|-3| = 3$ $|2| = 2$ $3 - 2 = 1$

$|-3| > |2|$, so $-3 + 2 = -1$.

Apply the Pennsylvania Academic Standards

Draw a picture to find each sum.

1. $-5 + (-2) =$ _____

2. $-6 + 1 =$ _____

3. $7 + (-3) =$ _____

4. $5 + (-6) =$ _____

Tell whether each sum will be positive, negative, or zero.

5. $-9 + 9$

6. $-2 + (-6)$

7. $-4 + 8$

8. $3 + (-10)$

_____

_____

_____

_____

Use the rules for adding integers to find each sum.

9. $-4 + (-6) =$ _____

10. $-9 + 5 =$ _____

11. $-1 + 9 =$ _____

12. $7 + (-11) =$ _____

13. $-9 + 18 =$ _____

14. $-8 + 8 =$ _____

15. $-20 + 10 =$ _____

16. $9 + (-17) =$ _____

17. $0 + (-12) =$ _____

18. $-14 + 3 =$ _____

19. $18 + (-5) =$ _____

20. $-15 + (-20) =$ _____

Solve each problem.

21. The temperature at 6 A.M. was $-5°$C. By 9 A.M. the temperature had risen 8 degrees. What was the temperature at 9 A.M.? Explain your answer.

_____

22. The price of a stock opened at $50.00. It fell $6.00, rose $3.00, and then fell another $2.00. What was the closing price of the stock? Explain your answer.

_____

Directions: Read each question. Then circle the letter for the best answer.

1. Lila withdrew $13.00 from the bank. Later that day, she deposited $8.00 into the bank. Which expression represents her banking activity for the day?

   A   13 + 8   B   −13 + 8

   C   13 − 8   D   −13 − 8

2. A submarine at −20 feet descends 30 feet. Which represents the location of the submarine after the descent?

   A   10 feet   B   −20 feet

   C   −10 feet   D   −50 feet

3. At 6 A.M., the temperature was −5°F. By noon, the temperature had risen 25°F. What was the temperature at noon?

   A   −30°F   B   20°F

   C   −20°F   D   30°F

4. Which addition expression is modeled by the counters below?

   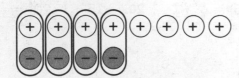

   A   4 + (−8)

   B   −4 + (−8)

   C   −8 + (−4)

   D   8 + (−4)

5. Which of the following expression do **not** have a negative value?

   A   −12 + 6

   B   7 + (−9)

   C   −8 + (−8)

   D   4 + (−4)

6. Which equation is modeled below?

   A   12 + 5 = 17

   B   12 + (−5) = 7

   C   12 − 7 = 5

   D   −12 + 5 = −7

7. Allison had 19 dollars. She spent 11 d at the movies and was then paid 15 d for doing work for her mother. How much money did she have after her m paid her?

   A   −7 dollars

   B   15 dollars

   C   23 dollars

   D   45 dollars

Apply the Pennsylvania Academic Standards

Draw a picture to find each sum.

1. $-5 + (-2) =$ _____

2. $-6 + 1 =$ _____

3. $7 + (-3) =$ _____

4. $5 + (-6) =$ _____

Tell whether each sum will be positive, negative, or zero.

5. $-9 + 9$

6. $-2 + (-6)$

7. $-4 + 8$

8. $3 + (-10)$

_____   _____   _____   _____

Use the rules for adding integers to find each sum.

9. $-4 + (-6) =$ _____

10. $-9 + 5 =$ _____

11. $-1 + 9 =$ _____

12. $7 + (-1) =$ _____

13. $-9 + 18 =$ _____

14. $-8 + 8 =$ _____

15. $-20 + 10 =$ _____

16. $9 + (-17) =$ _____

17. $0 + (-12) =$ _____

18. $-14 + 3 =$ _____

19. $18 + (-5) =$ _____

20. $-15 + (-20) =$ _____

Solve each problem.

21. The temperature at 6 A.M. was $-5°C$. By 9 A.M. the temperature had risen 8 degrees. What was the temperature at 9 A.M.? Explain your answer.

_____

22. The price of a stock opened at $50.00. It fell $6.00, rose $3.00, and then fell another $2.00. What was the closing price of the stock? Explain your answer.

_____

PSSA Practice Directions: Read each question. Then circle the letter for the best answer.

1. Lila withdrew $13.00 from the bank. Later that day, she deposited $8.00 into the bank. Which expression represents her banking activity for the day?

   A $13 + 8$

   B $-13 + 8$

   C $13 - 8$

   D $-13 - 8$

2. A submarine at -20 feet descends 30 feet. Which represents the location of the submarine after the descent?

   A 10 feet

   B -20 feet

   C -10 feet

   D -50 feet

3. At 6 A.M., the temperature was $-5°$F. By noon, the temperature had risen $25°$F. What was the temperature at noon?

   A $-30°$F

   B $20°$F

   C $-20°$F

   D $30°$F

4. Which addition expression is modeled by the counters below?

   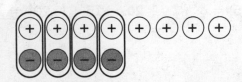

   A $4 + (-8)$

   B $-4 + (-8)$

   C $-8 + (-4)$

   D $8 + (-4)$

5. Which of the following expression does **not** have a negative value?

   A $-12 + 6$

   B $7 + (-9)$

   C $-8 + (-8)$

   D $4 + (-4)$

6. Which equation is modeled below?

   A $12 + 5 = 17$

   B $12 + (-5) = 7$

   C $12 - 7 = 5$

   D $-12 + 5 = -7$

7. Allison had 19 dollars. She spent 11 dollars at the movies and was then paid 15 dollars for doing work for her mother. How much money did she have after her mom paid her?

   A -7 dollars

   B 15 dollars

   C 23 dollars

   D 45 dollars

   Measuring Up® to the Pennsylvania Academic Standards

Assessment Anchors/Eligible Content: M7.A.1.2.2 Locate/identify decimals, fractions, mixed numbers and/or integers on a number line (a mix of these number forms may be on the same number line).

M7.A.3.2.2 Solve problems involving addition and subtraction of integers.

Academic Standards: 2.1.8.F, 2.2.8.B, 2.4.8.B, 2.4.8.D

The **opposite** of a number is a number that is the same distance from zero on a number line as the given number, but in the opposite direction. For example, −4 and 4 are opposites.

To model the subtraction of integers, you can use a number line. You can also use the following rule to subtract integers: To subtract an integer, add its opposite.

Guided Instruction

Problem   At 6 P.M. the temperature is −2°F. At 8 P.M. the temperature is 3°F. What is the change in temperature from 6 P.M. to 8 P.M.?

Use a number line to solve 3 − (−2).

Step 1   Begin at zero. Move to the right 3 units to show 3.

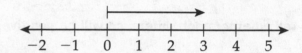

Step 2   To add −2, you would move to the left 2 units. So *to subtract −2, do the opposite*, and move to the right 2 units.

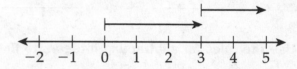

Step 3   What is the value on the number line? _____

So 3 − (−2) = _____.

Solution   What is the change in temperature from 6 P.M. to 8 P.M.?

_____

Another Example

Subtract. −4 − (−1)

To subtract, add the opposite.   −4 − (−1) = −4 + (1) = −4 + 1

Find the sum. Use the rules for |−4| = 4
the addition of integers. |1| = 1
                                         4 − 1 = 3

                                         So −4 + 1 = _____,
                                         and −4 − (−1) = _____.

Apply the Pennsylvania Academic Standards

Draw a picture to find each difference

1. $2 - 6 =$ _____

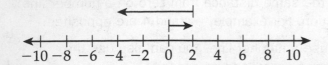

2. $-2 - (-6) =$ _____

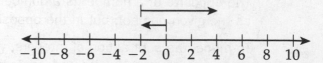

3. $2 - (-6) =$ _____

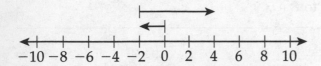

4. $-2 - 6 =$ _____

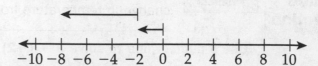

Tell whether each difference will be positive, negative, or zero.

5. $-8 - 8$

_____

6. $-2 - (-3)$

_____

7. $-4 - (-4)$

_____

8. $5 - (-5)$

_____

Use the rules for subtracting integers to find each difference.

9. $-4 - (-8) =$ ____

10. $-9 - 3 =$ ____

11. $-2 - 9 =$ ____

12. $7 - (-5) =$ ____

13. $-9 - 4 =$ ____

14. $-6 - 6 =$ ____

15. $7 - 10 =$ ____

16. $9 - (-8) =$ ____

17. $0 - (-10) =$ ____

18. $-3 - (-3) =$ ____

19. $4 - (-5) =$ ____

20. $-15 - (-20) =$ __

Solve each problem.

21. A woman got on the elevator on the fourth floor. The elevator went down 2 floors, then up 12 floors. The woman got off the elevator. On which floor did the woman exit the elevator? Explain how you found your answer.

_____

22. At 6 P.M., the temperature was 16°C. By midnight, the temperature had dropped 18 degrees. What was the temperature at midnight? Explain how you found your answer.

_____

 Measuring Up® to the Pennsylvania Academic Standards

PSSA Practice Directions: Read each question. Then circle the letter for the best answer.

1. Kirsten added 8 beads to her bracelet on Monday. She lost 6 beads on Tuesday. What was the net gain or loss?

A   14

B   2

C   −2

D   −14

2. Which expression has a negative value?

A   4 − (−4)

B   −5 − 3

C   3 − (−5)

D   5 − (−3)

3. At midnight, the temperature was 8°F. By 4 A.M., the temperature had dropped 14 degrees. What was the temperature at 4 A.M.?

A   −14°F

B   −6°F

C   6°F

D   22°F

4. Which expression has a positive value?

A   −8 − 5

B   8 − (−5)

C   5 − 8

D   −5 − (−5)

 5. Which of the following equations is **not** true?

A   −2 − 6 = −8

B   2 − 7 = −5

C   −2 − (−6) = −4

D   −6 − (−7) = 1

6. Which equation is modeled below?

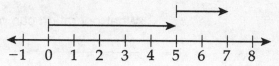

A   5 − 2 = 3

B   7 − 2 = 5

C   2 − 7 = −5

D   5 − (−2) = 7

7. A quarterback ran the football for a gain of 55 yards. A penalty moved the ball back 10 yards. Which integer represents how many yards were gained on the play?

A   65

B   45

C   −10

D   −45

Assessment Anchors/Eligible Content: M7.A.3.2.1 Solve problems involving operations ($+$, $-$, $\times$, $\div$) of whole numbers, decimals, fractions, or mixed numbers (straight computation or word problems).

M7.A.3.2.2 Solve problems involving addition and subtraction of integers.

Academic Standards: 2.1.8.F, 2.2.8.B, 2.4.8.B, 2.4.8.D

Sometimes you have to use more than one operation to solve a problem.

Guided Instruction

Problem

Over a 6-hour period, the temperature dropped from 36°F to -12°F. What integer represents the average number of degrees the temperature dropped each hour?

First you need to find the total temperature change. Then you must find the average number of degrees the temperature dropped per hour.

Step 1 To find the average change in temperature per hour, you need to make two calculations.

What operation can you use to find the total change in temperature?

_____

What operation can you use to find the average temperature change each hour? _____

Step 2 Use the operations to solve the problem.

Write an expression that shows the change in temperature. _____

By how many degrees did the temperature change? _____

How many hours did it take for the temperature to change that much?

_____

Write an expression to find the average change in temperature per hour. _____

What was the average change in temperature per hour? _____

Solution

What integer represents the average number of degrees the temperature dropped per hour? _____

Measuring Up® to the Pennsylvania Academic Standards

Apply the Pennsylvania Academic Standards

Write the operation(s) needed to solve each problem. Then solve each problem.

1. This week, Sara spent 4 hours at dance practice. Last week she spent half as long at dance practice. How many hours fewer did she spend at dance practice last week?

Work Space

_____

2. Zach buys 3 pounds of apples for $0.98 per pound, 2 pounds of grapes for $1.79 per pound, and 1 bag of oranges for $2.59. How much does he spend on the fruit in all?

_____

3. Setsuko had $256.00 in her account at the beginning of the month. The table below shows the 4 transactions she made during the month. What was her balance at the end of the month?

Date	Transaction
10/8	−$32.00
10/17	$45.00
10/23	−$14.00
10/29	−$7.00

_____

4. A bookshelf is 15 inches long. There are 8 books in a set of adventure books that are each $\frac{5}{6}$-inch thick. If Pablo puts the set of books on the shelf, how much space will be left for other books?

_____

5. A scuba diver swimming at a depth of 25 feet below sea level dives down an additional 48 feet. What integer represents the total depth the diver reaches?

_____

PSSA Practice Directions: Read each question. Then circle the letter for the best answer.

1. The football team starts the play at the 15-yard line. In three plays, they lose 12 yards, gain 7 yards, and then lose another 4 yards. What is the team's position relative to where they started?

   A   −9 yards

   B   −6 yards

   C   −1 yard

   D   5 yards

2. Philip wants to make 3 pounds of trail mix. He has $\frac{3}{4}$ pound almonds, $1\frac{1}{8}$ pounds peanuts, and $\frac{1}{2}$ pound raisins. How much dried fruit does he need to complete the trail mix?

   A $\frac{3}{4}$ pound

   B $\frac{5}{8}$ pound

   C $\frac{3}{8}$ pound

   D $\frac{1}{2}$ pound

 3. Jared raised $8.50 for the animal shelter. Vanessa raised half as much as Jared. Rosa raised $2.25 more than Jared. How much did they raise altogether?

   A $6.25

   B $12.75

   C $15.00

   D $23.50

4. The temperature dropped from 16°F to −12°F over a 4-hour period. Which integer represents the average temperature change per hour?

   A   −28°F

   B   −7°F

   C   −4°F

   D   4°F

 5. A cab company charges $3.50 for the first mile traveled and then $0.85 for each additional mile. How much would it cost to travel 8 miles in the cab?

   A $4.35

   B $9.45

   C $10.30

   D $12.35

 6. From the trailhead, Kylie hiked 1.4 miles to the first overlook. Then she hiked 0.7 mile to the fork and another 1.25 miles to the summit. She hiked back the same way she had come. How many miles did Kylie hike?

   A   1.65 miles

   B   3.35 miles

   C   4.30 miles

   D   6.70 miles

Directions: Read each question. Then circle the letter for the best answer.

1. Use the number line below to help answer the question.

   If the integers $-3, -2, 1, 5,$ and -4 are listed in order from least to greatest, which integer will come **first** in the list?

   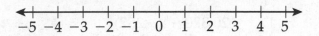

   A -1

   B 1

   C -3

   D 5

2. Catalina's teacher has challenged the students to compare integers. Which of the following is **not** a true statement?

   A $-4 > -5$

   B $3 < -2$

   C $5 > -7$

   D $-3 < 0$

3. Sandy was playing a game with friends. She scored 3 on the first round and -4 on the second round. What was her score after the two rounds?

   A -7

   B -1

   C $+1$

   D $+7$

4. $|7| + |-17| =$

   A -10

   B -1

   C 10

   D 24

5. Ms. Dederman asked Tom to find the value of $|-7| - |-2|$. Then she asked Tom to find the value of $|11| + |-4|$. Which of the following will Tom get when he adds the two values?

   A -20

   B 5

   C 7

   D 20

6. Which explains how to find the absolute value of -10?

   A   Remove the negative sign. Write 10.

   B   Write -10.

   C   Add 10 to -10. Write 0.

   D   Take half the distance between -10 and 0 on the number line. Write 5.

7. Which statement is **not** true?

   A   –3 is less than 0.

   B   –1 is greater than –2.

   C   0 is greater than –5.

   D   –1 is less than –5.

8. Which two numbers each have an absolute value of 17?

   A   −17 and 0

   B   −17 and 17

   C   0 and 17

   D   −289 and 289

9. Which of the expressions is equivalent to the following expression?

   $$-7 - (-2)$$

   A   −7 + (−2)

   B   −7 + 2

   C   7 − 2

   D   −2 − 7

10. The temperature outside is −5°F. The wind is blowing at 15 miles per hour, which makes the wind chill feel 21°F **colder** than the temperature. What temperature does the wind chill feel like?

    A   −26°F

    B   −20°F

    C   10°F

    D   16°F

11. Alaska's Mt. McKinley is 20,320 feet above sea level. California's Death Valley is 282 feet below sea level. Which expression could be used to find the difference between their heights?

    A   20,320 − 282

    B   20,320 − (−282)

    C   −20,320 − (−282)

    D   −20,320 + (−282)

12. Which of the following numbers is **not** an integer?

    A   −2.4   B   −1

    C   3   D   16

13. What is the sum of the expression shown below?

    $$3 + (-4) + |-11|$$

    A   −18

    B   −12

    C   4

    D   10

14. The high temperature was 3°F on Monday, −6°F on Tuesday, and −2°F on Wednesday. What was the difference between the **greatest** high temperature and the **least** high temperature during those three days?

    A   4°F

    B   5°F

    C   9°F

    D   11°F

Open-Ended Items

15. The table below shows the locations and depths of four of the lowest points on the Earth.

Location of Depths Below Sea Level

Continent	Location	Depth
Africa	Lake Assal	−156 meters
Asia	Dead Sea	−411 meters
Europe	Caspian Sea	−28 meters
North America	Death Valley	−86 meters

A. List the continents in order from greatest to least distance below sea level. Explain your answer.

B. How much farther below sea level is the Dead Sea than the Caspian Sea? Show your work.

16. Michelle had $326.00 in her account at the beginning of a 30-day month. The table shows five transactions she made during the month.

Date	Transaction
June 1	−$42.00
June 10	$36.00
June 20	−$105.00
June 25	$95.00
June 30	−$65.00

A. What was Michelle's balance at the end of the month? Show your work.

B. What is the total amount of money Michelle withdrew from her account during this month? Show your work.

16. *Continued.*

C. If the data in the table represents Michelle's typical spending habits for each month, about how much to the nearest dollar does Michelle spend on average per day? Explain your answer.

Assessment Anchors/Eligible Content: M7.D.2.2.1 Identify expressions, equations or inequalities that model mathematical situations (using whole numbers or decimals, no more than two operations and one variable).

Academic Standards: 2.8.8.C

A **variable** is a letter or symbol that represents a quantity.

A **coefficient** is the number by which a variable is multiplied.

A **constant** is a symbol or number whose value does not change.

An **expression** is a mathematical phrase that may include constants, variables, and operation symbols.

> x is a variable.
> $24x + 3$ is an expression.
> 24 is the coefficient of x.
> 24 and 3 are constants.

Sometimes you need to write and evaluate an algebraic expression to solve a problem. To evaluate an expression, substitute an appropriate number for each variable and perform the indicated operations.

Guided Instruction

Problem

After Cassie bought 2 audio cassettes for 3 dollars each, she had 8 dollars left. To keep track of her spending, she wrote "cost of 2 audio cassettes plus 8." What algebraic expression represents what Cassie wrote? How much money did Cassie have before she made her purchase?

Step 1   Choose a letter to represent the variable in the expression.

Let c represent the cost of 1 audio cassette.

Step 2   Decide which operations you need to perform. Then write an expression using these operations.

2 times c plus 8

Times means _____.

Plus means _____.

____ • c + ____ or ____ c + ____

Step 3   To evaluate the expression, substitute the given value for the variable and perform the indicated operations.

$2 • 3 + 8 =$ ____

Solution

What algebraic expression represents what Cassie wrote? _____

How much money did she have before she made her purchase? _____

Another Example

Write an expression for the value in cents of x quarters and y nickels.
Let $x = 3$ and $y = 7$, and evaluate the expression.
A quarter is worth 25 cents and a nickel is worth 5 cents.
Write $25x$ to represent the value of the quarters and $5y$ to represent the value of the nickels.
Use the expression $25x + 5y$ to represent the total value.
Substitute 3 for x and 7 for y to evaluate the expression.

$$25x + 5y = 25 • 3 + 5 • 7 = 75 + 35 = 110$$

So the value of x quarters and y nickels, when $x = 3$ and $y = 7$, is 110 cents.

Apply the Pennsylvania Academic Standards

Write an expression for each phrase.

1. eight increased by a number *n*

2. the product of a number *n* and a number *d*

3. the quotient of a number *n* and four

_____   _____   _____

Match the expression to the phrase and write the correct letter.

4. $6 - n$ _____

5. $2n \cdot c$ _____

6. $n - 6$ _____

7. $n + c + 2$ _____

8. $\frac{n}{6}$ _____

    a. 6 less than a number *n*

    b. 2 more than a number *n* plus a number *c*

    c. the quotient of a number *n* and 6

    d. twice a number *n* times a number *c*

    e. 6 decreased by a number *n*

Evaluate each expression.

9. $x - 12$, for $x = 51$

10. $\frac{144}{n}$, for $n = 3$

11. $6.3 + a + r$, for $a = 1.7$ and $r = 2$

_____   _____   _____

Solve each problem.

12. Phil told his aunt that he likes to collect stamps. "I have 4 South African stamps, 20 French stamps, some Spanish stamps, and a number of stamps from Croatia," he said. Write an expression to show the total number of stamps that Phil has.

_____

13. The sign in the bookstore window said, "Half-price sale! Buy any book in the store for half its regular price!" Write an expression to show the sale price of a book. What is the sale price of a book that cost $12.50 before the sale? Explain your answer.

_____

14. Movie tickets cost $5 for students and $7 for adults. Write an expression for the cost of tickets for a group of students and adults. Identify the constants and the variables in your expression and explain your choices.

_____

_____

_____

1. Which expression represents the phrase "ten less than a number *n*"?

   A $\frac{n}{10}$

   B $n - 10$

   C $\frac{10}{n}$

   D $10 - n$

2. Which phrase represents the expression $n + 5$?

   A the product of a number and 5

   B the quotient of a number and 5

   C a number increased by the constant 5

   D 5 times a number

3. Every CD at Melody Music is the same price. If one CD costs $9, what is the cost of three CDs?

   A $12

   B $21

   C $24

   D $27

4. Which expression uses 7 as a coefficient?

   A $7n$

   B $\frac{n}{7}$

   C $n - 7$

   D $7 + n$

5. To go to school, Janet walks two more blocks than Barbara walks. If Barbara walks eight blocks to school, how many blocks does Janet walk to school?

   A 16

   B 12

   C 10

   D 4

6. Hank caught six fewer fish than Sam. Which expression represents the number of fish Sam caught?

   A $h - 6$

   B $6h$

   C $h + 6$

   D $\frac{h}{6}$

Assessment Anchors/Eligible Content: M7.A.2.1.1 Use the order of operations to simplify numerical expressions (may use parentheses, brackets, $+$, $-$, $\times$, $\div$, squares up to 10^2 and cubes up to 4^3; whole numbers only).

M7.D.2.1.2 Use substitution of one and/or two variables to simplify expressions (whole numbers only — use order of operations).

M7.D.2.2.1 Identify expressions, equations or inequalities that model mathematical situations (using whole numbers or decimals, no more than two operations and one variable).

Academic Standards: 2.1.8.B, 2.1.8.E, 2.8.8.C

A power is an expression of the form x^n. An **exponent** tells how many times the **base** is used as a factor. For example, in the expression 10^2, the base is 10 and the exponent is 2. So $10^2 = 10 \times 10$, or 100.

The Order of Operations tells you how to simplify and evaluate expressions with more than one operation:

1. Work within the parentheses.
2. Work with exponents.
3. Multiply and divide from left to right.
4. Add and subtract from left to right.

Guided Instruction

Problem What is the value of the expression $12 + 4 \div 2 \cdot (5 - 3)^2$?

Follow the order of operations.

Step 1 Work within the parentheses.

$$12 + 4 \div 2 \cdot (5 - 3)^2$$
$$= 12 + 4 \div 2 \cdot (\underline{})^2$$

Step 2 Work with exponents.

$$12 + 4 \div 2 \cdot (2)^2$$
$$= 12 + 4 \div 2 \cdot \underline{}$$

Step 3 Multiply and divide from left to right.

$$12 + 4 \div 2 \cdot 4$$
$$= 12 + \underline{} \cdot \underline{}$$
$$= 12 + \underline{}$$

Step 4 Add and subtract from left to right.

$$12 + 8 = \underline{}$$

Solution What is the value of the expression, $12 + 4 \div 2 \cdot (5 - 3)^2$? $\underline{}$

Another Example

Evaluate the expression: $18 \div 3^2 + 4(a + b)$, for $a = 3$ and $b = 6$.

Substitute given values for the variables. $18 \div 3^2 + 4(a + b) = 18 \div 3^2 + 4(3 + 6)$

Work within the parentheses. $= 18 \div 3^2 + 4(9)$

Work with exponents. $= 18 \div 9 + 4(9)$

Multiply and divide from left to right. $= 2 + 36$

Add and subtract from left to right. $= 38$

So $18 \div 3^2 + 4(a + b) = 38$, for $a = 3$ and $b = 6$.

Apply the Pennsylvania Academic Standards

Simplify each expression.

1. $3 + 2(4 \cdot 3)$

2. $12 - 15 \div 3$

3. $6 + 7^2$

4. $64 \div 8 + 8$

_____

_____

_____

_____

5. $(22 + 14) \div 6^2$

6. $(3 + 5)^2 \div 4$

7. $4 \cdot (24 \div 4)^2$

8. $12^2 + (145 - 5) \cdot 3$

_____

_____

_____

_____

Evaluate each expression for $a = 3$, and $b = 2$.

9. $2a + 5b$

10. $100 - 20b$

11. $4^2 \div 4 + a + b$

12. $\frac{7a}{3} \cdot (4 - b)$

_____

_____

_____

_____

13. $a^2 + 9(a + 6) - 10$

14. $\frac{72}{9} + 3(b + 4)$

15. $(4 + a) \div (3 + b^2)$

16. $\frac{4b + 10}{3^3}$

_____

_____

_____

_____

Solve each problem.

17. During their vacation, Jim, Hank, and Phil took turns driving. Jim drove 50 miles. Hank drove 10 miles less than Jim. Phil drove twice as many miles as both Jim and Hank. Write and evaluate an expression for the total number of miles they drove.

_____

18. Nia had 6^2 boxes of cards. She gave away 10 boxes and then got 4 boxes from a friend. Each box contains 8 cards. How many cards does Nia have now? Show your work.

_____

_____

19. Jules has $48.00 in her savings account. She works 40 hours each week and makes $7.00 per hour. If she works for 4 weeks and puts $\frac{1}{4}$ of the money she earns into her saving account, how much will she have in her account? Show your work.

_____

_____

PSSA Practice Directions: Read each problem. Then circle the letter for the best answer.

1. Which expression equals 15?

    A $2 \cdot 12 \div 3 + 2$

    B $2 + 6 \cdot 2 - 3$

    C $12 + 3 \cdot 2 \div 2$

    D $6 + 6 \cdot 2 + 1$

2. If $u = 4$, then what is the value of $3(a + 2) - 6$?

    A   15

    B   12

    C   10

    D   6

3. Susan bought 2 books for $12.00 each, a calendar for $6.50, and a bookmark that cost half as much as the calendar. How much did Susan spend?

    A $43

    B $35.50

    C $34

    D $33.75

4. Which statement is **not** true?

    A $12(3 + 5) = 96$

    B $(2^3 + 6) \div 2 = 7$

    C $8 - 32 \div 8 + 2 = 2$

    D $25 \cdot 3 + 2 = 77$

5. Which expression equals 18?

    A $8 \cdot 3 - 4 \div 2$

    B $9 \cdot 2 + 3 - 1$

    C $6 + 3 \cdot 2 + 3$

    D $4^2 + 8 \div 2 - 2$

6. If $x = 4$ and $y = 2$, what is the value of $x(3x - 2y) + y$?

    A   46

    B   34

    C   10

    D   5

7. Mark has forty-six coins. Three of the coins are pennies, 10 are nickels, 23 are dimes, and 10 are quarters. Which of the expressions shown can be used to find the amount of money that Mark has?

    A $3(0.01) + 10(0.05) + 23(0.10) + 10(0.25)$

    B $3(0.01) + 10(0.10) + 23(0.05) + 10(0.25)$

    C $3(0.10) + 10(0.01) + 23(0.25) + 10(0.05)$

    D $3(0.25) + 10(0.05) + 23(0.10) + 10(0.01)$

8. If $a = 3$ and $b = 6$, what is the value of $a^3 \cdot (b + 2)$?

    A   24

    B   72

    C   164

    D   216

Lesson 22 Use Properties to Simplify Expressions

Assessment Anchors/Eligible Content: M7.D.2.1.2 Use substitution of one and/or two variables to simplify expressions (whole numbers only – use order of operations)

M7.D.2.2.1 Identify expressions, equations or inequalities that model mathematical situations (using whole numbers or decimals, no more than two operations and one variable).

Academic Standards: 2.1.8.B, 2.1.8.E, 2.8.8.C

You can use any combination of the associative, commutative, distributives, identity, or inverse properties to simplify expressions.

Associative Property

Changing how numbers are grouped does not change the sum or product.

Addition: $(a + b) + c = a + (b + c)$ Multiplication: $(ab)c = a(bc)$

Commutative Property

Changing the order of the numbers does not change the sum or product.

Addition: $a + b = b + a$ Multiplication: $a \cdot b = b \cdot a$

Distributive Property

If one factor is a sum, multiplying before adding does not change the result.

$a(b + c) = ab + ac$

Identity Property

Adding zero or multiplying by one does not change a number.

Addition: $0 + a = a$ Multiplication: $1 \cdot a = a$

Inverse Property

Addition: $a + (-a) = 0$ Multiplication: $a \cdot \frac{1}{a} = 1$

Note: The number 0 does not have a multiplicative inverse.

Guided Instruction

Problem   Simplify the expression $b + 4 - b$, and justify each step.

Use properties of numbers to simplify expressions.

Step 1	Rewrite subtraction as addition.	$b + 4 - b$
		$= b + 4 + (-b)$
Step 2	Commutative Property of _____	$= b + (-b) + 4$
Step 3	_____ Property of Addition	$= (b + (-b)) + 4$
Step 4	_____ Property of Addition	$= 0 + 4$
Step 5	_____ Property of Addition	$= 4$

Solution $b + 4 - b =$ _____

Apply the Pennsylvania Academic Standards   Identify the property used to simplify each expression.

1. $a \cdot 5 + b = 5a + b$

_____

2. $6 + \frac{2}{a}\left(\frac{a}{2}\right) = 6 + 1$

_____

3. $4b + (6b + 3) = (4b + 6b) + 3$

_____

Simplify each expression.

4. $2(x + 2) - x$

_____

5. $3a - 4 + 2a$

_____

6. $8 \cdot a \cdot 2$

_____

7. $5x + x - 2 - 2x$

_____

8. $a + 6 + a$

_____

9. $9 + x - 2$

_____

10. $6b + 4 - 2b + 2$

_____

11. $5x + 4y + 3x - y$

_____

12. $3(a + y) + 2a + y$

_____

Solve each problem.

13. The perimeter of a triangle is the sum of the lengths of its sides. A triangle has sides that measure s, $2s$, and 4. Write an expression to show the perimeter of the triangle. Simplify the expression.

_____

14. Lisa sold magazine subscriptions to four families. Each subscription costs $6. She sold 5 subscriptions to the Jones family, 4 to the Rivera family, 2 to the Darren family, and 1 to the Smith family. Use the distributive property to write an expression for the cost of the subscriptions that Lisa sold. Evaluate the expression.

_____

15. Use properties of numbers to explain why $(2m + 4) + 4m = 6m + 4$.

_____

_____

_____

_____

_____

PSSA Practice **Directions: Read each question. Then circle the letter for the best answer.**

1. Which property tells you that $(6 + b) + b$ and $6 + (b + b)$ are equivalent expressions?

   A Commutative Property of Addition

   B Identity Property of Addition

   C Associative Property of Addition

   D Distributive Property

2. $16x + 10 + 4x + 2 =$

   A $18x + 14$

   B $20x + 12$

   C $22x + 10$

   D $16x + 16$

 3. $2m + 6m + 5 =$

   A $6(m) + 5$

   B $m(2 + 6 + 5)$

   C $2(m + 3m + 5)$

   D $m(2 + 6) + 5$

4. Which property tells you that $5 \cdot 6 \cdot b$ and $6 \cdot 5 \cdot b$ are equivalent expressions?

   A Associative Property of Addition

   B Commutative Property of Multiplication

   C Multiplicative Inverse

   D Associative Property of Multiplication

 5. If $a = 5$ and $x = 2$, then what is the value of $ax + ax - x$?

   A 22

   B 18

   C 16

   D 12

6. Which of the following does **not** equal the expression $4m + 2m$?

   A $6m$

   B $m(4 + 2)$

   C $(4 + 2)m$

   D $2(4m)$

Focus on the Pennsylvania Academic Standards

Lesson 23 — Write Equations or Inequalities

Assessment Anchors/Eligible Content: M7.D.2.2.1 Identify expressions, equations or inequalities that model mathematical situations (using whole numbers or decimals, no more than two operations and one variable).

Academic Standards: 2.8.8.C

An **equation** is a mathematical sentence with an equal sign.

An **inequality** is a mathematical sentence with one of these symbols: $<$, $\leq$, $>$, or $\geq$.

You can write an equation or an inequality to help you solve a word problem. An equation shows that two expressions are equivalent. An inequality shows how two expressions compare. You can use the symbols below to write inequalities.

$<$	less than	$>$	greater than
$\leq$	less than or equal to	$\geq$	greater than or equal to

Guided Instruction

Problem

William spent $32 to buy 2 CDs and 1 book. The CDs cost $24.

What equation can you write to represent this situation?

Step 1 Choose a variable to represent the unknown value.

Let b represent the cost of 1 book.

Step 2 Write an equation to represent the situation.

Cost of 2 CDs + cost of 1 book = $32

_____ + b = _____

Solution What equation can you write to represent this situation? _____.

Another Example

Write an inequality for each mathematical sentence.
Use the correct symbol to represent each relationship.

A number n divided by 8 is less than 12.

$n \div 8 < 12$

A number n added to -8 is at least 35.

$n + (-8) \geq 35$

When the difference between 6 and 4 is subtracted from a number n, the result is greater than 5.

$n - (6 - 4) > 5$

Apply the Pennsylvania Academic Standards

Write a mathematical equation or inequality for each statement.

1. Five more than two times a number *n* is twenty-five.

_____

2. Twenty decreased by 4 times a number *n* is 4.

_____

3. Six times a number *n* is greater than thirty-six.

_____

Match each equation or inequality to the correct statement.

4. $10 < n + 6$ _____

5. $2 + 5n = 55$ _____

6. $n - (5 + 10) \leq 12$ _____

7. $6 + \dfrac{n}{8} = 14$ _____

8. $n + 3 \geq -8$ _____

9. $-3n + 6 = 15$ _____

a Two increased by five times a number *n* is 55.

b Three more than a number *n* is greater than or equal to −8.

c The product of a number *n* and −3 increased by 6 is 15.

d A number *n* decreased by the sum of 5 and 10 is less than or equal to 12.

e Ten is less than a number *n* increased by 6.

f Six more than the quotient of a number *n* and 8 is 14.

Solve each problem.

10. Barbara gave the cashier $15 for the posters she bought. The cashier gave her $3 in change. What equation represents this situation? Let *p* represent the cost of the posters.

_____

11. Ethan carried 3 boxes of books that weighed at most 60 pounds altogether. If the weight of each box was the same, what inequality represents this situation? Let *b* represent the weight of 1 box.

_____

12. During their vacation, Michelle and Janet decided to share equally the cost of renting a canoe for the day. Janet's share of the cost was $25. What equation represents this situation? Let *c* represent the cost of the canoe.

_____

13. Explain the difference in meaning between $n - 6$ and $6 - n$.

_____

_____

 Measuring Up to the Pennsylvania Academic Standards

PSSA Practice **Directions: Read each question. Then circle the letter for the best answer.**

1. Which equation could be used to solve this problem?

   Tanya bought 5 rolls of wrapping paper for $30. Each roll was the same price, p. What was the cost of 1 roll?

   A $5p = 30$

   B $5 + p = 30$

   C $\frac{30}{p} < 5$

   D $5 - p = 30$

2. Which inequality represents this statement?

   The product of a number n and 5 is less than 20.

   A $5 + n > 20$

   B $\frac{n}{5} < 20$

   C $5 - n < 20$

   D $5n < 20$

 3. Which of the following statements represents the inequality $12 - n \geq 5$?

   A A number n decreased by 12 is 5.

   B The quotient of a number n and 12 is less than 5.

   C Twelve decreased by a number n is at least 5.

   D The product of 12 and a number n is greater than 5.

4. Which statement represents the equation $n - 10 = 45$?

   A The quotient of a number n and 10 is 45.

   B A number n decreased by 10 is 45.

   C A number n increased by 10 is 45.

   D The product of a number n and 10 is 45.

 5. Which equation could be used to solve this problem?

   There are 3 feet in 1 yard. How many yards are there in 51 feet?

   A $\frac{y}{3} = 51$

   B $3y = 51$

   C $y - 3 = 51$

   D $y + 3 = 51$

6. Which mathematical statement says that the product of a number n and -2 is less than or equal to 8?

   A $n + (-2) < 8$

   B $2n \leq 8$

   C $n - 2 \geq 8$

   D $-2n \leq 8$

Lesson 24 Use Models to Solve Equations

Assessment Anchors/Eligible Content: M7.D.2.1.1 Select and/or use appropriate strategies to solve one-step equations (no negative numbers).

M7.D.2.2.1 Identify expressions, equations or inequalities that model mathematical situations (using whole numbers or decimals, no more than two operations and one variable).

Academic Standards: 2.1.8.G, 2.8.8.C, 2.8.8.D, 2.8.8.E, 2.8.8.J

You can use a model for an equation to find its solution.

Guided Instruction

Problem Brian biked 6 miles on Saturday and x miles on Sunday. If he biked a total of 8 miles over the weekend, how many miles did he bike on Sunday?

To solve, use an equation and a model.

Step 1 Write an equation using the information in the problem. Let x = the number of miles that Brian biked on Sunday.

Step 2 Model the equation using a balance scale. The tall rectangular block represents x. Each square block represents one mile.

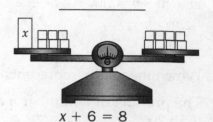

$$x + 6 = 8$$

Step 3 Solve the equation by isolating the variable. To isolate the variable, cross out the same number of square blocks from each side of the scale.

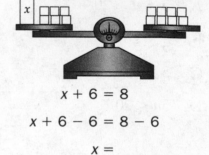

$$x + 6 = 8$$

$$x + 6 - 6 = 8 - 6$$

$$x = \underline{\hspace{1cm}}$$

Solution How many miles did he bike on Sunday? _____

Another Example

Solve the equation $y - 2 = 6$.

Subtracting is the same as adding a negative.
Write the equation as an addition problem.

$$y + (-2) = 6$$

Model the equation using tiles.
The tall rectangle represents y.
The plus-tiles represent positive integers.
The minus-tiles represent negative integers.

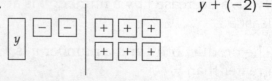

Add 2 plus-tiles to each side and remove the zero pairs. Then simplify.

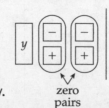

zero pairs

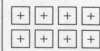

$$y + (-2) = 6$$

$$y + (-2) + 2 = 6 + 2$$

$$y = \underline{\hspace{1cm}}$$

Write and solve each equation modeled below.

1.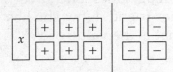

_____

_____

2.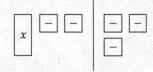

_____

_____

3.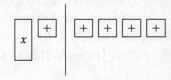

_____

_____

Use a model to solve each equation.

4. $6 = x - 9$

_____

5. $7 = y - 2$

_____

6. $14 = 7 + t$

_____

7. $m - 3 = 11$

_____

8. $n + 7 = 13$

_____

9. $8 + x = 9$

_____

Solve each problem.

10. Terry walked 7 miles on Monday and m miles on Tuesday. She walked a total of 12 miles on Monday and Tuesday. Write an equation to show how many miles she walked altogether, and then solve for m. Explain your answer.

_____

_____

11. Jorge had 13 trading cards. His friend gave him x more trading cards. Jorge now has 18 trading cards. Write an equation to show how many trading cards Jorge received from his friend, and then solve for x. Explain your answer.

_____

_____

PSSA Practice

Directions: Read each question. Then circle the letter for the best answer.

1. Georgia completed 8 paintings during May. In June, she completed *x* paintings. She completed a total of 14 paintings in May and June. What is the value of *x*?

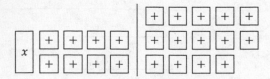

A $x = 6$

B $x = 8$

C $x = 14$

D $x = 22$

 2. Walter had 9 trading cards. He gave 4 trading cards to his friend and received *x* cards back from his friend. He now has 12 cards. What is the value of *x*?

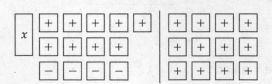

A $x = 13$

B $x = 12$

C $x = 9$

D $x = 7$

3. Penelope had 15 magazines. She gave *x* magazines to her friend. Now she has 7 magazines. What is the value of *x*?

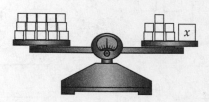

A $x = 7$

B $x = 8$

C $x = 15$

D $x = 22$

 4. Bill had $16.00. He gave a cashier $10.00 to pay for his movie ticket. He received *x* dollars in change. He now has $8.00. What is the value of *x*?

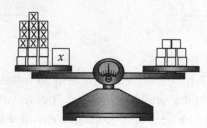

A $x = 2$

B $x = 6$

C $x = 8$

D $x = 10$

Focus on the Pennsylvania Academic Standards

Lesson 25   Solve One-Step Equations

Assessment Anchors/Eligible Content: M7.D.2.1.1 Select and/or use appropriate strategies to solve one-step equations (no negative numbers).

M7.D.2.2.1 Identify expressions, equations or inequalities that model mathematical situations (using whole numbers or decimals, no more than two operations and one variable).

Academic Standards: 2.1.8.G, 2.8.8.C, 2.8.8.E, 2.8.8.J

To solve an equation, you need to get the variable alone on one side of the equals sign. You can use a model or an inverse operation to solve a one-step equation.

Guided Instruction

Problem   Rick received 3 boxes. Each box contains an equal number of bottles. If Rick received a total of 24 bottles, how many bottles does each box contain?

To solve, use an equation and a model.

Step 1   Write an equation using the information. Let x = the number of bottles that each box contains.

Step 2   Model the equation by using a balance scale. The tall rectangular blocks represent x. Each square block represents one bottle.

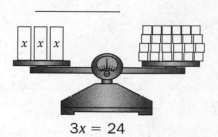

$3x = 24$

Step 3   Solve the equation. Divide the items on each side of the scale into 3 equal groups.

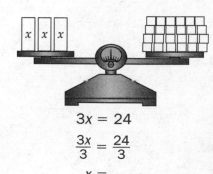

$3x = 24$

$$\frac{3x}{3} = \frac{24}{3}$$

$x =$ _____

Solution   How many bottles does each box contain? _____

Other Examples

A. Solve the equation $n + \frac{2}{3} = 5$.

The inverse of addition is subtraction.

$$n + \frac{2}{3} = 5$$

$n + \frac{2}{3} - \frac{2}{3} = 5 - \frac{2}{3}$ To get n alone on one side, subtract $\frac{2}{3}$ from both sides.

$n = 4\frac{1}{3}$ Simplify.

Check: $4\frac{1}{3} + \frac{2}{3} = 5$

B. Solve the equation $\frac{b}{2} = 10$.

The inverse of division is multiplication.

$$\frac{b}{2} = 10$$

$\frac{b}{2} \cdot 2 = 10 \cdot 2$ To get b alone on one side, multiply both sides by 2.

$b = 20$ Simplify.

Check: $\frac{20}{2} = 10$

Write and solve the equation modeled below.

1.

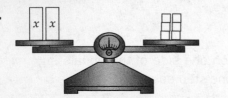

_____

_____

Solve each equation.

2. $x - 7 = 20$

3. $3x = 18$

4. $x \div 6 = 7$

5. $14 = x - 5$

6. $x + 9 = 13$

7. $16x = 48$

8. $x + \frac{2}{3} = 4$

9. $x \div \frac{3}{4} = \frac{1}{3}$

10. $0.7x = 4.2$

11. $1.2x = 6$

12. $x - 3.5 = 7.2$

13. $x \div 0.3 = 12$

14. $\frac{4}{5}x = \frac{7}{8}$

15. $x + 4.8 = 11.7$

16. $x \div 1.5 = 3.25$

Solve each problem.

17. Wendy has 6 boxes of cat food. Altogether, the boxes weigh 36 pounds. Write and solve an equation that shows how many pounds each box weighs.

_____

18. Harriet buys 4 gallons of juice for a party. After the party, she has $1\frac{5}{8}$ gallons of juice left. Write and solve an equation that shows how many gallons of juice were used for the party.

_____

PSSA Practice

Directions: Read each question. Then circle the letter for the best answer.

Use the information below to answer questions 1–2.

Angelina has 5 boxes of markers. Each box contains an equal number of markers. She has a total of 40 markers.

1. If x represents the number of markers in each box, which equation represents this situation?

   A $5 \cdot x = 40$

   B $5 \div x = 40$

   C $40 - x = 5$

   D $5 + x = 40$

2. How many markers are in each box?

   A   5

   B   8

   C   35

   D   40

3. Mary has 2.75 gallons of orange juice. She has x cups. She pours an equal amount of juice into each cup using all of the juice. Each cup holds 0.0625 gallon. What is the value of x?

   A $x = 6.5$

   B $x = 13.25$

   C $x - 44$

   D $x = 44.625$

Use the information below to answer questions 4–5.

Henri spent $8.43 on a new pair of jeans at a going-out-of-business sale. He used a $20 bill to pay the cashier.

4. If x represents the amount of change that Henri will receive, which equation represents this situation?

   A $8.43 = 20.00 + x$

   B $20.00 = 8.43 + x$

   C $20.00 = 8.43 - x$

   D $20.00 = x - 8.43$

5. How much change will the cashier give to Henri?

   A $28.57

   B $28.43

   C $11.57

   D $11.43

6. Alex has 4 bags of peppermints. Each bag contains x number of peppermints. If Alex has 60 peppermints total, how many peppermints does each bag hold?

   A $x = 240$

   B $x = 64$

   C $x = 56$

   D $x = 15$

Lesson 26 Find and Extend Patterns

Assessment Anchors/Eligible Content: M7.D.1.1.1 Describe, extend or find a missing element of a pattern (show 3 repetitions of the pattern)

- fractions or decimals – may use only one operation from +, − or ×
- whole numbers – may use only one operation from +, −, ×, ÷ or squares

Academic Standards: 2.1.8.E, 2.8.8.A, 2.8.8.B

Sometimes you can solve a problem by extending a pattern that you might observe. A **pattern** is the rule that an ordered set of terms follows. A **term** is a number, a variable, or a product of numbers and/or variables. A **sequence** is an ordered set of terms.

Guided Instruction

Problem

Greg made a series of deposits to his bank account that resulted in the following balances: $1.00, $3.00, $9.00, $27.00, and $81.00. If the pattern continues, what would be the balance after the sixth deposit?

To solve, find a rule to the pattern.

Step 1 Look for a pattern in the data.

What operations could you perform on $1.00 to get $3.00?

_____

Step 2 Check these operations with the next term in the sequence.

$3.00 + $2.00 = _____

$3.00 × 3 = _____

Which operation produced the next term? _____

Step 3 Test the operation with the next term.

$9.00 × 3 = _____

Did the operation give the next term of the sequence? _____

Step 4 Use the operation to find the 6th term in the sequence.

$81.00 × 3 = _____

Solution

If the pattern continues, what would be the balance after the sixth deposit?

_____

Another Example

Find the next two terms in the following sequence: 3, 0, −3, −6, ...

Find the rule that relates one term to the next.

3,	0,	−3,	−6
3 − **3** = 0	0 − **3** = −3	−3 − **3** = −6	−6 − **3** = _____

Write the next two terms.

3, 0, −3, −6, _____, _____

Apply the Pennsylvania Academic Standards

Identify the operation used in each pattern.

1. 30, 27, 24, 21, ...

_____

2. 2, 4, 16, 256, ...

_____

3. 7, 13, 19, 25, ...

_____

4. 160, 80, 40, 20, ...

_____

Write the next two numbers in each pattern.

5. 4, 11, 18, 25, ...

_____

6. 2.75, 3.50, 4.25, 5.00, ...

_____

7. 4, 12, 36, 108, ...

_____

8. $\frac{1}{64}, \frac{1}{32}, \frac{1}{16}, \frac{1}{8}, \ldots$

_____

Write a sequence of eight numbers using the given operation.

9. Add 8, starting with 7.

_____

10. Multiply by 5, starting with 1.

_____

11. subtract 0.6, starting with 10.

_____

12. Add $\frac{1}{2}$, starting with 1.

_____

Solve each problem.

13. Harriet makes a series of withdrawals from her savings account, resulting in the following balances: $67.00, $61.00, $55.00, $49.00, and $43.00. If the pattern continues, what will the balance be after her eighth withdrawal? Explain your answer.

_____

_____

_____

14. Doug is saving for a new bike. He saves the same amount each week, resulting in the following totals at the end of each of the first six weeks: $55.00, $70.00, $85.00, $100.00, $115.00, and $130.00. If the pattern continues, how many weeks altogether will it take him to save enough for a bike that costs $220.00? Explain your answer.

_____

_____

_____

Directions: Read each question. Then circle the letter for the best answer.

1. Larry has $90.00 in his savings account. Larry makes a series of withdrawals from his savings account, resulting in the following balances: $81.00, $72.00, $63.00, and $54.00. If the pattern continues, what will the balance be after his **sixth** withdrawal?

A $46.00

B $45.00

C $36.00

D $27.00

2. Grace is saving for new stereo speakers. Each week, Grace puts an additional $21 into her savings account. The weekly balance in her savings account for five weeks is $21.00, $42.00, $63.00, $84.00, and $105.00. If the pattern continues, how many weeks will it take her to save enough if her father will give her $80 for the speaker and if the speakers cost $290.00?

A 8 weeks

B 9 weeks

C 10 weeks

D 11 weeks

3. Melanie writes the following pattern: 5.5, 5.1, 4.7, 4.3, 3.9, and 3.5. Which of the following operations match the pattern?

A add 0.8

B subtract 2

C divide by 0.4

D subtract 0.4

4. Orin opens a savings account with $8.00. Each week afterwards, he makes a series of weekly deposits into his account. The first four weekly balances after his initial deposit are $22.50, $37.00, $51.50, and $66.00. If the pattern continues, what will the balance be after his **sixth** deposit?

A $124.00

B $109.50

C $95.00

D $80.50

5. Jackson challenges his friend Sarah to write a pattern. He tells her to use the operation "multiply by 6." Which sequence of numbers could Sarah choose?

A 6, 36, 96, 126

B $\frac{1}{36}, \frac{1}{6}, 1, 6$

C 1, 7, 13, 19

D 36, 30, 24, 18

6. Joseph is saving for a new acoustic guitar. He opened a savings account with $150.00. After each week of saving, his account had the following balances: $171.00, $192.00, $213.00, $234.00, and $255.00. If the pattern continues, how many **more** weeks will it take him to save enough money if the guitar costs $335.00?

A 4 weeks

B 5 weeks

C 9 weeks

D 10 weeks

 Measuring Up® to the Pennsylvania Academic Standards

Assessment Anchors/Eligible Content: M7.D.1.1.1 Describe, extend or find a missing element of a pattern (show 3 repetitions of the pattern)

- fractions or decimals – may use only one operation from +, − or ×
- whole numbers – may use only one operation from +, −, ×, ÷ or squares

M7.D.2.1.2 Use substitution of one and/or two variables to simplify expressions (whole numbers only – use order of operations).

Academic Standards: 2.1.8.E, 2.8.8.A, 2.8.8.B

Guided Instruction

Problem

Erin is collecting plastic bottles. On Monday she has 7 bottles, on Tuesday she has 14 bottles, on Wednesday she has 21 bottles, and on Thursday she has 28 bottles. If the pattern continues, how many bottles will she have on Friday? Explain your answer.

Find the pattern to solve the problem.

Step 1   Write the numbers in the pattern that you are given.

_____

Step 2   Write the different operations that you can perform on 7 to get 14.

_____

Step 3   Check these operations with the next term in the pattern.

$14 + 7 =$ _____

$14 \times 2 =$ _____

Which operation produced the next term? _____

Step 4   Check with the next term in the pattern.

$21 + 7 =$ _____

Step 5   Solve the problem.
Find the next term in the pattern to determine how many bottles Erin will have on Friday.

$28 + 7 =$ _____

If the pattern continues, how many bottles will she have on Friday? Explain your answer.

Solution

_____

_____

Apply the Pennsylvania Academic Standards

Solve each problem.

Work Space

1. Morris was trying to find the sixth term in the pattern shown below:

    3, 12, 48, 192, …

    His answer was 210. Is his answer correct? If not, find the correct answer for the sixth term and explain how you found the pattern.

    _____

    _____

    _____

    _____

2. Erin works at the grocery store. On Monday she worked for 2 hours. By the end of Tuesday, she had worked a total of 8 hours. By the end of Wednesday, she had worked a total of 14 hours, and by the end of Thursday, she had worked a total of 20 hours. If the pattern continues, how many total hours will she have worked by the end of Friday? Explain your answer.

    _____

    _____

    _____

3. Lynne makes the following weekly deposits into her bank account during the first five weeks: $11.00, $12.00, $13.00, $14.00, $15.00. She started with $40.00 in her account. If the pattern continues, what will be the total balance in her account after the seventh week? Explain your answer.

    _____

    _____

    _____

    _____

 Measuring Up® to the Pennsylvania Academic Standards

Directions: Read each question. Then circle the letter for the best answer.

1. Faun is collecting stones. She counts her total at the end of each week and writes down the following totals: 3, 8, 13, 18, 23, and 28. If this pattern continues, what will the total be after the ninth week?

   A   38 stones

   B   40 stones

   C   43 stones

   D   48 stones

2. David is recording the growth of a certain plant every morning. On the first day, the plant was $\frac{1}{2}$ inch tall. On the second day, the plant was $1\frac{1}{4}$ inches tall. On the third day, the plant was 2 inches tall, and on the fourth day, it was $2\frac{3}{4}$ inches tall. If the pattern continues, how tall will the plant be on the fifth day?

   A   4 inches

   B $3\frac{3}{4}$ inches

   C $3\frac{1}{2}$ inches

   D $3\frac{1}{4}$ inches

3. Natalie makes the following withdrawals from her bank account over 5 weeks: $3.00, $6.00, $9.00, $12.00, $15.00. She started with $100.00 in her account. If the pattern continues, what will be the balance in the account after the sixth week?

   A $34.00

   B $37.00

   C $63.00

   D $163.00

4. Maggie was trying to find the pattern for the numbers shown:

   90, 75, 60, 45, …

   What is the pattern?

   A   Add 15.

   B   Multiply by 15.

   C   Divide by 15.

   D   Subtract 15.

5. George makes the following weekly deposits into his bank account over 5 weeks: $4.00, $8.00, $12.00, $16.00, $20.00. If the pattern continues and his balance after the seventh week is $159.00, how much was his initial deposit?

   A $163.00

   B $100.00

   C $75.00

   D $47.00

6. Alan is collecting marbles. He counts his total at the end of each week and wrote down the following totals: 7, 11, 15, 19, 23, and 27. What will the total be after the eighth week?

   A   28 marbles

   B   31 marbles

   C   35 marbles

   D   39 marbles

Directions: Read each question. Then circle the letter for the best answer.

1. At swimming practice, Michelle swam 4 more laps around the pool than Andy. If Andy swam sixteen laps around the pool, how many laps did Michelle swim?

   A   24 laps

   B   20 laps

   C   18 laps

   D   12 laps

2. Tuesday night, every movie ticket at Tony's Theater is $4.00. If Jason goes to the movies on Tuesday night with 11 friends, what is the total cost of their tickets?

   A $52.00

   B $48.00

   C $46.00

   D $44.00

3. If $b = 6$, what is the value of $5(17 - b)$?

   A   115

   B   79

   C   60

   D   55

4. Which property tells you that $14(b + 2)$ and $14b + 28$ are equivalent expressions?

   A   Associative Property

   B   Commutative Property

   C   Distributive Property

   D   Inverse Property

5. Which of the following expressions does **not** have the same value as the expression $3g + 8g + 4$?

   A $8 + 3g + 8g - 4$

   B $4 + 8g + 3g$

   C $g(3 + 8) + 4$

   D $5g + 8$

6. Danny gave the cashier $20 for a baseball cap he purchased. The cashier gave him $7 in change. Which equation represents this situation?

   A $7 - x = 20$

   B $20 - x = 7$

   C $20 + x = 7$

   D $20 + 7 = x$

7. Which of the statements below represents the following inequality?

   $$3 + t > 12$$

   A   12 is less than the sum of 3 and a number t.

   B   12 minus a number t is more than 3.

   C   A number t decreased by 3 is less than or equal to 12.

   D   The sum of 12 and 3 is more than a number t.

8. What is the value of the following expression when $a = 2$ and $b = 1$?

$$a(7 - b)^2 \div 3$$

A 72

B 24

C 12

D 3

9. Alicia has 3 boxes of movies. Each box contains x movies. If Alicia has a total of 39 movies, how many movies does each box hold?

A 27

B 24

C 16

D 13

10. Starting from 3 feet above ground, Roger dropped a ball and recorded its height after each bounce:

$$3, \ 1, \ \frac{1}{3}, \ \frac{1}{9}, \ \dots$$

If the pattern continues, what will be the height the ball bounces up to on the sixth bounce?

A $\frac{1}{3}$

B $\frac{1}{64}$

C $\frac{1}{81}$

D $\frac{1}{27}$

11. Sanura is creating patterns for a puzzle book her school is publishing. What is the rule for the following pattern?

$$1, 1, 2, 3, 5, 8, 13, 21, \dots$$

A Multiply the previous number by 2.

B Multiply the previous number by $1\frac{1}{2}$.

C Add the previous two numbers.

D Square the previous number.

12. George has recorded his height every 2 years since he was 8, in the table below. If George's growth pattern continues, how tall will he be when he is 18?

Age (years)	Height (inches)
8	50
10	54
12	58
14	62

A 72 inches

B 70 inches

C 68 inches

D 66 inches

13. Emily made 23 bracelets. She gave x bracelets to her friends. If she has 8 bracelets left, what is the value of x?

A 31

B 15

C 13

D 7

Open-Ended Items

14. Kofi must simplify the following expression: $5 \times (4 - 1)^3 + 85$.

> Suppose Kofi says that the value of the expression is 104. Explain what Kofi might have done incorrectly. Then find the correct value of the expression. Explain each step.

15. Michael has 43 marbles in a bag. The marbles were red, blue, green, yellow or orange. There were 8 red marbles, 4 blue marbles, 9 green marbles, 14 yellow marbles, and x orange marbles.

A. Write an equation that shows the total number of marbles.

B. Find the number of orange marbles. Explain your answer.

15. *Continued*

C. Michael went to the store and bought more marbles. Of the marbles he bought, 20 were orange, red, blue or yellow. The rest were green. If he now has 68 marbles in all, how many are green? Explain your answer.

 Measuring Up® to the Pennsylvania Academic Standards

Assessment Anchors/Eligible Content: M7.A.2.2.1 Write ratios to compare quantities (e.g., ratio of boys to girls).
Academic Standards: 2.1.8.D, 2.3.8.D

You can use a ratio to make comparisons. A **ratio** compares two numbers called **terms**. Ratios can be written in three different forms. Examples are 2 to 3, 2:3, and $\frac{2}{3}$. Ratios that compare quantities of different units are called **rates**. Examples are a rate of pay, such as $40 in 5 hours, or a rate of speed, such as 120 miles in 2 hours.

Different ratios that have equal values are called **equivalent ratios**. Examples are 12:20 and 3:5. Multiply or divide the terms of a ratio by the same number to find equivalent ratios. For cxample, 12:20 = 3:5 – 6:10. A ratio is in **simplest form** when its terms have no common factors other than 1. For example, 6:10 = 3:5 in simplest from.

Guided Instruction

Problem

When Mr. Thomas made Swedish meatballs for his anniversary party, he used 2 cups of cream in a recipe that made 20 servings. Today, Mr. Thomas wants to make his recipe for a dinner party. How many cups of cream will he need for 10 servings?

Use division to find an equivalent ratio.

Step 1   Identify the ratio for the larger quantity.
Compare the number of cups of cream to the number of servings.

_____

Step 2   Find an equivalent ratio for the smaller quantity.

$$\frac{2 \text{ cups of cream}}{20 \text{ servings}} \overset{?}{=} \frac{\text{cups of cream}}{10 \text{ servings}}$$

$$\frac{2 \div 2}{20 \div 2} = \frac{1}{10}$$

Solution   How many cups of cream will he need for 10 servings? _____

Other Examples

In Emilio's class, there are 24 students. Of these students, 9 are boys.

A. Find the ratio of boys to total students, in simplest form.

$$\frac{\text{boys}}{\text{total students}} = \frac{9}{24} = \frac{3}{8}$$

There are 3 boys to 8 students in the class.

B. Find the ratio of girls to boys, in simplest form.

There are 9 boys and 24 students in the class. So there are
24 − 9 = 15 girls in the class.

girls : boys = 15:9 = 5:3

Write each ratio in two other forms.

1. 4:7 = _____

2. 9:24 = _____

3. $\frac{2}{11}$ = _____

4. 16 to 18 = _____

Write each ratio three different ways, in simplest form.

5. 50 inches to 75 inches

_____

_____

_____

6. 162 jelly beans to 45 jelly beans

_____

_____

_____

Write each rate in simplest form.

7. a recipe that calls for 8 cups of bananas to 6 cups of strawberries

_____

8. the speed of a car that travels 273 miles in 6 hours

_____

9. a population density of 6 people per 120 square miles

_____

10. the student-teacher ratio in a special education program that has 21 students to 6 teachers _____

Solve each problem.

11. A box of chocolates contains pieces wrapped in silver foil and pieces wrapped in gold foil. In all, there are 10 silver-foiled pieces and 15 gold-foiled pieces. What is the ratio of silver-foiled pieces to the total number of candies in the box? Write your answer in simplest form. _____

12. In Suzanne's class, the ratio of girls to boys is 3:2, and the total number of students is 20. Explain how to find the ratio of girls to the total number of students.

_____

_____

Explain how to check your result.

_____

_____

Directions: Read each problem. Then circle the letter for the best answer.

1. In Mr. Todd's class, 12 students are right-handed only, 4 are left-handed only, and 2 students are both left- and right-handed. What is the ratio of students who are both left- and right-handed to the total number of students?

   A 1:9

   B 9:1

   C 8:9

   D 1:8

2. A nursery school program has 16 students and 2 teachers. If 24 students are added to the program, how many teachers should be added in order to maintain the same student-teacher ratio?

   A 1

   B 3

   C 5

   D 8

3. John is a data-entry professional. His typing rate is 70 words per minute. At this rate, how long will it take John to complete a memo of 665 words?

   A 9.5 min

   B 9 min

   C 8.5 min

   D 8 min

4. If 1 decaminute is equivalent to 10 minutes of time, how many decaminutes are equivalent to 2 hours of time?

   A 20 decaminutes

   B 16 decaminutes

   C 12 decaminutes

   D 10 decaminutes

5. Power laundry detergent claims that 0.25 ounce of its concentrated detergent has the same cleaning power as 4 ounces of Blando detergent. Which is the **best** representation of this ratio?

   A $\frac{0.25}{1}$

   B $\frac{1}{4}$

   C $\frac{1}{8}$

   D $\frac{1}{16}$

6. Megan is going to run in a 26-mile race. She plans to run each mile in 7 minutes. At this pace, how long will it take Megan to complete the race?

   A 3 hours 18 minutes

   B 3 hours 2 minutes

   C 2 hours 58 minutes

   D 2 hours 42 minutes

Focus on the Pennsylvania Academic Standards

Lesson 29 | Unit Rates

Assessment Anchors/Eligible Content: M7.A.2.2.4 Calculate and/or apply unit rates or unit prices (terminating decimals through the hundredth place only).

Academic Standards: 2.1.8.D, 2.3.8.B, 2.3.8.D, 2.5.8.A, 2.5.8.D

As a consumer, you can use unit rates to make decisions about purchases.

When the second term of a rate is 1, the rate is called a **unit rate**. A unit rate often includes the word *per*. For example, $8 per hour is a rate of pay, and 55 miles per hour is a rate of speed.

Guided Instruction

Problem

The Sock Shop is selling 8 pairs of white socks for $10. Mrs. Simms wants to buy only 5 pairs. If the cost per pair is the same for any number of pairs, how much will Mrs. Simms pay for 5 pairs of white socks?

Find the unit price.

Step 1 Identify a ratio to represent the cost per pair.
Compare the selling price to the number of pairs of socks.

_____

Step 2 Simplify the ratio so that the denominator is 1.

Divide the numerator and the denominator by 8.

$$\frac{\$10}{8 \text{ pairs of socks}}$$

unit price = _____

Step 3 Multiply the unit price by the number of pairs to be purchased.

$1.25 · 5 = _____

Solution

How much will Mrs. Simms pay for 5 pairs of white socks?

_____

Another Example

Estimate which is the better buy: a 12-pack of juice for $9.99 or a 6-pack of juice for $5.99?

Estimate by rounding each dollar amount to the nearest ten cents.

Unit price for a 12-pack: $10 ÷ 12 is about $0.80 per can

Unit price for a 6-pack: $6 ÷ 6 is exactly $1.00 per can

So, the _____ is the better buy.

Measuring Up® to the Pennsylvania Academic Standards

Apply the Pennsylvania Academic Standards

Write each ratio as a unit rate.

1. $\dfrac{25,000}{5}$

_____

2. $\dfrac{0.36}{6}$

_____

3. $\dfrac{2}{\frac{1}{8}}$

_____

4. $\dfrac{8.5}{0.25}$

_____

Find each unit rate.

5. $\dfrac{25,000 \text{ people}}{5 \text{ square miles}}$

_____

6. $\dfrac{255 \text{ lines}}{3 \text{ pages}}$

_____

7. $\dfrac{75 \text{ miles}}{4 \text{ days}}$

_____

Find each unit price to the nearest cent.

8. $\dfrac{\$3.60}{4 \text{ pens}}$

_____

9. $\dfrac{\$2.21}{8 \text{ ounces}}$

_____

10. $\dfrac{\$5.60}{4 \text{ pounds of grapes}}$

_____

Solve each problem.

11. Rabbitton has 34 rabbits for every 8 gardens. Rabbitville has 48 rabbits for every 14 gardens. Which town has more rabbits per garden?

_____

_____

12. At Camp Monongahela, there are 18 campers for every 4 counselors. If there are 45 campers, how many counselors are needed?

_____

13. NET is charging $9.95 for 5 hours of online time, and WEB is charging $11.95 for 7 hours of online time. Determine the better buy.

_____

_____

14. Hank is refueling his truck with diesel fuel that costs $3.109 per gallon. The fuel tank of the truck, which holds 25 gallons, is nearly empty. Hank has $51 to spend. Estimate how many gallons of fuel Hank will be able to buy. (Hint: Round to the nearest dollar.)

_____

How many gallons can he buy to the nearest tenth of a gallon?

_____

PSSA Practice

Directions: Read each question. Then circle the letter for the best answer.

1. Which is a unit rate?

   A   150 words in 3 minutes

   B   150 miles in 3 hours

   C $150 in 3 days

   D   50 miles per hour

2. A food market offers 2 specials on corn on the cob. The first is 6 ears for $1.68 and the second is 10 ears for $2.80. Which of the following statements is true?

   A   The offer for 6 ears is the better deal.

   B   The offer for 10 ears is better deal.

   C   Both offer are equivalent.

   D   The offer for 6 ears is the same as a price of $ 0.20 per ear.

3. Bianca buys a 12-pack of apple juice for $4.32. What is the unit cost of the apple juice?

   A $0.12

   B $0.32

   C $0.36

   D $51.84

4. Julien bought a 5-pound bag of potatoes for $2.70. The bag contained 10 potatoes. If each potato weighed about the same, which is the most reasonable estimate of the unit price per potato?

   A $3.70

   B $2.70

   C $0.54

   D $0.27

5. A recipe for cookies uses $\frac{1}{4}$ teaspoon of vanilla extract with $\frac{1}{2}$ stick of butter. Which represents a unit rate for this recipe?

   A $\frac{1}{2}$ teaspoon of vanilla extract per stick of butter

   B $\frac{1}{4}$ teaspoon of vanilla extract per stick of butter

   C $\frac{1}{8}$ teaspoon of vanilla extract per stick of butter

   D $\frac{1}{16}$ teaspoon of vanilla extract per stick of butter

6. Rachel started her road trip with 16 gallons of fuel in the tank of her car. After traveling a total of 324 miles, Rachel had to refuel her car. How many miles did Rachel's car get per gallon?

   A   17.90 miles per gallon

   B   20.25 miles per gallon

   C   21.38 miles per gallon

   D   25.20 miles per gallon

Lesson 30 Proportions

Assessment Anchors/Eligible Content: M7.A.2.2.2 Solve for a variable in a given proportion.
M7.A.2.2.3 Use proportions to determine if two quantities are equivalent (e.g., similar figures, prices of different sized items, etc.).
M7.A.2.2.5 Select and/or use ratios or proportions to solve problems.
Academic Standards: 2.1.8.D, 2.3.8.B, 2.5.8.A, 2.5.8.D

You can use a proportion to represent situations involving equal ratios.

A **proportion** is an equation stating that two ratios are equal.
When you know values for three of the four terms of a proportion,
you can find the value of the fourth term.

In some situations, it may be appropriate to estimate an answer. When an exact answer is needed, you can use **cross-products** to solve a proportion.

$\frac{8}{12} \diagdown\!\!\!\diagup \frac{2}{3}$ is a true proportion because $8 \times 3 = 12 \times 2$.

Guided Instruction

Problem 1

A soup kitchen that feeds the needy uses 6.6 pounds of ground beef every 3 days. The cook wants to know about how many pounds of ground beef this kitchen will use in the month of March. About how many pounds will the cook need? What is the exact number needed?

Estimate by rounding and using compatible numbers. Use cross-products to solve.

Step 1 Write a proportion. Use p for the number of pounds used in 31 days.

$$\frac{\text{number of pounds}}{\text{number of days}} = \frac{\text{number of pounds}}{\text{number of days}}$$

$$\frac{6.6}{3} = \frac{p}{31}$$

Step 2 Use rounding and compatible numbers to estimate.
Round the decimal 6.6 to a whole number. _____

Find a number that is close to 31
and is a multiple of 3. _____

$$\frac{7}{3} = \frac{p}{30}$$

Write a proportion using the rounded and compatible numbers. Since 30 is 10 times 3, p must be 10 times 7.

$$\frac{7 \cdot 10}{3 \cdot 10} = \frac{70}{30}$$

The cook will need about _____ pounds of ground beef in March.

Step 3 To find the exact amount, solve the proportion.
Use cross-products. $\frac{6.6}{3} \diagdown\!\!\!\diagup \frac{p}{31}$

$$3 \times p = \text{_____} \cdot \text{_____}$$

$$3p = 204.6$$

$$p = \text{_____}$$

The cook will need exactly _____ pounds of ground beef in March.

Solution

About how many pounds will the cook need? _____

What is the exact number needed? _____

Guided Instruction

Lila is a data-entry operator. In 6 minutes, she keys in 360 words. Working at the same rate, how many words can Lila type in 20 minutes? Working at the same rate, how long does it take her to complete a report that has 4,860 words?

Write and solve two proportions using the given rate.

Step 1 Identify the rate. Then set up the first proportion.

Compare words to minutes.

The first rate is $\frac{360 \text{ words}}{6 \text{ minutes}}$.

Let $n =$ the number of words.

The second rate is $\frac{n \text{ words}}{20 \text{ minutes}}$.

So the proportion is _____.

Step 2 Use cross-products to solve the proportion.

$$\frac{360}{6} = \frac{n}{20}$$

$$6 \cdot n = \underline{\hspace{1cm}} \cdot \underline{\hspace{1cm}}$$

$$6n = \underline{\hspace{1cm}}$$

$$6n \div 6 = 7{,}200 \div \underline{\hspace{1cm}}$$

$$n = \underline{\hspace{1cm}}$$

Step 3 Write the second proportion using the same rate and solve.

Let $m =$ the number of minutes for typing 4,860 words.

$$\frac{360}{6} = \frac{4{,}860}{m}$$

$$360 \cdot m = \underline{\hspace{1cm}} \cdot \underline{\hspace{1cm}}$$

$$360m = \underline{\hspace{1cm}}$$

$$360m \div 360 = 29{,}160 \div \underline{\hspace{1cm}}$$

$$m = \underline{\hspace{1cm}}$$

How many words can Lila type in 20 minutes? _____

Solution How long does it take her to type a report that has 4,860 words?

_____

Apply the Pennsylvania Academic Standards

Use cross-products to determine if each is a proportion.
Write *yes* or *no*.

1. $\frac{12}{18} \overset{?}{=} \frac{20}{30}$

2. $\frac{45}{30} \overset{?}{=} \frac{36}{24}$

3. $\frac{9}{16} \overset{?}{=} \frac{3}{4}$

4. $\frac{72}{52} \overset{?}{=} \frac{52}{72}$

_____

Use cross-products to solve each proportion.

5. $\frac{40}{12} = \frac{60}{t}$

6. $\frac{36}{n} = \frac{35}{70}$

7. $\frac{20}{240} = \frac{x}{12}$

8. $\frac{w}{180} = \frac{30}{90}$

_____

Use proportions to find the missing numbers in each table.

9. The table below shows the growth of a strain of virus over a period of hours. If the growth rate is constant, how many virus cells will there be after 15 hours?

Number of Hours	5	9	12	15
Number of Cells	3,000	5,400	7,200	

10. The table below shows the distance covered on an automobile trip. If the average speed of the car is constant, how far will the car have traveled after 15 hours?

Driving Time (hours)	3	5	8	12	15
Distance (miles)	159	265	424		

Solve each problem.

11. A cook at a hotel is using a recipe that makes 100 servings.
This recipe calls for 37 pounds of flour and 115 cups of milk.
The cook needs to serve 250 people.
How many pounds of flour are needed? _____
How many cups of milk are needed? _____
To the nearest gallon, about how many gallons of milk are needed? _____

12. John's Jewelry Supply is selling 7 hand-crafted silver beads for $2.49.
Jan has $10 to spend. Use *n* to represent the number of beads for $10.

Write a proportion that can be used to find *n*. _____

Explain how to use your proportion to estimate an answer.

_____

_____

Solve your proportion to find the exact number of beads that Jan can buy for $10.
Explain your result.

_____

_____

PSSA Practice Directions: Read each question. Then circle the letter for the best answer.

1. A clock loses 3 minutes every 4 hours. At this rate, how many minutes will the clock lose in one day?

A 16 min

B 18 min

C 24 min

D 32 min

2. Joe drove for 5 hours and traveled a distance of 240 miles. Which is the **best** estimate of the number of miles that Joe will travel in 7.2 hours?

A 400 mi

B 375 mi

C 350 mi

D 325 mi

3. To make a fruit drink for 6 people, Yolanda mixed $\frac{1}{2}$ liter of concentrate with $4\frac{1}{2}$ liters of water. How many liters of concentrate will Yolanda need to serve 20 people?

A 2 L

B $1\frac{2}{3}$ L

C $1\frac{1}{2}$ L

D $\frac{2}{3}$ L

4. Joey can buy 6 jelly beans for 5 cents. He uses the following proportion to determine how many jelly beans he can buy for 75 cents: $\frac{6}{5} = \frac{x}{75}$. If x is the number of jelly beans he can buy, what is the value of x?

A 60

B 65

C 81

D 90

5. An experimental rocket travels at the rate of 50 miles every 2 seconds. How many **minutes** will it take the rocket to cover a distance of 7,500 miles?

A 5 min

B 150 min

C 300 min

D 600 min

6. Janice wants to buy a new bike that costs $153. If Janice babysits for 5 hours for $42.50, how many more hours does she need to babysit in order buy the bike she wants?

A 13

B 18

C 30

D 22

Focus on the Pennsylvania Academic Standards

Lesson 31   Scaling

Assessment Anchors/Eligible Content: M7.A.2.2.1 Write ratios to compare quantities (e.g., ratio of boys to girls).

M7.A.2.2.2 Solve for a variable in a given proportion.

M7.A.2.2.5 Select and/or use ratios or proportions to solve problems.

M7.B.2.2.1 Interpret and/or apply scales shown on maps, blueprints, models, etc.

Academic Standards: 2.3.8.F

You can use proportions to solve problems involving scale drawings.

A **scale** is the ratio of the measurements of a drawing, a model, a map, or a floor plan to the actual size of the objects or distances. A scale drawing is similar in shape to the object it represents. For a very small object, such as a microchip, a scale drawing would be larger than the actual object.

Guided Instruction

Problem

An architect's floor plan for a museum exhibit hall uses a scale of 0.5 inch : 2 feet. On this drawing, a passageway between exhibits is represented by a rectangle 3.75 inches long. What is the actual length of the passageway?

To find an actual length from a scale drawing, identify and solve a proportion.

Step 1   Identify two ratios in the same order.

$$\frac{\text{drawing}}{\text{actual}} = \frac{\text{drawing}}{\text{actual}}$$

Let p = the actual length in feet of the passageway.

$$\frac{0.5 \text{ inch}}{2 \text{ feet}} = \underline{\hspace{3cm}}$$

Step 2   Use cross-products to solve the proportion.

$$\frac{0.5}{2} = \frac{3.75}{p}$$

$$0.5 \cdot p = \underline{\hspace{2cm}} \cdot \underline{\hspace{1.5cm}}$$

$$0.5p = \underline{\hspace{2cm}}$$

$$p = \underline{\hspace{2cm}}$$

Solution   What is the actual length of the passageway? _____

Another Example

Pittsburgh and Philadelphia are about 300 miles apart.
On Porforio's Pennsylvania map, the distance between these cities is represented by a line that is 4 inches long.
What is the scale on this map?
Write a ratio in simplest form.

$$4 \text{ inches} : 300 \text{ miles} = (4 \div 4) \text{ inches} : (300 \div 4) \text{ miles}$$
$$= 1 \text{ inch} : 75 \text{ miles}$$

Apply the Pennsylvania Academic Standards   Write a scale for each map or drawing.

1. The map distance between two cities is 4.5 inches. The actual distance between these cities is 900 miles.

A scale for this map is 1 inch: _____.

2. On a scale drawing, the width of a room is 3.5 inches. The actual width of the room is 24.5 feet.

A scale for this drawing is 1 inch: _____.

3. On a scale drawing, the distance between two elements in a microchip is 1.5 inches. The actual distance between these elements is 0.3 millimeter.

A scale for this drawing is 1 inch: _____.

4. In a drawing of two similar triangles, one side of the smaller triangle measures 8 inches. The corresponding side of the larger triangle measures 24 inches.

A scale ratio for these similar triangles is _____.

Solve each problem.

5. An artist is making a mural on a building, using a photo that is 5 inches by 7 inches. First he practices painting the photo in 3 different sizes. Use the table to find the length of the mural. Then write the dimensions in feet.

	Photo	Size 1	Size 2	Size 3	Mural
Width, w (in.)	5	15	45	135	405
Length, l (in.)	7	21	63	189	

_____

6. Two seventh graders want to build a sandcastle at the beach. They begin by making a sketch of their sandcastle in the sand. If the sketch shows that the towers of the castle are 4.4 inches tall, estimate how tall the actual towers will be if the scale is 1 inch : 1 foot. Explain your answer.

_____

_____

_____

         Measuring Up to the Pennsylvania Academic Standards

Directions: Read each question. Then circle the letter for the best answer.

1. The scale on a map is 1 inch : 75 miles. The map distance between Harrisburg and Scranton is about 1.4 inches. About how many miles is the actual distance?

   A   About 25 miles

   B   About 50 miles

   C   About 75 miles

   D   About 100 miles

2. Rob is designing an outdoor billboard. The rectangular billboard is 16 feet by 48 feet. Using a scale of $\frac{5}{8}$ inch : 1 foot, what are the dimensions of Rob's design model?

   A   5 in. by 12.5 in.

   B   7.5 in. by 18.75 in.

   C   10 in. by 30 in.

   D   15 in. by 37.5 in.

3. The scale ratio for two similar regular pentagons is 3:8. Let l represent the measure of a side of the larger regular pentagon and s represent the measure of a side of the smaller regular pentagon. Which equation is true for this situation?

   A $l = \frac{3s}{8}$

   B $l = \frac{8s}{3}$

   C $l = \frac{3}{8s}$

   D $l = \frac{8}{3s}$

Use the information below to answer questions 4–5.

A scale drawing of a recreation center is $1\frac{3}{8}$ inches wide and $2\frac{5}{8}$ inches long.

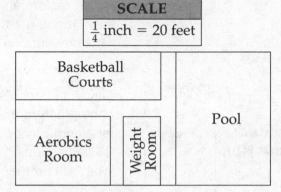

4. What is the actual length of the recreation center?

   A   80 feet   B   120 feet

   C   160 feet   D   210 feet

5. How much longer than the actual width of the recreation center is the actual length?

   A   50 feet   B   80 feet

   C   100 feet   D   200 feet

6. Jasper is making a scale drawing of an airplane that is 38 meters long. He is using the scale 2 centimeters : 5 meters. How long should he make the airplane in his drawing?

   A   7.6 centimeters

   B   15.2 centimeters

   C   25 centimeters

   D   95 centimeters

Focus on the Pennsylvania Academic Standards

Lesson 32 **Use Proportions to Enlarge or Reduce**

Assessment Anchors/Eligible Content: M7.A.2.2.1 Write ratios to compare quantities (e.g., ratio of boys to girls).

M7.A.2.2.2 Solve for a variable in a given proportion.

M7.A.2.2.5 Select and/or use ratios or proportions to solve problems.

M7.B.2.2.1 Interpret and/or apply scales shown on maps, blueprints, models, etc.

M7.B.2.2.2 Determine and/or apply an appropriate scale for reduction or enlargement.

Academic Standards: 2.3.8.G

In mathematics, a **scale factor** is used to describe an enlargement or reduction. A scale factor can be expressed using a ratio. A scale factor that is between 0 and 1 represents a reduction of the original. A scale factor that is greater than 1 represents an enlargement of the original.

Guided Instruction

Problem

Mindy and her sisters want to make an enlargement of a photograph of their parents. The original photograph is 5 inches long and 3 inches wide. They would like the enlargement to be 35 inches long. What is the scale factor of the enlargement? What will be the width of the enlargement?

Step 1 Find the scale factor.

The original length is 5 inches and the enlargement length is 35 inches.

As a ratio: $\dfrac{\text{enlargement length}}{\text{original length}} = \dfrac{35 \text{ inches}}{5 \text{ inches}}$ or $\dfrac{7}{1}$.

The scale factor is $\dfrac{7}{1}$ or 7 times the original.

Step 2 Use a proportion to find the width of the enlargement.

Let x represent the width of the enlargement.

Scale factor → $\dfrac{7}{1} = \dfrac{x}{3}$ ← enlargement width
← original width

Step 3 Find the cross products. $1 \cdot x = 7 \cdot 3$

$x = \underline{\hspace{1cm}}$

Solution

What is the scale factor of the enlargement? What will be the width of the enlargement? _____

_____

Directions: Read each question. Then circle the letter for the best answer.

1. The scale on a map is 1 inch : 75 miles. The map distance between Harrisburg and Scranton is about 1.4 inches. About how many miles is the actual distance?

A   About 25 miles

B   About 50 miles

C   About 75 miles

D   About 100 miles

2. Rob is designing an outdoor billboard. The rectangular billboard is 16 feet by 48 feet. Using a scale of $\frac{5}{8}$ inch : 1 foot, what are the dimensions of Rob's design model?

A   5 in. by 12.5 in.

B   7.5 in. by 18.75 in.

C   10 in. by 30 in.

D   15 in. by 37.5 in.

3. The scale ratio for two similar regular pentagons is 3:8. Let l represent the measure of a side of the larger regular pentagon and s represent the measure of a side of the smaller regular pentagon. Which equation is true for this situation?

A $l = \frac{3s}{8}$

B $l = \frac{8s}{3}$

C $l = \frac{3}{8s}$

D $l = \frac{8}{3s}$

Use the information below to answer questions 4–5.

A scale drawing of a recreation center is $1\frac{3}{8}$ inches wide and $2\frac{5}{8}$ inches long.

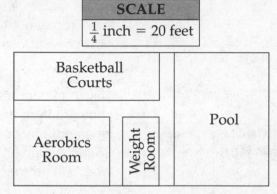

4. What is the actual length of the recreation center?

A   80 feet   B   120 feet

C   160 feet   D   210 feet

5. How much longer than the actual width of the recreation center is the actual length?

A   50 feet   B   80 feet

C   100 feet   D   200 feet

6. Jasper is making a scale drawing of an airplane that is 38 meters long. He is using the scale 2 centimeters : 5 meters. How long should he make the airplane in his drawing?

A   7.6 centimeters

B   15.2 centimeters

C   25 centimeters

D   95 centimeters

Assessment Anchors/Eligible Content: M7.A.2.2.1 Write ratios to compare quantities (e.g., ratio of boys to girls).

M7.A.2.2.2 Solve for a variable in a given proportion.

M7.A.2.2.5 Select and/or use ratios or proportions to solve problems.

M7.B.2.2.1 Interpret and/or apply scales shown on maps, blueprints, models, etc.

M7.B.2.2.2 Determine and/or apply an appropriate scale for reduction or enlargement.

Academic Standards: 2.3.8.G

In mathematics, a **scale factor** is used to describe an enlargement or reduction. A scale factor can be expressed using a ratio. A scale factor that is between 0 and 1 represents a reduction of the original. A scale factor that is greater than 1 represents an enlargement of the original.

Guided Instruction

Problem

Mindy and her sisters want to make an enlargement of a photograph of their parents. The original photograph is 5 inches long and 3 inches wide. They would like the enlargement to be 35 inches long. What is the scale factor of the enlargement? What will be the width of the enlargement?

Step 1   Find the scale factor.

The original length is 5 inches and the enlargement length is 35 inches.

As a ratio: $\dfrac{\text{enlargement length}}{\text{original length}} = \dfrac{35 \text{ inches}}{5 \text{ inches}}$ or $\dfrac{7}{1}$.

The scale factor is $\dfrac{7}{1}$ or 7 times the original.

Step 2   Use a proportion to find the width of the enlargement.

Let x represent the width of the enlargement.

Scale factor $\rightarrow \dfrac{7}{1} = \dfrac{x}{3}$ $\begin{matrix}\leftarrow \text{enlargement width}\\ \leftarrow \text{original width}\end{matrix}$

Step 3   Find the cross products. $1 \cdot x = 7 \cdot 3$

$$x = \underline{\hspace{2cm}}$$

Solution

What is the scale factor of the enlargement? What will be the width of the enlargement? _____

_____

Apply the Pennsylvania Academic Standards

Use the scale factor of 4 to find each missing dimension.

1. enlargement: _____ inches

   actual: 6 inches

2. enlargement: _____ inches

   actual: 9 inches

3. enlargement: _____ inches

   actual: 4.3 inches

4. enlargement: 80 inches

   actual: _____ inches

5. enlargement: 68 inches

   actual: _____ inches

6. enlargement: 127.2 inches

   actual: _____ inches

Use the scale factor of $\frac{1}{3}$ to find each missing dimension.

7. reduction: _____ inches

   Actual: 27 inches

8. reduction: _____ inches

   Actual: 39 inches

9. reduction: _____ inches

   Actual: 56.1 inches

10. reduction: 3 inches

    Actual: _____ inches

11. reduction: 117 inches

    Actual: _____ inches

12. reduction: 25.6 inches

    Actual: _____ inches

Solve the problem.

13. Jeremy is making a photocopy of an original drawing. The dimensions of the drawing are $8\frac{1}{2}$ inches long and 11 inches wide. The scale factor of the enlargement is $\frac{3}{2}$. What are the dimensions of the enlarged copy? Explain your answer.

   _____

   _____

   _____

1. Clare is making a sketch of an ant for science class. She is using a scale factor of 20, and the length of the ant is actually 1.7 centimeters. How long is the sketch?

   A   21.7 cm

   B   27 cm

   C   34 cm

   D   37 cm

2. Jasper is making a model airplane with a scale factor of $\frac{1}{250}$. If the base of the model is 15.2 centimeters long, what is the actual length of the airplane?

   A   1,900 cm

   B   3,800 cm

   C   6,250 cm

   D   7,600 cm

3. Rita wants to make a scale drawing of a tower that is 150 feet tall. She decides the drawing should be as large as possible and fit on a sheet of paper that is $8\frac{1}{2}$ inches by 11 inches. Which is a reasonable scale to use for the drawing?

   A $\frac{1}{2}$ in. = 5 ft

   B   1 in. = 15 ft

   C   1 in. = 20 ft

   D   1 in. = 100 ft

4. A rectangular painting has a length of 48 inches and a width of 36 inches. A reduced copy of the painting has a length of 32 inches and a width of 24 inches. What is the scale factor of the reduction?

   A $\frac{1}{2}$

   B $\frac{2}{3}$

   C $\frac{3}{2}$

   D   2

5. A photograph that is 5 inches long and 7 inches wide is enlarged. The copy has a *width* of 25 inches. If x is the length of the copy, which of the following proportions could determine x?

   A $\frac{x}{25} = \frac{5}{7}$

   B $\frac{x}{25} = \frac{7}{5}$

   C $\frac{x}{7} = \frac{25}{5}$

   D $\frac{25}{x} = \frac{5}{7}$

Focus on the Pennsylvania Academic Standards | Lesson 33 | Understand Percent

Assessment Anchors/Eligible Content: M7.A.1.1.1 Convert between fractions, decimals and/or percents (e.g., 20% = 0.2 = 1/5) (terminating decimals only).

Academic Standards: 2.1.8.A

A **percent** is a special kind of ratio that compares a number to 100. You can write a percent as a fraction or a decimal. Sometimes you need to relate percents, decimals, and fractions to solve problems.

Here are some common fractions and their equivalent decimals and percents:

$\frac{1}{4}$ = 0.25 = 25% $\frac{1}{2}$ = 0.5 = 50% $\frac{3}{4}$ = 0.75 = 75%

$\frac{1}{8}$ = 0.125 = 12.5% $\frac{1}{5}$ = 0.2 = 20% $\frac{1}{10}$ = 0.1 = 10%

Guided Instruction

Problem

For a class project, Cindy mailed a survey to 8 students. One week later, 5 out of 8 students sent back the survey. What percent of the students returned the survey?

Step 1   Change the ratio "5 out of 8" to fraction form.   "5 out of 8" can be written as $\frac{5}{8}$.

Then write the fraction as a decimal by dividing the numerator by the denominator. $\frac{5}{8}$ = 5 ÷ 8 = _____

Step 2   Multiply the result by 100.   0.625 · 100 = _____
Then write the % symbol.   0.625 = 62.5%

Solution   What percent of the students returned the survey? _____

Other Examples

A. Write 125% as a decimal

Divide by 100.
125 ÷ 100 = 1.25
125% = 1.25

B. Write 6% as a fraction.

Write a fraction with a denominator of 100.
Then simplify.
6% = $\frac{6}{100}$ = $\frac{3}{50}$

C. Write 0.5% as a fraction.

Write the decimal as a fraction.
Then divide by 100.

0.5% = $\frac{\frac{1}{2}}{100}$ = $\frac{1}{200}$

Apply the Pennsylvania Academic Standards

Write each percent as a decimal.

1. 9%   **2.** 23%   **3.** 16.5%   **4.** 240%

_____   _____   _____   _____

Write each decimal as a percent.

5. 0.03   **6.** 1.92   **7.** 0.1725   **8.** 35

_____   _____   _____   _____

Write each percent as a fraction or mixed number in simplest form.

9. 80%   **10.** 0.25%   **11.** 37%   **12.** 210%

_____   _____   _____   _____

Write each fraction or mixed number as a percent.

13. $\frac{1}{2}$ **14.** $\frac{5}{8}$ **15.** $1\frac{3}{5}$ **16.** $\frac{3}{2}$

_____   _____   _____   _____

Write _equivalent_ if all three ratios are equivalent. Otherwise, write _not equivalent_.

17. $\frac{1}{20}$, 0.20, 20%   **18.** $\frac{3}{5}$, $\frac{6}{10}$, 60%   **19.** $1\frac{3}{8}$, 137.5%, $\frac{11}{8}$ **20.** 7.7, $70\frac{7}{10}$%, 770%

_____   _____   _____   _____

Solve each problem.

21. Complete the table. Fractions should be in simplest form.

Percent	Decimal	Fraction
60%		
	1.40	
		$\frac{7}{8}$

22. José made 33 of the 88 baskets for his basketball team. What percent did he not make? _____

23. Emilio got 14 out of 16 questions right on his science test. What percent did he get right? _____

24. Put in order from least to greatest: 0.03, $\frac{5}{4}$, $\frac{1}{20}$, 70%, 2, 0.03%.

_____

25. Explain how to estimate a percent equivalent to the ratio $\frac{344}{513}$.

_____

_____

Directions: Read each question. Then circle the letter for the best answer.

1. Which of the following shows three equivalent numbers?

   A $\frac{6}{8}$, 0.68, 68%

   B 0.15, 15%, $\frac{1}{5}$

   C 7, 7%, $\frac{7}{100}$

   D 40%, $\frac{2}{5}$, 0.4

2. Which is the **best** estimate of the fraction $\frac{57}{182}$?

   A 3%

   B 13%

   C 30%

   D 36%

3. What percent is equivalent to the ratio 7:700?

   A 1%

   B 10%

   C 100%

   D 110%

4. Which is the **best** description of a mental math method that can be used to change a decimal to a percent?

   A Move the decimal point to the left.

   B Move the decimal point two places to the left and write the % symbol.

   C Move the decimal point to the right.

   D Move the decimal point two places to the right and write the % symbol.

5. What is the percent equivalent to the whole number 2?

   A 2%

   B 20%

   C 200%

   D 2,000%

6. Which of the following shows three numbers that are **not** equivalent?

   A $\frac{19}{50}$, 0.38, 38%

   B 20%, $\frac{3}{15}$, 0.20

   C 0.652, $\frac{5}{8}$, 65.2%

   D 0.84, 84%, $\frac{21}{25}$

Assessment Anchors/Eligible Content: M7.D.3.1.1 Solve problems involving a constant rate of change (e.g., word problems, graphs or data tables).

M7.D.3.1.2 Describe and/or use the relationship of data displayed on a rate of change graph (e.g., how does the *x*-axis data relate to the *y*-axis data).

Academic Standards: 2.1.8.A, 2.3.8.B, 2.5.8.A, 2.5.8.D

A **rate** is a ratio that compares quantities involving two different units.

The formula that relates distance, rate, and time is *distance = rate • time*. Speed is an example of a rate.

$$speed = \frac{distance\ traveled}{time\ spent\ traveling}$$

When James says he drives at a speed of 50 miles per hour, he means that he would travel a distance of 50 miles *if* he drove for 1 hour (and 25 miles if he drove for half an hour, etc.).

Guided Instruction

Problem

The graph shows the rate Amanda bicycled at a recent competition. The total length of the competition was 120 miles. Amanda finished in 6 hours. If Amanda maintained a constant speed, how long did it take her to bicycle 60 miles? Use the graph to verify.

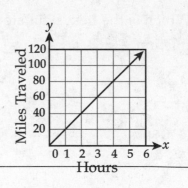

Step 1 Use the formula that relates distance, rate (speed), and time.

distance = rate • time

Step 2 Substitute the known values into the formula. Let *r* = Amanda's rate (miles per hour).

_____ = r • _____

Step 3 Solve for the rate.

$$\frac{120}{6} = \frac{\cancel{6}r}{\cancel{6}}$$

_____ = r

Step 4 Use the rate or the graph to determine how long it took Amanda to travel 60 miles. So it took Amanda _____ hours to travel 60 miles.

distance = rate • time

60 = _____ t

_____ = t

Step 5 You can use the graph to verify your answer. Find 3 hours on the *x*-axis, and then go up on the *y*-axis to verify. At 3 hours, Amanda had traveled 60 miles.

Solution

If Amanda maintained a constant speed, how long did it take her to bicycle 60 miles? _____

Apply the Pennsylvania Academic Standards

Simplify each ratio to find the missing rate.

1. Ed drove 420 miles in 7 hours. His speed is $\dfrac{420 \text{ miles}}{7 \text{ hours}}$ = _____

2. Dimitri earned $40 for 4 hours of work. His wage is $\dfrac{\$40}{4 \text{ hours}}$ = _____

3. Sugar costs $2.40 for 5 pounds. Sugar costs $\dfrac{\$2.40}{5 \text{ pounds}}$ = _____

Find each product. Use the correct measure.

4. $\dfrac{60 \text{ mi}}{1 \text{ hr}} \cdot 4 \text{ hr}$ = _____   5. $\dfrac{\$18.40}{1 \text{ hr}} \cdot 40 \text{ hr}$ = _____

6. $\dfrac{1.2 \text{ lb}}{1 \text{ in.}^3} \cdot 20 \text{ in.}^3$ = _____   7. $\dfrac{1,250 \text{ people}}{1 \text{ mi}^2} \cdot 400 \text{ mi}^2$ = _____

Use the information below to solve problems 8–9.

Every two hours since leaving home at 7 A.M. Hedwig recorded the distance he had traveled in the table to the right.

Time	Distance (mi)
9 A.M.	50
11 A.M.	100
1 P.M.	150
3 P.M.	200
5 P.M.	250

8. According to the table, what was Hedwig's speed

   throughout the day? _____

9. If Hedwig decided to continue driving until 6 P.M.,

   how many miles would he have traveled? _____

Solve each problem.

10. Ms. Demitan drove 630 miles in 12 hours. To the
    nearest tenth, at what speed did she drive? _____

11. Mr. Gonzalez drove 630 miles on 25 gallons of gas. At that rate,
    how many miles can he drive on 40 gallons of gas? _____

12. Mr. Kendall can type 920 words in 20 minutes. Ms. Kinoke can type 1,260 words
    in 30 minutes. Which office worker can type a 2,000-word document in less time? Explain.

    _____

    _____

    _____

PSSA Practice Directions: **Read each question. Then circle the letter for the best answer.**

1. In 3 hours, a pipe can put 400 gallons of water into a storage tank. At this rate, about how long will it take to put 1,500 gallons of water into the tank?

   A 3 hours

   B $9\frac{1}{2}$ hours

   C $9\frac{2}{3}$ hours

   D $11\frac{1}{4}$ hours

2. The graph below shows the distance that Rosemary has bicycled over time.

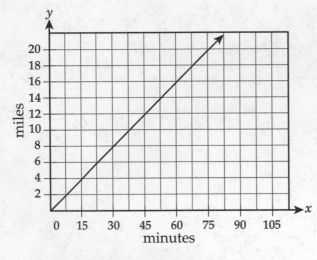

   At about what speed is Rosemary bicycling?

   A 15 miles per hour

   B 12 miles per hour

   C 9 miles per hour

   D 6 miles per hour

Use the table below to answer questions 3–4.

Number of Apples	Price Paid
7	$3.50
10	$5.00
13	$6.50
16	$8.00

3. How much does one apple cost?

   A $0.25

   B $0.50

   C $0.75

   D $1.25

4. How much will 20 apples cost?

   A $5.00

   B $10.00

   C $15.00

   D $25.00

5. The best buy is the least cost per orange. Which is the best buy?

   A $3.60 for 6 oranges

   B $4.50 for 8 oranges

   C $6.00 for 12 oranges

   D $8.60 for 12 oranges

     Measuring Up® to the Pennsylvania Academic Standards

Directions: Read each question. Then circle the letter for the best answer.

1. A car traveled a distance of 195 miles in 3 hours 15 minutes. What is the speed?

    A   60 miles per hour

    B   61.9 miles per hour

    C   62.5 miles per hour

    D   65 miles per hour

2. There are 13 boys and 14 girls in Mrs. Green's class. If 3 of the students are absent today, what is the ratio of students absent to students present?

    A   1:8

    B   1:9

    C   1:10

    D   1:27

3. Which of the following lists the ratios from **least** to **greatest**?

    A $\frac{3}{8}$, 35%, 0.3

    B   0.3, 35%, $\frac{3}{8}$

    C $\frac{3}{8}$, 0.3, 35%

    D   0.3, $\frac{3}{8}$, 35%

4. Boxes of trash bags are sold in 4 different sizes. Which box size has the least unit price?

    A   10-count box for $1.29

    B   25-count box for $3.09

    C   45-count box for $5.99

    D   85-count box for $10.79

5. A catering hall uses 11 heads of iceberg lettuce and 7 heads of Romaine lettuce to make a green salad for 70 people. How many heads of lettuce would be needed for 175 people?

    A   7 heads of lettuce

    B   10 heads of lettuce

    C   28 heads of lettuce

    D   45 heads of lettuce

6. Which of the following is **not** equivalent to 400%?

    A $6 \div 1\frac{1}{2}$

    B $2\frac{2}{3} \times 1\frac{1}{2}$

    C $0.24 + 0.16$

    D $5.2 \div 1.3$

7. If *b* books cost *d* dollars, which expression represents the unit cost per book?

   A $\frac{b}{d}$

   B $\frac{d}{b}$

   C bd

   D $b + d$

8. An architect has built a model of a new housing complex. The graph below is used to calculate the scale from the model to the building.

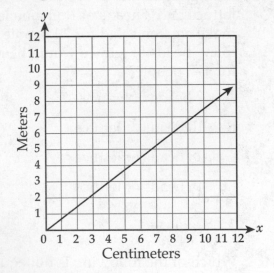

Which statement is true?

   A The building measures 4 centimeters for every 3 meters of the model.

   B The building measures 3 centimeters for every 4 meters of the model.

   C The building measures 4 meters for every 3 centimeters of the model.

   D The building measures 3 meters for every 4 centimeters of the model.

9. A group consisting of 126 students and 7 chaperones is going on a field trip. Which of the following groups does **not** have the same ratio of students to chaperones?

   A 36 students and 2 chaperones

   B 54 students and 3 chaperones

   C 90 students and 4 chaperones

   D 108 students and 6 chaperones

10. Consuelo wants to enlarge a photograph that is 3 inches wide and 5 inches high to make a poster that is 2 feet wide. What will be the height of the poster?

   A 3 ft

   B 3 ft 2 in.

   C 3 ft 3 in.

   D 3 ft 4 in.

11. In a drawing, the length of an amoeba is 65 millimeters. The actual length of the amoeba is 0.65 millimeters. What is the scale factor of the drawing?

   A $\frac{1}{100}$

   B $\frac{1}{10}$

   C 10

   D 100

12. The table below shows the reading speeds of four students. Use the information from the table to answer the questions.

Student	Reading Speed
Naomi	364 words in 7 minutes
Kaitlin	333 words in 6 minutes
Enrique	265 words in 5 minutes
Jordan	420 words in 8 minutes

A. Write the rates for each of the students in words per minute. Explain how you found your answers.

B. Arrange the students according to their reading speeds from least to greatest. Explain your answer.

13. The graph below shows the progress of a certain car along the highway during a ten-hour trip. Use the graph to help you answer the questions.

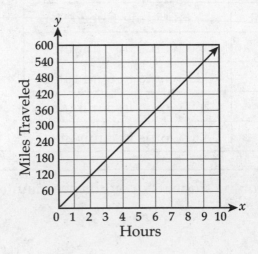

A. What is the speed of the car? Explain.

13. *Continued.*

B. A second car traveled the same distance. If the car was traveling at 50 miles per hour, how many more hours did it take for that car to travel 600 miles? Explain your answer.

C. A third car made the same trip in 8 hours. What was the average speed for the third car? Explain your answer.

Directions: Read each question. Then circle the letter for the best answer

1. Use the number line below to determine which of the following statements is true.

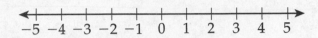

   A   −2 is greater than −1.

   B   0 is greater than 2.

   C   3 is greater than −1.

   D   4 is greater than 5.

2. What is the sum represented in the number line below?

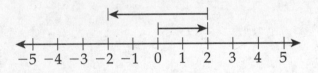

   A   0 + (−4) = −2

   B   2 + 4 = 6

   C   2 − (−4) = 2

   D   2 + (−4) = −2

3. When shipping her homemade cakes for sale at local shops, Sarah packs 14 cakes to a box. Which of the following expressions shows how many cakes would fill 15 boxes?

   A   14 + 15

   B   15 − 14

   C   14 · 15

   D   15 · 15

4. Which of the numbers listed has the **greatest** value?

   A   0.707   B $\frac{7}{10}$

   C   0.077   D   0.77

5. Without using a calculator, which of the following is equivalent to $10\frac{3}{4} \div 8\frac{1}{2}$?

   A $\frac{43}{4} \div \frac{2}{17}$

   B $\frac{43}{4} \cdot \frac{2}{17}$

   C $\frac{34}{4} \div \frac{2}{17}$

   D $\frac{34}{4} \cdot \frac{2}{17}$

6. Which of the statements that follows is equivalent to this subtraction statement?

$$-2 - (-6) = 4$$

   A   −2 + 6 = 4

   B   −2 − 6 = −4

   C   6 − (−2) = 4

   D   −6 − (−2) = 4

7. What is the rule to find the next term in this sequence?

$$7, 8.1, 9.2, 10.3, \ldots$$

   A   Subtract 1.1

   B   Add 0.1

   C   Add 1.01

   D   Add 1.1

8. Last month, Fiona's household used 41 thermal units of gas. The basic service charge, which included the cost of the first 2.9 thermal units, was $11.35. The remaining thermals units were charged at $0.476 per thermal unit. What is a reasonable estimate for the cost of the remaining thermal units?

A $190

B $90

C $19

D $9

9. Joanne bought a box of 12 donuts, which cost $6.24. If each donut cost the same amount, what was the cost of 1 donut?

A $0.92

B $0.72

C $0.52

D $0.20

10. Which of the following fractions is **not** equivalent to $\frac{14}{18}$?

A $\frac{7}{9}$

B $\frac{56}{72}$

C $\frac{28}{38}$

D $\frac{42}{54}$

11. Which set of numbers is in order from **least** to **greatest**?

A $-1, \frac{1}{10}, \frac{1}{4}, 0.2, 1.1$

B $-1, \frac{1}{10}, 0.2, \frac{1}{4}, 1.1$

C $\frac{1}{10}, -1, \frac{1}{4}, 0.2, 1.1$

D $\frac{1}{10}, -1, 0.2, \frac{1}{4}, 1.1$

12. The table shows the amount of weight a kitten gained over a 5-month period.

Weight Gained Per Month

Month	Pounds
May	$\frac{1}{4}$
June	0.24
July	0.54
August	$\frac{3}{8}$
September	0.3

Without using a calculator, what was the total weight the kitten gained at the end of this period?

A 1.505 lb

B 1.605 lb

C 1.705 lb

D 1.805 lb

13. Herbert pays $8.67 for some apples. If the apples cost $2.89 per pound, how many pounds did Herbert buy?

A 2　　　　　B 3

C 4　　　　　D 5

14. Harry has a piece of ribbon that is $\frac{3}{4}$ meter long. He cut the ribbon into 6 equal pieces. How long is each piece?

    A $4\frac{1}{2}$ m

    B   2 m

    C $\frac{1}{6}$ m

    D $\frac{1}{8}$ m

15. Which of the calculations that follows will produce the 7th term?

$$3,\ 9,\ 81,\ 6{,}561,\ \dots$$

    A   Add 6 to the 6th term.

    B   Multiply 3 by the 6th term.

    C   Multiply 9 by the 6th term.

    D   Square the 6th term.

16. The prices of 4 different cans of tomato sauce are given in the table.

Tomato Sauce

Size (oz)	Price
6	$0.39
11	$0.70
12	$0.76
18	$1.14

Which size can(s) has the **least** price per ounce?

    A   The 18-oz can only

    B   The 18-oz and the 12-oz cans only

    C   The 18-oz, the 12-oz, and the 11-oz cans

    D   The 6-oz can

17. At the rate of 4 mints for 5 cents, how many mints can you buy for d dollars?

    A $80d$

    B $\frac{80}{d}$

    C $\frac{8}{d}$

    D $8d$

18. What is the result when the sum of -9 and -2 is subtracted from the sum of 4 and -1?

    A   14

    B   10

    C -4

    D -8

19. What is the value of the expression if $m = 5$ and $n = -2$?

$$5(m + n) + 9$$

    A   44

    B   24

    C   14

    D   4

20. There are 75 adults and 35 children who participate in a local theater group. What is the ratio of children to total participants for this group?

    A $\frac{7}{22}$

    B $\frac{7}{15}$

    C $\frac{15}{22}$

    D $\frac{22}{15}$

21. Mark is driving 30 miles per hour on his motorcycle. If he continues at this speed, how many miles can he travel in 2.5 hours?

A   45 miles

B   60 miles

C   75 miles

D   85 miles

22. Which of the following statements is **not** a true statement?

A   1.33 > 1.333 > 1.3333

B   1.33 < 1.333 < 1.3333

C   1.2 < 1.204 < 1.21

D   1,092 < 1,902 < 1,912

23. A car rental company charges customers a daily rate. If a customer was charged $161.70 for a 6-day rental, how much did he pay per day?

A $23.10

B $26.95

C $32.34

D $40.43

24. Attendance at a concert at a local stadium was recorded as 10,254 adults and 3,845 children. Which is the **best** estimate for concert attendance?

A   12,000

B   13,000

C   14,000

D   15,000

25. The sales for a computer company for two months are shown below.

Month	Sales
August	$45,086
September	$68,903

How much **more** did the company make in sales in the month of September?

A $114,000

B $113,989

C $23,914

D $23,817

 26. Which of the following fractions is **not** equivalent to $\frac{4}{9}$?

A $\frac{8}{18}$

B $\frac{16}{36}$

C $\frac{12}{72}$

D $\frac{20}{45}$

27. Richard had $80.14 when he returned from a concert. He bought a T-shirt for $25.60 and spent $18.79 on refreshments. **About** how much money did he have before he went to the concert?

A $36

B $90

C $125

D $150

28. Boxes of cereal are sold in different sizes. Which box size has the **greatest** unit price?

    A   14-ounce box for $4.29

    B   15-ounce box for $4.29

    C   18-ounce box for $4.89

    D   27-ounce box for $5.69

29. What is the value of $14(b + 28)$, if $b = 3$?

    A   70

    B   395

    C   434

    D   476

30. Josephine bought some bamboo shoots because she heard it was the fastest growing plant in the world. Josephine charted the height of the plant each morning. If the bamboo continues to follow the same pattern, how tall will the plant be on the sixth morning?

Morning	Height (inches)
1	18
2	36
3	54
4	72

    A   90

    B   96

    C   104

    D   108

31. Barbara has 7 books of stamps. Each book contains x number of stamps. If Barbara has 147 stamps, how many stamps does each book hold?

    A   12   B   17

    C   21   D   27

32. León has a picture that is 5 inches wide and 9 inches long. If he wants to enlarge the picture to be 30 inches wide, what will be the length of the enlarged picture?

    A   45 inches

    B   48 inches

    C   54 inches

    D   63 inches

33. Which of the following expressions equals the expression $5g + 14g + 3$?

    A $8g + 14g$

    B $19g + 3$

    C $5g + 17g$

    D $9g + 3$

34. Carol and Jim are working on a research project. Carol has done 0.40 of the project and Jim has completed 38% of the project. What fraction of the project has **not** been completed?

    A $\frac{11}{50}$ B $\frac{13}{50}$

    C $\frac{37}{50}$ D $\frac{39}{50}$

35. Miguel is trying to decipher a code his brother gave him. What is the rule for the following pattern?

…9, 27, 81, 243, 729, …

A Multiply the previous term by 3.

B Divide the previous term by 3.

C Subtract 3 from the previous term.

D Add 3 to the previous term.

36. Allen has a bag of stones. In the bag are 4 blue stones, 3 red stones, 7 black stones, and 2 white stones. What is the ratio of blue stones to black stones?

A 1:4

B 4:1

C 4:7

D 7:4

37. If $c = 4$ and $d = 6$, what is the value of the expression $7d \div (2 + c)$?

A 7   B 9

C 25   D 21

38. On October 14, 1947, Chuck Yeager became the first person in flight to break the sound barrier by flying faster than Mach 1. This is equivalent to 660 miles per hour. If Yeager accelerated to a speed of 699.6 miles per hour, how many Machs was he flying?

A 1.02   B 1.04

C 1.06   D 1.08

39. If $c = 6$ and $d = 4$, what is the value of the expression $8d - (18 \div c)$?

A 26

B 29

C 35

D 45

40. Which set of numbers is in order from **greatest** to **least**?

A $1.33, \frac{5}{4}, 2\frac{2}{5}, 2$

B $2\frac{2}{5}, 2, 1.33, \frac{5}{4}$

C $\frac{5}{4}, 2\frac{2}{5}, 2, 1.33$

D $2, 1.33, \frac{5}{4}, 2\frac{2}{5}$

41. After a 25% discount, and an additional $5 discount, Tami paid $57 for running shoes. If p represents the original price of the running shoes, which equation can be used to find p?

A $p - 0.25p - 5 = 57$

B $p - 0.25p + 5 = 57$

C $p - 25p - 5 = 57$

D $p - 0.5p - 5 = 57$

42. Holly can swim one lap around the pool in 4 minutes. If she continues at this pace, how many laps can Holly swim in 64 minutes?

   A   13 laps   B   14 laps

   C   15 laps   D   16 laps

43. Of the 132 people who sent in their resumes to apply for a job, 47 people were granted interviews. Which ratio represents the number of applicants to the number of people that did **not** get an interview?

   A   132 : 85

   B   132 : 47

   C   47 : 132

   D   47 : 85

44. Julie walks $1\frac{9}{10}$ miles a day. **About** how far does Julie walk in 31 days?

   A   60 miles   B   55 miles

   C   50 miles   D   45 miles

45. What is the next term in the pattern given below?

$$\frac{1}{9}, \frac{2}{9}, \frac{1}{3}, \frac{4}{9}, \frac{5}{9}, \cdots$$

   A $\frac{1}{9}$

   B $\frac{2}{3}$

   C $\frac{3}{2}$

   D $\frac{9}{1}$

46. If $s = 5$ and $t = 8$, what is the value of the expression $100 + s \cdot t \div 2$?

   A   60

   B   75

   C   120

   D   142

47. 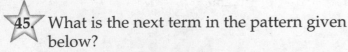 Stefan's pineapple casserole, which serves 6 people, uses $2\frac{3}{4}$ cups of pineapples. If Stefan is planning on serving his casserole to 22 people, how much pineapple does he need?

   A $10\frac{1}{2}$ cups

   B $10\frac{1}{12}$ cups

   C $11\frac{3}{4}$ cups

   D $12\frac{1}{10}$ cups

48.  Sal is building a model railroad using models that follow the N scale (1:160). If he has a model locomotive that is 10.7 centimeters long, how long is the actual locomotive to the nearest meter?

   A   7 m

   B   17 m

   C   27 m

   D   37 m

49. Mason went to the supermarket and bought 6 pounds of grapes for $9.00. Judy bought 2 pounds of the same grapes for $3.00. Using the graph, what is the cost of grapes per pound?

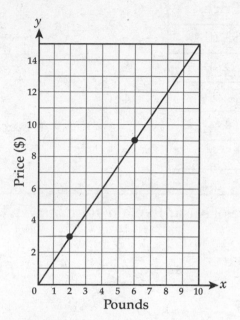

A $1.00 per 1.5 pounds

B $1.50 per pound

C $1.00 per pound

D $0.50 per pound

50. Jacob loves to kayak. He can travel 2 miles in 30 minutes. If Jacob continues to kayak at the same pace, how far will he travel in 75 minutes?

A   8 miles

B   7 miles

C   6 miles

D   5 miles

51. At Dave's Summer Sport camp there are 5 camp counselors that supervise 31 boys and 24 girls. What is the ratio of camp counselors to campers?

A   1:11

B   5:24

C   5:31

D   11:1

52. Mauna Kea, a volcano on the island of Hawaii, begins below sea level at the ocean floor, and ascends upwards 10,203 meters. The Summit of Mauna Kea is 4,205 meters above sea level. How many meters of Mauna Kea are **below** sea level?

A   5,898 m

B   5,998 m

C   6,098 m

D   6,998 m

53. Donald had 27 books. He returned x books to the library. If Donald still has 12 books left, what is the value of x?

A $x = 15$

B $x = 14$

C $x = 13$

D $x = 12$

Open-Ended Items

54. The prices for 5 different salsa jars are given in the table below.

Ounces of Salsa	Price
6	$2.10
8	$4.40
10	$3.00
12	$4.80
16	$5.76

A. Which size jar has the least price per ounce of salsa? Explain your answer.

B. Which size jar has the greatest price per ounce of salsa? Explain your answer.

55. Michael bikes 9 miles in 45 minutes.

A. What is his rate of speed in miles per hour? Explain your answer.

B. If he biked 4 hours at that speed, how many miles did he travel? Explain your answer.

56. The Schuylkill River Theater company encourages boys and girls, ages 8 through 15, to participate in their annual theater festival. This year, the ratio of boys to girls in the festival is 11:14.

A. Last year, 84 girls participated. How many boys participated? Explain your answer.

B. This year the company decided to hire 1 director for every 10 children. If 44 of the children are boys, how many directors did they hire?

Copying is illegal.   Measuring Up® to the Pennsylvania Academic Standards

57. The table shows the number of miles Shauna walked each day last week.
What is the total number of miles she walked? Record your answer in decimal form.
Show your work.

Day of the week	Number of miles walked
Monday	0.25
Tuesday	$\frac{1}{2}$
Wednesday	1.3
Thursday	0.96
Friday	$\frac{6}{8}$
Saturday	2.3
Sunday	$\frac{3}{2}$

Chapter 6 Measurement
In Chapter 6, you will study and practice:

- how to use and convert units of length;
- how to use and convert units of weight and mass;
- how to use and convert units of capacity;
- how to use and convert units of time.

★ **Building Stamina®:** This section gives you a chance to sharpen your measurement skills and to strengthen your test-taking ability.

Chapter 7 7 Perimeter, Circumference, and Area
In Chapter 7, you will study and practice:

- how to find the area of triangles and parallelograms;
- how to find the perimeter and area of compound figures;
- how to find the circumference and area of circles;
- how to use formulas to solve problems.

★ **Building Stamina®:** This section gives you a chance to sharpen your skills with perimeter, circumference, and area, and to strengthen your test-taking ability.

Chapter 8 Geometry
In Chapter 8, you will study and practice:

- how to work with circles;
- how to classify lines;
- how to identify congruent and similar figures;
- how to plot points on the coordinate grid;
- how to solve problems using similar figures.

★ **Building Stamina®:** This section gives you a chance to sharpen your geometric skills and to strengthen your test-taking ability.

Chapter 9 Statistics and Data Analysis

In Chapter 9, you will study and practice:

- how to find mean, median, mode, and range;
- how to select an appropriate statistical measure;
- how to analyze data;
- how to use stem-and-leaf plots and graphs to display data;
- how to choose the appropriate representation.

★ **Building Stamina®:** This section gives you a chance to sharpen your skills with statistics and data analysis, and to strengthen your test-taking ability.

Chapter 10 Probability

In Chapter 10, you will study and practice:

- how to find the probability of simple events;
- how to use experimental probability;
- how to find the probability of independent events.

★ **Building Stamina®:** This section gives you a chance to sharpen your probability skills and to strengthen your test-taking ability.

Chapter 6
Focus on the Pennsylvania Academic Standards
Lesson 35   Use and Convert Units of Length

Assessment Anchors/Eligible Content: M7.B.1.1.1 Add, subtract, or convert measurements, using only the units below, with and without regrouping (e.g., 4 ft − 2 ft 5 in. = 1 ft 7 in.) Answer should be converted to the largest whole unit (e.g., 37 oz = 2 lb 5 oz or 39 in. = 1 yd 3 in.). Conversion chart provided on the reference sheet.

- in., ft, yd
- fl oz, cup, pint, quart, gallon
- oz, lb
- sec, min, hours, days
- metric units including milli, centi and kilo (m, g or L)

Academic Standards: 2.3.5.D, 2.3.8.D, 2.4.8.B

You can measure the length of an object in either customary or metric units.

Customary Units of Length	Metric Units of Length
1 yard (yd) = 3 feet (ft) = 36 inches (in.)	1 meter = 100 centimeters (cm)
1 mile = 1,760 yards = 5,280 feet	1 meter = 1,000 millimeters (mm)
	1 kilometer (km) = 1,000 meters (m)

Guided Instruction

Problem   Evan had 2 feet 4 inches of wire. He used 10 inches for a science project. How much wire does he have left?

Convert the measurements to a single customary unit to find the difference.

Step 1   Convert 2 feet to inches. $2 \times \underline{\hspace{1cm}} = \underline{\hspace{1cm}}$

To find the number of inches, multiply 2 by _____ .

Step 2   Add to find how many inches of wire Evan had altogether. $24 + 4 = \underline{\hspace{1cm}}$ inches

Step 3   Subtract the number of inches of wire he used. $28 - 10 = \underline{\hspace{1cm}}$ inches

Step 4   Convert the difference into feet and inches.

To find the number of feet and inches, divide by 12. Then write the decimal as a mixed number in simplest form. $\underline{\hspace{1cm}} \div 12 = \underline{\hspace{1cm}}$ feet

$1.5 = 1 \underline{\hspace{1cm}} = \underline{\hspace{1cm}}$ feet

1 foot is 12 inches, so $\frac{1}{2}$ foot is _____ inches.

So 18 inches equals _____.

Solution   How much wire does he have left? _____

Another Example

By how many meters do 7,000 millimeters and 7.55 meters differ?

Convert 7,000 millimeters to meters:
1,000 millimeters = 1 meter. So 7,000 millimeters = 7 meters.
Subtract to find the difference. 7.55 meters − 7 meters = 0.55 meter

Apply the Pennsylvania Academic Standards

Convert each measure to the given unit.

1. 5,000 millimeters = _____ meters

2. 4 miles = _____ feet

3. 8 centimeters = _____ millimeters

4. 5 feet = _____ inches

5. 18 feet = _____ yards

6. 7.8 kilometers = _____ meters

7. 144 inches = _____ feet

8. 7 yards = _____ feet

9. 4 millimeters = _____ centimeter

10. 5,280 yards = _____ miles

11. 39 feet = _____ yards

12. 16 meters = _____ kilometers

Complete each equation.

13. 20 in. × 9 = _____ yd

14. 2 m − 85 cm = _____ cm

15. 1 mile − 2,080 ft = _____ ft

16. 4 ft · 3 = _____ yd

17. 6 km − 4,700 m = _____ m

18. 20 in. + 4 ft = _____ in.

Solve each problem.

19. Ernest lives 0.7 mile from school and Mei lives 1,300 yards from school. Which student lives closer to school? Explain how you found your answer.

    _____

    _____

20. Fran bought 3 packages of lace. Each package contains 2 feet 8 inches of lace. How many feet of lace did Fran buy? Explain how you found your answer.

    _____

    _____

    _____

PSSA Practice Directions: Read each question. Then circle the letter for the best answer.

1. Mattie measured one side of the patio shown below in yards. Jimmy measured the longer side in feet.

24 feet

5 yards

By how much does Jimmy's measurement **exceed** Mattie's measurement?

A   9 ft

B   9 yd

C   19 ft

D   19 yd

2. Paula has 15 feet of yarn. If she uses 1 yard 2 feet, how much yarn does she have left?

A   2 yd

B   3 yd 1 ft

C   2 ft 5 in.

D   1 yd 14 in.

3. Frank has a piece of wood that is 5 feet long. How many 8-inch pieces can he cut from the wood?

A   9

B   8

C   7

D   6

4. Bev has 38 inches of red trim, 2.5 feet of white trim, and 1 yard of blue trim. How would you list the trims from **least** to **greatest** length?

A   red, white, blue

B   blue, white, red

C   red, blue, white

D   white, blue, red

5. Rico jogs 3.5 kilometers, 3 times a week. How many meters does he jog each week?

A   10,500 m

B   1,050 m

C   10.5 m

D   0.0105 m

6. Jon used a centimeter ruler to measure the width of a leaf. He recorded the width as 47 centimeters. What is the width expressed in meters?

A   0.047 m

B   0.47 m

C   470 m

D   4,700 m

Assessment Anchors/Eligible Content: M7.B.1.1.1 Add, subtract, or convert measurements, using only the units below, with and without regrouping (e.g., 4 ft − 2 ft 5 in. = 1 ft 7 in.). Answer should be converted to the largest whole unit (e.g., 37 oz = 2 lb 5 oz or 39 in. = 1 yd 3 in.). Conversion chart provided on the reference sheet.

- in., ft, yd
- fl oz, cup, pint, quart, gallon
- oz, lb
- sec, min, hours, days
- metric units including milli, centi and kilo (m, g or L)

Academic Standards: 2.3.5.D, 2.3.8.D, 2.4.8.B

You can measure the weight or mass of an object in either customary or metric units.

Customary Units of Weight	Metric Units of Mass
1 pound (lb) = 16 ounces (oz)	1 gram (g) = 1,000 milligrams (mg) 1 kilogram (kg) = 1,000 grams

Guided Instruction

Problem

The weight of rock sample A is 24 ounces. The weight of rock sample B is 2 pounds. What is the combined weight of the rock samples?

Convert both measurements to a single unit.

Step 1   Convert 2 pounds to ounces. $2 \cdot 16 = $ _____

Step 2   Add the weight of both samples. $32 + 24 = $ _____ ounces

Step 3   Convert the answer to pounds. $56 \div 16 = $ _____

So 56 ounces equals _____ pounds _____ ounces.

Solution

What is the combined weight of the rock samples?

_____

Another Example

Which is greater, 820 grams or 0.48 kilograms?

Convert 0.48 kilograms to grams.
To convert from a larger unit to a smaller unit, multiply.

0.48 kilograms × 1,000 = 480 grams

480 < 820

So 820 grams is greater than 0.48 kilograms.

Apply the Pennsylvania Academic Standards

Convert each measure to the given unit.

1. 3 pounds =

_____ ounces

2. 20 pounds =

_____ ounces

3. 5 grams =

_____ milligrams

4. 10,000 grams =

_____ kilograms

5. 2,160 ounces =

_____ pounds

6. 800 milligrams =

_____ gram

7. 27 grams =

_____ kilogram

8. 9,000 ounces =

_____ pounds

9. 112 ounces =

_____ pounds

10. 5.4 kilograms =

_____ grams

11. 6,200 milligrams =

_____ grams

12. 208 ounces =

_____ pounds

Complete each equation.

13. 5 lb − 1 lb 2 oz = _____ lb _____ oz

14. 3.5 kg − 275 g = _____ kg

15. 4 lb 3 oz − 26 oz = _____ lb _____ oz

16. 65 g + 1,935 g = _____ kg

17. 5 lb 7 oz − 39 oz = _____ lb

18. 12 lb − 4 lb 8 oz = _____ lb _____ oz

Solve each problem.

19. Josie has two packages of cheese. Each of them weighs 28 ounces. Todd has one package of cheese that weighs 24 ounces. What is the weight of all 3 packages together, in pounds? Explain how you found the answer.

_____

_____

20. Gayle bought 4.5 pounds of chopped meat. She used 48 ounces of it for dinner. How much meat does she have left? Explain how you found the answer.

_____

_____

 Measuring Up® to the Pennsylvania Academic Standards

PSSA Practice

Directions: Read each question. Then circle the letter for the best answer.

 1. Wendy used 12 ounces of strawberries, 1.5 pounds of melon, and 28 ounces of blueberries to make a fruit salad. How many pounds of fruit did she use?

A   2.5 lb

B   3 lb

C   3.2 lb

D   4 lb

2. Jason has a package he wants to send from London to his sister Chloë in Pittsburgh. If the package has a mass of 3.24 kilograms, what is the mass of Jason's package expressed in grams?

A   3.24 g

B   32.4 g

C   324 g

D   3,240 g

 3. If 3 computer discs have a mass of 384 grams, what is the mass of 10 discs, in kilograms?

A   3.84 kg

B   1.92 kg

C   1.28 kg

D   6.4 kg

 4. Josh needs 32 ounces of sugar. He only has 1 pound 3 ounces. How many ounces does he need to borrow?

A   16 oz

B   13 oz

C   10 oz

D   6 oz

 5. Manuel and three friends buy a watermelon. Suppose Manuel then cuts the watermelon approximately into fourths and gives each fourth to a friend. If the watermelon originally weighed 6 pounds, about how much will each piece weigh?

A   1.5 oz

B   8 oz

C   16 oz

D   24 oz

6. Justin used a scale to measure the mass of a soil sample. He recorded the measure as 155 grams. What is the mass expressed in kilograms?

A   0.155 kg

B   1.55 kg

C   15.5 kg

D   1,550 kg

Assessment Anchors/Eligible Content: M7.B.1.1.1 Add, subtract, or convert measurements, using only the units below, with and without regrouping (e.g., 4 ft − 2 ft 5 in. = 1 ft 7 in.). Answer should be converted to the largest whole unit (e.g., 37 oz = 2 lb 5 oz or 39 in. = 1 yd 3 in.). Conversion chart provided on the reference sheet.

- in., ft, yd
- fl oz, cup, pint, quart, gallon
- oz, lb
- sec, min, hours, days
- metric units including milli, centi and kilo (m, g or L)

Academic Standards: 2.3.5.D, 2.3.8.D, 2.4.8.B

You can measure capacity in either customary or metric units.

Customary Units of Capacity	Metric Units of Capacity
1 cup = 8 fluid ounces (fl oz) 1 pint = 2 cups (c) 1 quart = 2 pints (pt) 1 gallon (gal) = 4 quarts (qt)	1 liter = 1,000 milliliters (mL) 1 kiloliter (kL) = 1,000 liters (L)

Guided Instruction

Problem Meg made a fruit punch by mixing 1 pint of apple juice, 8 fluid ounces of orange juice, and 1 quart of ginger ale. How many cups of punch did she make?

Convert the measurements to a single customary unit to find the total.

Step 1 Convert 1 pint to cups.

How many cups equal 1 pint? _____

Step 2 Convert 8 fluid ounces to cups.

How many cups equal 8 fluid ounces? _____

Step 3 Convert 1 quart to cups.

How many cups equal 1 quart? _____

Step 4 Add to find the total number of cups.   2 + 1 + 4 = _____

Solution How many cups of punch did she make? _____

Another Example

Which is greater, 1,367 milliliters or 1.3 liters?

Convert 1,367 milliliters to liters
To Convert from a smaller unit to a larger unit, divide.

1,367 ÷ 1,000 = 1,367 liters

1.367 > 1.3

So 1,367 milliters is greater than 1.3 liters.

Apply the Pennsylvania Academic Standards

Convert each measure to the given unit.

1. 22 pints = _____ quarts

2. 1.5 gallons = _____ cups

3. 8 liters = _____ milliliters

4. 600 liters = _____ kiloliter

5. 160 fluid ounces = _____ quarts

6. 7 gallons = _____ quarts

7. 32 cups = _____ quarts

8. 18 cups = _____ pints

9. 3,000 milliliters = _____ liters

10. 4.5 liters = _____ milliliters

11. 48 fluid ounces = _____ pints

12. 256 fluid ounces = _____ gallons

Complete each equation.

13. 3 qt − 5 pt = _____ pt

14. 2 qt + 10 qt = _____ gal

15. 3 pt + 1 qt = _____ fl oz

16. 4 L + 28 L = _____ mL

17. 7 kL − 350 L = _____ L

18. 2 gal − 30 c = _____ fl oz

19. A chef made 4 gallons of soup. He stored the soup in 1-quart containers. How many of the containers did he fill? Explain how you found your answer.

_____

_____

20. Guy poured 275 milliliters of water from a full 1-liter bottle. How many milliliters of water were left in the bottle?

_____

_____

PSSA Practice **Directions: Read each question. Then circle the letter for the best answer.**

1. Ester's water cooler uses a five-gallon water bottle. How many cups of water will she be able to get a full bottle?

A 16 cups

B 20 cups

C 40 cups

D 80 cups

2. Meredith is making lemonade. A large pitcher holds 2.5 quarts of liquid. How many fluid ounces does the pitcher hold?

A 95 fl oz

B 80 fl oz

C 76 fl oz

D 75 fl oz

3. What fact do you need to know in order to find the mass of 3 liters of water?

A 3 kiloliters equals 3,000 liters.

B 1 liter equals 1,000 milliliters.

C 1 milliliter equals 0.001 liter.

D 1 milliliter of water has a mass of 1 gram.

4. Rico's sports bottle holds 1.5 quarts of water, Dave's sports bottle holds 50 fluid ounces of water, and Bill's bottle holds 5 cups of water. How would you list the names in the same order as their sports bottles from **least** to **greatest** capacity?

A Rico, Bill, Dave

B Bill, Rico, Dave

C Bill, Dave, Rico

D Dave, Rico, Bill

5. Randy drinks 6 cups of water a day. How many quarts of water does she drink in a week?

A 336 qt

B 48 qt

C 10.5 qt

D 2.25 qt

6. Beth filled a watering can with 1 liter of water. She used 755 milliliters to water her plants. How many milliliters of water were left in the watering can?

A 245 mL

B 255 mL

C 355 mL

D 455 mL

Assessment Anchors/Eligible Content: M7.B.1.1.1 Add, subtract, or convert measurements, using only the units below, with and without regrouping (e.g., 4 ft − 2 ft 5 in. = 1 ft 7 in.). Answer should be converted to the largest whole unit (e.g., 37 oz = 2 lb 5 oz or 39 in. = 1 yd 3 in.). Conversion chart provided on the reference sheet.

- in., ft, yd
- fl oz, cup, pint, quart, gallon
- oz, lb
- sec, min, hours, days
- metric units including milli, centi and kilo (m, g or L)

Academic Standards: 2.3.8.D, 2.4.8.B

You can use conversion equations to convert units of time.

$$1 \text{ day} = 24 \text{ hours (hr)}$$
$$1 \text{ hour} = 60 \text{ minutes (min)}$$
$$1 \text{ minute} = 60 \text{ seconds (sec)}$$

Guided Instruction

Problem Karla needs to leave the house in 2 hours to go to her basketball practice. She will also need 117 minutes to finish her homework. If Karla must finish her homework before she leaves, how many seconds does Karla have left to get ready?

Step 1 Convert 2 hours to minutes.   2 • _____ = _____

Step 2 Subtract to find the time she has left.   120 − 117 = _____ minutes

Step 3 Convert the difference into seconds.   3 • _____ = _____ seconds

Solution How many seconds does Karla have left? _____

Other Examples

A. How many hours are there in 54,000 seconds?
Use the conversion equations.

Convert 54,000 seconds to minutes. $54{,}000 \div 60 = 900$ minutes

Convert 900 minutes to hours. $900 \div 60 = 15$ hours

So there are 15 hours in 54,000 seconds.

B. Ismael studied from 10:25 A.M. till 1:37 P.M. How many minutes did he study?

Find the difference of the two times.
Since 1:37 P.M. comes after 12 P.M.,
add 12 hours to 1:37 P.M. Write the
time in terms of hours and minutes.

$$\begin{array}{ll} 1\text{:}37 \text{ P.M.} \rightarrow & 13\text{:}37 \\ -\ 10\text{:}25 \text{ A.M.} \rightarrow & -\ 10\text{:}25 \\ \hline & 3\text{:}15 = 3 \text{ hr } 15 \text{ min} \end{array}$$

Convert hours to minutes. Then find
the sum of the minutes.

$$3 \times 60 = 180 \text{ minutes}$$
$$180 + 15 = 195 \text{ minutes}$$

Convert each measure to the given unit.

1. 3.5 hr = _____ min

2. 36 days = _____ hr

3. 3,120 sec = _____ min

4. 15 min = _____ sec

5. 0.4 hr = _____ sec

6. 90 min = _____ hr

7. 7 days = _____ min

8. 36 hr = _____ days

9. 2.5 hr = _____ sec

10. 2.5 days = _____ min

11. 3,600 sec = _____ hr

12. 4 weeks = _____ hr

Complete each equation.

13. 3 hr − 45 min = _____ hr _____ min

14. 2 days + 48 hr = _____ days

15. 420 sec − 3 min = _____ min

16. 22 min + 1.5 hr = _____ hr _____ min

17. 1.5 hr − 90 min = _____ sec

18. 33 hr + 10,800 sec = _____ days

Solve each problem.

19. There are two printers in Sofia's office. One of the printers can print a maximum of 8 black-and-white copies per minute. The second printer can print a maximum of 6 black-and-white copies per minute. What is the maximum number of black-and-white pages that Sofia can print from the hours of 9 to 5 at her office? Explain how you found your answer.

_____

_____

_____

20. Three machines are needed to construct a chair. The first machine takes 4 hours 39 minutes. The second machine takes 46 minutes, and the third, 35 minutes. If only one of the machines can be in operation at a time, how many hours does it take to finish one chair? Explain how you found your answer.

_____

_____

_____

PSSA Practice Directions: Read each question. Then circle the letter for the best answer.

1. Jamie is flying from New York City to Orlando, Florida. His flight departs New York City at 3:25 P.M. and arrives in Orlando at 6:19 P.M. How long will Jamie's flight be in hours and minutes?

   A   3 hr 22 min

   B   2 hr 54 min

   C   2 hr 24 min

   D   1 hr 43 min

2. Willis needs 1,740 seconds to walk to school. His brother Justin takes 36.5 minutes and his sister Wendy 0.5 hour. In what order would they arrive at school if they leave at the same time?

   A   Wendy, Justin, Willis

   B   Justin, Willis, Wendy

   C   Justin, Wendy, Willis

   D   Willis, Wendy, Justin

 Todd is timing Matt in running 100 yards. It took Matt 0.1875 minute to complete 100 yards. How many seconds did it take him?

   A   0.003125 sec

   B   11.25 sec

   C   18.75 sec

   D   31.25 sec

4. Suzie has a clock that runs too fast. Her clock gained 48 minutes in 64 days. At this rate, how many seconds did Suzie's clock gain in one day?

   A   45 sec

   B   51.2 sec

   C   75 sec

   D   80 sec

 A cheetah can run 60 miles per hour for short distances. At that rate, how long would it take the cheetah to run 88 miles?

   A   1 hr 33 min

   B   1 hr 28 min

   C   45 min

   D   28 min

6. Gloria studies 96 minutes every day. How many hours does she study in 5 days?

   A   5 hr

   B   6 hr

   C   7 hr

   D   8 hr

Directions: Read each question. Then circle the letter for the best answer.

1. Mr. Henderson is 6 feet 4 inches tall. How many inches tall is he?

    A   64 in.

    B   68 in.

    C   76 in.

    D   88 in.

2. Paolo measures his pen and finds that it is 15 centimeters long. What is the length of the pen measured in meters?

    A   0.015 m

    B   0.15 m

    C   1.5 m

    D   150 m

3. Diana jogs 2.8 kilometers each day from Monday through Friday. She jogs 4.5 kilometers on Saturday. If she does **not** run on Sunday, how many meters does she run each week?

    A   7.3 m

    B   18.5 m

    C   7,300 m

    D   18,500 m

 4. Darren is flying from Newark, New Jersey, to San Juan, Puerto Rico. His flight departs Newark at 10:55 A.M. and arrives in San Juan at 3:05 P.M. How long is Darren's flight in minutes?

    A   270 min

    B   260 min

    C   250 min

    D   240 min

5. The minimum weight for a jockey and her equipment is 126 pounds. What is the minimum weight that a jockey must carry if she weighs 115 pounds 5 ounces?

    A   10 lb 11 oz

    B   10 lb 13 oz

    C   11 lb 10 oz

    D   13 lb 10 oz

 6. A vegetable platter contains 20 ounces of carrots, 8 ounces of celery and 14 ounces of cucumbers. How many pounds of vegetables does the platter contain?

    A   2.265 lb

    B   2.526 lb

    C   2.625 lb

    D   2.652 lb

7. A can of soda has a capacity of 354 milliliters. What is the capacity of a six-pack of soda?

A   31.24 L

B   21.24 L

C   3.124 L

D   2.124 L

8. Janelle is running in a 32,736-foot race. How long is the race in yards?

A   12,109 yd

B   11,902 yd

C   10,912 yd

D   10,291 yd

9. Pennsylvania has an average elevation of 13,200 inches. The highest point in Pennsylvania is Mt. Davis, at 3,213 feet.

Mount Davis is how much **higher** than Pennsylvania's average elevation?

A   1,100 ft

B   2,113 ft

C   2,413 ft

D   4,313 ft

10. Alexandra has a fan that makes 32 revolutions per second. Operating at that rate, how many revolutions can her fan make in 4 hours?

A   460,800

B   115,200

C   3,600

D   1,920

11. Anne ran a 26-mile marathon in 10,560 seconds. In how many hours and minutes did it take Anne to run the marathon?

A   3 hr 12 min

B   2 hr 56 min

C   3 hr 2 min

D   2 hr 26 min

12. Timothy wants to make lemonade to sell on a hot summer day. He only has enough to make 3.25 gallons of lemonade. How many cups of lemonade can he make?

A   32 cups

B   48 cups

C   25 cups

D   52 cups

13. Steven has 7 pints of water. He uses 64 fluid ounces to water the plants around the house. How many quarts of water does he have left after he waters the plants?

A   6 qt

B   4.5 qt

C   1.5 qt

D   1.12 qt

Open-Ended Items

14. Diana jogs 2.8 kilometers each day, Monday through Friday.

A. How many meters does Diana jog Monday through Friday? Explain your answer.

B. If Diana jogs 4.5 kilometers on Saturdays and 3.1 kilometers on Sundays, how many meters does she jog each week?

         Measuring Up® to the Pennsylvania Academic Standards

15. Maria, John, and Luke were trying to decide who studied more each day. Maria studies 90 minutes per day, John studies 4,500 seconds per day, and Luke studies 2 hours per day.

A. Who studies the most per day? Explain your answer.

B. How much does each student study in hours, Monday through Thursday? Explain your answer.

15. *Continued.*

C. How many more minutes does Luke study than John in four days?
Explain your answer.

D. How many more seconds does Maria study than John in four days?
Explain your answer.

Focus on the Pennsylvania Academic Standards

Chapter 7

Lesson 39   Find Area of Triangles

Assessment Anchors/Eligible Content: M7.B.2.1.3 Find the area of triangles and/or all types of parallelograms (formulas provided on the reference sheet).

Academic Standards: 2.3.8.A; 2.3.8.D; 2.9.8.D

You can use standard or metric units to measure the area of a triangle.

Area is the number of square units inside a figure. The area of a triangle can be found by finding half the product of base times height.

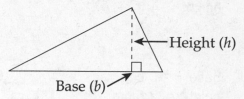

Height (h)

Base (b)

$$\text{Area} = \tfrac{1}{2}(\text{base} \times \text{height})$$
$$A = \tfrac{1}{2}bh$$

Guided Instruction

Problem

A triangle has a base that measures 24 inches and a height that measures 10 inches. What is the area?

Step 1   Write the formula for the area of a triangle.

$A =$ _____

Step 2   Find the area. Substitute b for 24 and h for 10 into the formula to solve for A.

$A = \frac{1}{2}bh$

$= \frac{1}{2} \cdot$ _____ $\cdot\ 10$

$= \frac{1}{2} \cdot$ _____

$=$ _____

Step 3   What units are used to measure the area of the triangle?

_____

Solution   What is the area? _____

Another Example

Find the area of the triangle shown.

$A = \frac{1}{2}bh$

$= \frac{1}{2}(4) \cdot (2)$

$= \frac{1}{2}(8)$

$= 4$

The area is 4 ft^2.

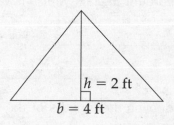

$h = 2$ ft

$b = 4$ ft

Apply the Pennsylvania Academic Standards Find the area of each triangle. Draw a diagram if you want.

1. base = 3 ft
height = 4 ft

_____

2. base = 7 in.
height = 3 in.

_____

3. base = 15 m
height = 16 m

_____

4. base = 10 cm
height = 2.5 cm

_____

5. base = 4.5 m
height = 9 m

_____

6. base = $\frac{1}{2}$ in.
height = 2 in.

_____

Find the area of each triangle.

7.

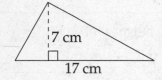

7 cm
17 cm

A = _____

8.

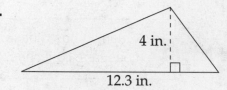

4 in.
12.3 in.

A = _____

9.

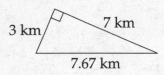

3 km   7 km
7.67 km

A = _____

10.

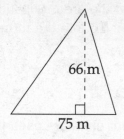

66 m
75 m

A = _____

Use the figure below to solve problems 11–12.

11. John has a new triangular garden. He wants to know the total area he has for planting. Find the area of John's triangular garden. Explain your answer.

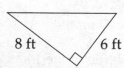

8 ft   6 ft

_____

_____

12. How will doubling the lengths of the sides change the area? Explain your answer.

_____

_____

_____

Directions: Read each question. Then circle the letter for the best answer.

1. A banner is shaped like the triangle shown below. What is the area of the banner?

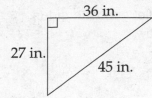

A   486 in.²

B   810 in.²

C   972 in.²

D   1,620 in.²

2.   Jessie draws the following figures. Which two have the same area?

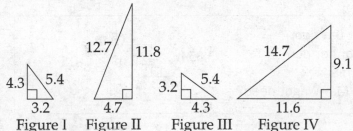

A   Figures I and II

B   Figures III and IV

C   Figures I and III

D   Figures II and IV

3. A triangle has a base that measures 30 inches and a height that measures 12 inches. What is the area of the triangle?

A   180 in.²

B   180 in.

C   360 in.²

D   360 in.

4. What is the area of the triangle below?

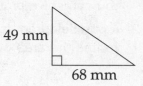

A   33.32 cm²

B   33.32 cm

C   16.66 cm²

D   16.66 cm

5. Which of the triangles shown appears to have the **greatest** area?

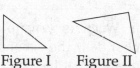

A   Figure I

B   Figure II

C   Figure III

D   Figure IV

6. A triangle has a base that measures 6 centimeters and a height that measures 2 centimeters. What is the area of the triangle?

A   6 cm

B   6 cm²

C   12 cm

D   12 cm²

Focus on the Pennsylvania Academic Standards

Lesson 40 **Find Area of Parallelograms**

Assessment Anchors/Eligible Content: M7.B.2.1.3 Find the area of triangles and/or all types of parallelograms (formulas provided on the reference sheet).

Academic Standards: 2.3.8.A; 2.3.8.D; 2.9.8.D

You can solve problems involving the area of parallelograms.

A **parallelogram** is a quadrilateral with two pairs of parallel opposite sides. To find the area of a parallelogram, use the formula below.

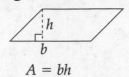

$$A = bh$$

Rectangles and **squares** are special parallelograms. The four angles of a rectangle or square are 90°. In addition to four right angles, a square also has four sides of equal length. You can find the areas of rectangles and squares by using the formulas below.

$$A = lw$$

$$A = s \cdot s$$

Guided Instruction

Problem

Ms. Wright is going to carpet the floor in her den. The dimensions of her den are shown at the right. How many square meters of carpet will Ms. Wright need?

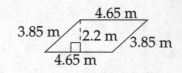

Step 1 Determine which formula to use.

_____

Step 2 Substitute the values needed in the formula.

$b =$ _____

$h =$ _____

Step 3 Use the formula to find the area of the parallelogram.

$A =$ _____ • _____ = _____

Solution How many square meters of carpet will Ms. Wright need? _____

Apply the Pennsylvania Academic Standards

Find the area for each figure.

1.

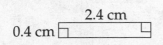

2.4 cm
0.4 cm

A = _____

2.

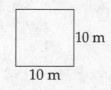

10 m

10 m

A = _____

3.

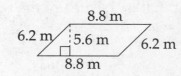

8.8 m
6.2 m 5.6 m 6.2 m
8.8 m

A = _____

4.

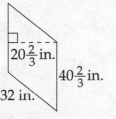

$20\frac{2}{3}$ in.
$40\frac{2}{3}$ in.
32 in.

A = _____

5.

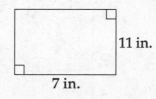

11 in.

7 in.

A = _____

6.

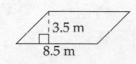

3.5 m
8.5 m

A = _____

Solve each problem.

7. A diagram of Mara's irregularly shaped flower garden is shown at the right. What is the area of the garden to the nearest tenth? _____

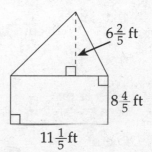

$6\frac{2}{5}$ ft

$8\frac{4}{5}$ ft

$11\frac{1}{5}$ ft

8. What is the area of the floor that is not covered by the carpet? The carpet is represented by the shaded area.

_____

Explain how you found the area.

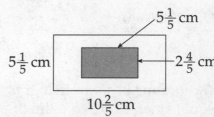

$5\frac{1}{5}$ cm

$5\frac{1}{5}$ cm

$2\frac{4}{5}$ cm

$10\frac{2}{5}$ cm

_____

_____

_____

Directions: Read each question. Then circle the letter for the best answer.

1. What is the area of the rectangle below?

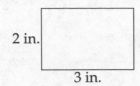

2 in.

3 in.

A   5 in.²

B   6 in.²

C   10 in.²

D   24 in.²

2. Which is the area of this parallelogram?

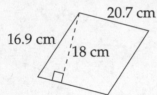

20.7 cm

16.9 cm

18 cm

A   349.83 cm

B   372.6 cm

C   349.83 cm²

D   372.6 cm²

3. A rhombus is a parallelogram with four equal sides and two pairs of equal angles. Which formula can be used to find the area of a rhombus?

A $A = bh$

B $A = 4s$

C $A = \frac{1}{2}bh$

D $A = b^2$

4. What is the area of the shaded figure?

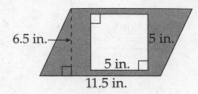

6.5 in.

5 in.

5 in.

11.5 in.

A   8 in.²

B   25 in.²

C   49.75 in.²

D   99.75 in.²

5. What is the area of the square below?

1 cm

1 cm

A   1 cm²

B   2 cm²

C   4 cm²

D   4 cm

6. A rectangular flower garden is 12 meters wide and 35 meters long. The garden must have a walkway that is 3 meters wide all the way around each side. What is the total area of the garden walkway?

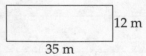

12 m

35 m

A   318 square meters

B   420 square meters

C   570 square meters

D   738 square meters

Focus on the Pennsylvania Academic Standards

Lesson 41 Find Perimeter and Area of Compound Figures

Assessment Anchors/Eligible Content: M7.B.2.1.1 Develop and/or use strategies to find the perimeter and/or area of compound figures (compound figures should only include quadrilaterals and triangles). Area formulas provided on the reference sheet.

Academic Standards: 2.3.8.A; 2.3.8.D; 2.9.8.D

You already know how to find the area of simple figures like triangles and parallelograms. Use what you know to find the area of more complex figures. Look at a figure to see if you can divide it into two or more simple figures with areas that are easy to find.

To find perimeter, find the sum of the lengths of the figure. **Perimeter** is the distance around a figure.

Guided Instruction

Problem

A construction crew wants to tile and fence the patio shown in the diagram at the right. What is the area of the patio? What is the perimeter of the patio?

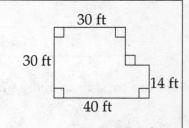

Step 1 Draw a dashed line segment to divide the figure into two rectangles. Use subtraction to find the length of each side.

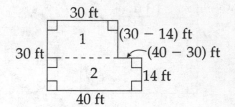

Step 2 Identify the dimensions of each rectangle.

Rectangle 1: length: _____ width: _____

Rectangle 2: length: _____ width: _____

Step 3 Use the area formula to find the area of each rectangle.
Area = length • width

Area of Rectangle 1 = _____

Area of Rectangle 2 = _____

Step 4 Add the areas to find the area of the complex figure.

Total Area = _____ + _____

= _____

Step 5 Find the sum of all the lengths of the figure to find the perimeter.

$P = 30 + 30 + 40 + 14 +$ _____ + _____ = _____

Solution

What is the area of the patio? What is the perimeter of the patio?

_____

Find the total area of each figure.

1.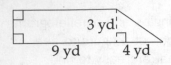

3 yd
9 yd   4 yd

2.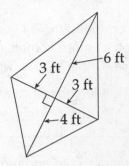

3 ft
6 ft
3 ft
4 ft

3.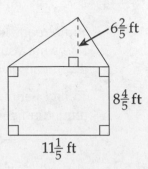

$6\frac{2}{5}$ ft

$8\frac{4}{5}$ ft

$11\frac{1}{5}$ ft

Find the total area and perimeter of each figure.

4.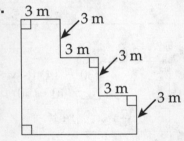

3 m   3 m
3 m   3 m
3 m
3 m

A = _____

P = _____

5.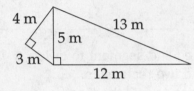

4 m   13 m
5 m
3 m
12 m

A = _____

P = _____

6.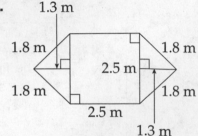

1.3 m
1.8 m   1.8 m
2.5 m
1.8 m   1.8 m
2.5 m
1.3 m

A = _____

P = _____

Solve each problem.

7. The white square represents a grassy area inside a square made of concrete. What is the area of the concrete?

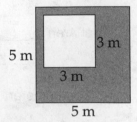

5 m
3 m
3 m
5 m

8. The diagram shows a rectangular piece of plastic with a triangle cut out. What is the area of the shaded region?

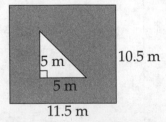

5 m   10.5 m
5 m
11.5 m

9. Katie has a piece of rectangular cardboard 13 inches long and 11 inches wide. She cuts out a square with sides equal to 3 inches. What is the area of the remaining cardboard after the square is cut out? Explain how you found your answer.

_____

_____

Directions: Read each question. Then circle the letter for the best answer.

1. A piece of sheet metal is a square 15 inches on a side. A square 6 inches on a side is cut from it. Which expression represents how many square inches of sheet metal remain?

   A $15 - 6$

   B $15^2 - 6^2$

   C $15^2 + 6^2$

   D $15^2 \times 6^2$

2. The square is 8 units on a side. The right triangle has legs 4 units long. What is the area of the shaded region?

   A 36 square units

   B 48 square units

   C 56 square units

   D 64 square units

3. The checkerboard square is 10 inches on a side. All small squares on the board are congruent. How many square inches are gray?

   A 13 in.^{2}

   B 50 in.^{2}

   C 52 in.^{2}

   D 100 in.^{2}

Use the figure below to answer questions 4–5.

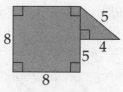

4. What is the area of the figure?

   A 6 square units

   B 64 square units

   C 70 square units

   D 80 square units

5. What is the perimeter of the figure?

   A 24 units

   B 30 units

   C 32 units

   D 38 units

6. What is the total area of the figure below?

   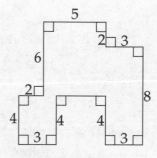

   A 44 square units

   B 48 square units

   C 66 square units

   D 88 square units

Focus on the Pennsylvania Academic Standards

Lesson 42 Circumference and Area of Circles

Assessment Anchors/Eligible Content: M7.B.2.1.2 Find the circumference and/or area of circles (formulas provided on the reference sheet).

M7.C.1.1.1 Identify, describe and/or define diameter, radius, chord and/or circumference in circles.

Academic Standards: 2.2.8.F; 2.3.8.A; 2.3.8.D; 2.9.8.D; 2.9.8.G

You can use the relationship between the distance around a circle and the length of its diameter to calculate circumference and area.

The distance around a circle is its **circumference**.

A line segment connecting two points on a circle and passing through the center is a **diameter**.

The ratio of a circle's circumference to its diameter is called **pi**. The decimal 3.14 and the fraction $\frac{22}{7}$ are approximations of pi. The symbol for pi is π.

A line segment from a point on a circle to the center of the circle is a **radius**.

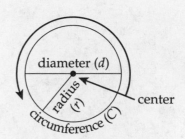

Guided Instruction

Problem 1

A round window has a radius of 12 inches. What is the approximate circumference of the window?

Use the formula $C = \pi d$ or $C = 2\pi r$ to calculate circumference.

Step 1 Select a formula.

Which measure are you given, diameter or radius? _____

Step 2 Identify the values you know.

Use 3.14 as an approximate value for π.

$r =$ _____

Step 3 Substitute into the formula $C = 2\pi r$ to calculate the circumference.

$C \approx 2(3.14)(12) =$ _____

$C \approx$ _____ in.

Solution

What is the approximate circumference of the window?

_____

Guided Instruction

Problem 2

A new circular fountain is planned for Kennedy Park. One plan calls for the circular fountain to have a diameter of 42 feet. Another plan calls for the fountain to have a diameter of 56 feet. About how many square feet greater is the area of the second fountain than the area of the first fountain?

Use the formula $A = \pi r^2$ to find the area of a circle.

Step 1 Find the radius for the first fountain.
The diameter is 42 feet.
Divide the diameter by 2.
What is its radius? _____

Step 2 Substitute into the formula $A = \pi r^2$.
Use $\frac{22}{7}$ as an approximate value for π.

$r = 21$

$A \approx$ _____

Step 3 Follow the order of operations to calculate the area.

$A \approx (\frac{22}{7}) (21)^2$

$A \approx \frac{22}{7} (441) =$ _____

$A \approx$ _____ ft^2

Step 4 Find the radius for the second fountain.
The diameter is 56 feet. Divide the diameter by 2.
What is its radius? _____

Step 5 Substitute into the formula $A = \pi r^2$.

Use $\frac{22}{7}$ as an approximate value for π.

$r = 28$

$A \approx$ _____

Step 6 Follow the order of operations to calculate the area.

$A \approx (\frac{22}{7}) (28)^2$

$A \approx (\frac{22}{7}) (784) =$ _____

$A \approx$ _____ ft^2

Step 7 Subtract to find the difference in the areas.

$2,464 - 1,386 =$ _____

Solution

About how many square feet greater is the area of the second fountain than the area of the first fountain? _____

Apply the Pennsylvania Academic Standards

Estimate the circumference and area of each circle. Use either 3.14 or $\frac{22}{7}$ for π.

1.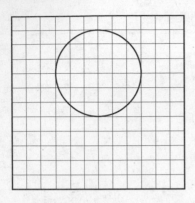

Circumference ≈ _____

Area ≈ _____

2.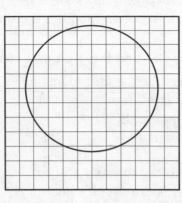

Circumference ≈ _____

Area ≈ _____

3.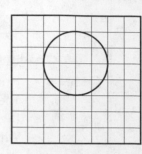

Circumference ≈ _____

Area ≈ _____

Find the circumference and area for a circle with the given radius or diameter. Use $\frac{22}{7}$ or 3.14 for π.

4. $r = 2$ cm

$C =$ _____

$A =$ _____

5. $r = 10$ ft

$C =$ _____

$A =$ _____

6. $d = 14$ mm

$C =$ _____

$A =$ _____

Solve each problem.

7. Rick is measuring the dimensions of his driveway. He is using a measuring wheel with a circumference of 36 inches. What is the diameter of the wheel to the nearest tenth?

_____

8. Mr. Perez built this circular garden. The inner circle has a diameter of 22 feet. The outer circle has a diameter of 44 feet. The circumference of section B is how many times as long as the circumference of Section A? _____

What is the area of section B (the shaded area) to the nearest whole number?

_____

9. Jonathan ordered a 6-inch-diameter pizza. Marie ordered a 12-inch-diameter pizza. How many times greater is the area of Marie's pizza than Jonathan's? _____

Explain your reasoning.

_____

_____

 Measuring Up® to the Pennsylvania Academic Standards

Directions: Read each question. Then circle the letter for the best answer.

1. A circle has a radius of 6.3 kilometers. What is the approximate circumference of the circle, to the nearest tenth of a kilometer?

   A   19.8 km

   B   39.6 km

   C   124.74 km

   D   498.96 km

2. The diameter of a circle is 14 feet. What is the approximate area of the circle, to the nearest whole foot?

   A   616 ft²

   B   154 ft²

   C   44 ft²

   D   22 ft²

3. In the diagram below, the inner circle has a radius of 4 meters. The outer circle has a radius of 11 meters.

   Which is the **best** estimate of the area of the shaded region?

   A   44 m²

   B   82 m²

   C   330 m²

   D   430 m²

Use the diagram below to answer questions 4–5.

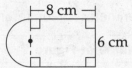

4. Which is the **best** estimate of the area of this figure?

   A   161 cm²

   B   104 cm²

   C   76 cm²

   D   62 cm²

5. Which is the **best** estimate of the perimeter of this figure?

   A   31 cm

   B   37 cm

   C   41 cm

   D   47 cm

6. A circle has a circumference of 63 miles. Which is the **best** estimate of the radius of the circle?

   A   10 mi

   B   20 mi

   C   30 mi

   D   40 mi

Assessment Anchors/Eligible Content: M7.B.2.1.1 Develop and/or use strategies to find the perimeter and/or area of compound figures (compound figures should only include quadrilaterals and triangles). Area formulas provided on the reference sheet.

M7.B.2.1.2 Find the circumference and/or area of circles (formulas provided on the reference sheet).

M7.B.2.1.3 Find the area of triangles and/or all types of parallelograms (formulas provided on the reference sheet).

Academic Standards: 2.3.8.A; 2.3.8.D

Perimeter, circumference, and area formulas can be used to solve problems.

Name of Figure	Figure	Perimeter	Area
Parallelogram		$P = 2a + 2b$	$A = bh$
Rectangle		$P = 2l + 2w$	$A = lw$
Square		$P = 4s$	$A = s \cdot s$
Triangle		$P = b + c + d$	$A = \frac{1}{2}bh$

Volume is the measure of space inside a solid figure. Volume is measured in cubic units.

The volume of a rectangular prism can be found using the formula $V = lwh$.

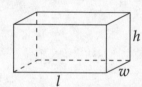

Guided Instruction

Problem

The Martin family is building a pool in their backyard. The pool is a rectangular prism that is 7 feet deep, 12 feet long, and 10 feet wide. What is the volume of the pool?

Step 1   Identify the dimensions of the pool.

Length = _____

Width = _____

Height = _____

Step 2   Use the formula to find the volume.

Volume = _____ • _____ • _____

$V =$ _____ cubic feet

Solution   What is the volume of the pool? _____

Solve each problem. Use 3.14 or $\frac{22}{7}$ for π where appropriate.

1. The area of a rectangular garden is 12 square feet. If the length of the garden is 4 feet, what is the width?

_____

2. Mary is painting a triangular banner. The banner has a height of 10 feet and a base of 12 feet. What is the area of the banner?

_____

3. Grace has a piece of rectangular plastic with a length of 3 feet and a width of 2 feet. She cuts a circular piece with a radius of 1 foot inside the plastic. What is the approximate area of the remaining plastic?

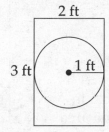

_____

4. A rectangle is 8 inches long and 5 inches wide. If each dimension is multiplied by 4, by what factor will the area change?

_____

_____

5. A rectangular pool is 6 feet long and 5 feet wide. If it is filled to a depth of 2 feet, what is the volume of the water in the pool?

_____

6. A cubic foot of water is about 7.5 gallons. If the pool in question 6 can be filled at a rate of about 10 gallons per minute, how long will it take to fill the pool to a depth of 2 feet? Explain your reasoning.

_____

_____

7. Mike's rectangular backyard has a circular pond. A sketch of his backyard with its dimensions is shown to the right. What is the area outside of the pond? Explain your answer.

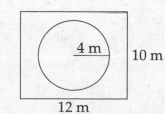

_____

_____

_____

Directions: Read each question. Then circle the letter for the best answer.

3. A shoe box is 12.4 inches long, 7.5 inches wide, and 4 inches deep. What is the volume of the shoebox?

A 1,008 in.^{3}

B 372 in.^{3}

C 88 in.^{3}

D 23 in.^{3}

2. Mary has a triangular garden inside her rectangular yard. What is the area surrounding the triangular garden?

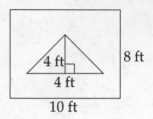

4 ft
4 ft
8 ft
10 ft

A 88 ft^2

B 72 ft^2

C 64 ft^2

D 24 ft^2

3. What is the approximate perimeter of the figure shown below?

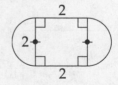

2
2
2

A 10.28 square units

B 10.28 units

C 7.14 square units

D 7.14 units

4. Bethany is designing a bathroom-floor tile. She decides that each tile will be composed of four black triangles and a white square, as shown below.

Scale
⊢—⊣ = 1 unit

What is the area of the white square?

A 12 square units

B 13 square units

C 19 square units

D 25 square units

5. The figure below is a trapezoid.

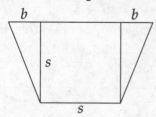

b   b
s
s

Which of the following formulas will give you the area of this trapezoid?

A $4s$

B $bs + b^2$

C $s^2 + bs$

D $b^2 + s^2$

Measuring Up® to the Pennsylvania Academic Standards

Directions: Read each question. Then circle the letter for the best answer.

1. In square inches, what is the area of this figure?

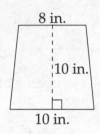

8 in.

10 in.

10 in.

A   800 in.²

B   90 in.²

C   30 in.²

D   14 in.²

2. The square below has an area of 100 square centimeters. Which is a reasonable estimate of the area of the shaded region?

A   25 cm²

B   45 cm²

C   65 cm²

D   85 cm²

3. What is the area of the triangle shown below?

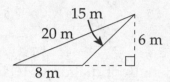

15 m

20 m

6 m

8 m

A   32 m²

B   43 m²

C   48 m²

D   60 m²

4. Look at the figures below.

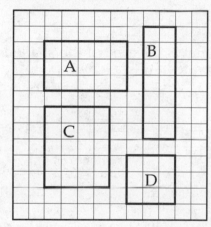

Which of the figures' area is **greater** than its perimeter?

A A   B B

C C   D D

5. If you double the diameter of a circle, how many times do you increase its circumference?

A 2   B 4

C 8   D 16

6. The figure below is a rhombus. Its diagonals intersect to form 4 right triangles.

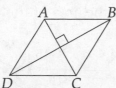

If the length of diagonal *AC* is *x* units, and the length of diagonal *BD* is *y* units, which formula gives the area of the rhombus?

A $x + y$

B $\frac{1}{2}xy$

C $2xy$

D xy

7. What is the area of the shaded part of this figure?

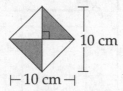

10 cm

⊢ 10 cm ⊣

A   200 m²   B   100 m²

C   50 m²   D   25 m²

8. What is the area of the shape shown below?

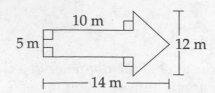

A   50 m²

B   74 m²

C   94 m²

D   118 m²

Use the figure below to answer questions 9–10.

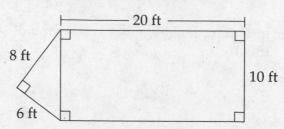

9. What is the perimeter of the figure?

A   64 ft

B   74 ft

C   84 ft

D   94 ft

10. What is the area of the figure?

A   514 ft²

B   278 ft²

C   224 ft²

D   200 ft²

11. A circle has a radius of 16 meters. Bill calculated the approximate area of the circle as 50.24 square meters. What step did he leave out of his calculations?

A   Multiply by 3.14.

B   Square the radius.

C   Multiply by 2.

D   Divide by 3.14.

Open-Ended Items

12. Find the approximate area of the shaded region. Let π = 3.14. Explain how you found your answer.

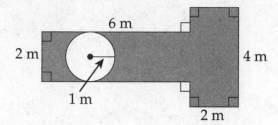

13. Samuel has decided to add a brick patio to his backyard. See the floor plan below.

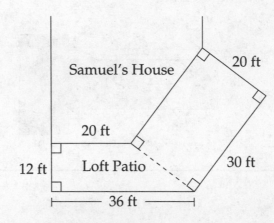

Samuel's House

20 ft

20 ft

12 ft   Loft Patio

30 ft

36 ft

A. Find the perimeter of Samuel's patio. Explain how you found your answer.

B. Find the area of Samuel's patio. Explain your answer.

13. *Continued*

> **C.** Suppose Samuel wants to put a square swimming pool on one side of his patio, and both a grill and picnic table on the other side. If the pool has a side of 15 feet, the grill is 18 inches by 21 inches, and the picnic table is 30 inches by 8 feet, how much floor space remains of the patio? Explain your answer.

Assessment Anchors/Eligible Content: M7.C.1.1.1 Identify, describe and/or define diameter, radius, chord and/or circumference in circles.

M7.C.1.1.2 Solve problems involving the relationship between the radius and diameter of the same circle.

Academic Standards: 2.9.8.D

The **diameter** of a circle is a line segment that connects two points on the circle, and passes through the center. For example, line segment BD ($\overline{BD}$) is a diameter.

The **radius** of a circle is half the diameter. It connects the center point of the circle to a point on the circle. For example, line segment FG ($\overline{FG}$) is a radius.

The **chord** of a circle is a line segment that connects two points on the circle. A chord does not have to pass through the center point. For example, line segment AE ($\overline{AE}$) is a chord.

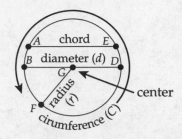

The **circumference** is the distance around the circle. You can calculate circumference by finding the product of pi and the diameter of the circle ($c = \pi d$ or $c = 2\pi r$). The decimal 3.14 and the fraction $\frac{22}{7}$ both approximate π.

Guided Instruction

Problem

Rita bought a new clock. She knows the minute hand of the clock is about 6 inches long. What is the approximate diameter of her clock?

Use what you know about diameter and radius to solve the problem.

Step 1   Draw a picture to help you solve the question. Draw the minute hand and the center point. Which measure does this approximate?

_____

Step 2   Determine the length of the radius. Let r equal radius.

$r \approx$ _____

Step 3   Find the length of the diameter. Let d equal diameter.

The radius of a circle is _____ its diameter.

So $r = \frac{1}{2}d$.

$r = \frac{1}{2}d$

$6 = \frac{1}{2}d$

_____ $= d$

Solution   What is the approximate diameter of Rita's clock? _____

Apply the Pennsylvania Academic Standards

Use the figure below to answer questions 1–6.

Identify each line segment either as a *chord*, *diameter*, *center point*, or *radius*.

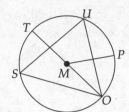

1. $\overline{TM}$ _____

2. $\overline{SU}$ _____

3. M _____

4. $\overline{TO}$ _____

5. $\overline{OU}$ _____

6. PM _____

Find the length of x.

7.

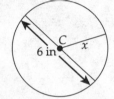

6 in   x

_____

8.

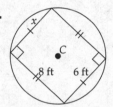

x   8 ft   6 ft

_____

9.

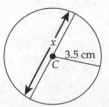

x   3.5 cm

_____

Solve the problem.

10. Julie cuts a piece out of the cake, pictured at the right. In terms of parts of a circle, what do the darkened lines represent?

_____

11. Triangle *ABD* has an area of 24 square inches. What are the lengths for triangle *ABD*? Show your work.

8 in.   5 in.

_____

_____

_____

1. What is the height of the triangle?

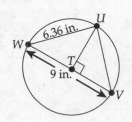

A   2.5 in.

B   4.5 in.

C   6.36 in.

D   9 in.

2. What is the length of x?

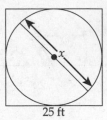

A   5 ft

B   12.5 ft

C   17.5 ft

D   25 ft

3. Matt's baseball bat has a maximum circumference of 345.4 millimeters. What is the approximate radius of this part of the bat?

A   11 mm

B   18 mm

C   36 mm

D   55 mm

4. Johnny's bicycle has wheels each with a diameter of 24 inches. If Johnny rides his bicycle 100 feet, how many revolutions will his wheels make?

A   12

B   14

C   15

D   17

5. The dome of the U.S. Capitol has a diameter of 96 feet. Approximately how **far** would you need to walk to circle the dome once?

A   151 ft

B   301 ft

C   452 ft

D   603 ft

6. A pizza has a diameter of 13 inches. What is its radius?

A   2.5 in.

B   6.5 in.

C   7.5 in.

D   13 in.

Focus on the Pennsylvania Academic Standards

Lesson 45 Classify Lines

Assessment Anchors/Eligible Content: M7.C.1.1.3 Identify parallel, perpendicular and/or skew line segments within three-dimensional figures.

Academic Standards: 2.9.8.A, 2.9.8.C, 2.9.8.E

When two lines meet at a point or cross each other, they are said to be **intersecting**. Intersecting lines occupy the same plane. They meet at only one point.

When two lines intersect and form 4 right angles they are called **perpendicular lines**. The symbol ⊥ means *perpendicular to*.

Parallel lines extend forever in both directions in the same plane and never intersect. The symbol ‖ means *parallel to*.

Skew lines are a pair of lines that are not parallel but never intersect. They occupy two different planes.

Guided Instruction

Problem

Highland Avenue and Lowell Street cross as shown in the picture below.

Which words describe these lines: intersecting, perpendicular, parallel, or skew?

Use the figure above to solve the problem.

Step 1   Determine if the lines intersect.

Do the lines meet at any point? _____

Can the lines be parallel? _____

Can the lines be skew? _____

Step 2   If the lines intersect, determine if they are also perpendicular.

Do the lines form right angles? _____

Are the lines perpendicular? _____

Solution

Which of these words describes these lines: intersecting, perpendicular, parallel, or skew?

_____

Apply the Pennsylvania Academic Standards

Identify each pair of lines as *intersecting*, *skew*, or *parallel*. If a pair of lines intersect perpendicularly, write *perpendicular*.

1.

_____

2.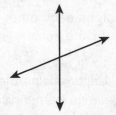

_____

3.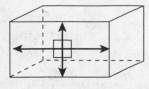

_____

4.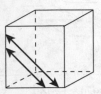

_____

5.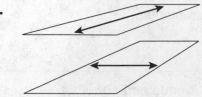

_____

6.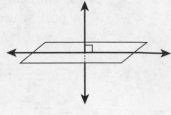

_____

Draw each pair of lines. Use a ruler.

7. $d \parallel e$

8. $a \perp b$

9. *Line r* intersects line *s*, but they are not perpendicular.

Solve each problem.

10. Phil made a drawing of his room. He has decided to paint the two darker walls on his drawing.

Phil's Room

What is the best description of these walls? _____

11. Dana drew a pair of lines on a cracker box. The lines did not intersect but were not parallel. Which type of lines did she draw? Explain your answer.

_____

_____

_____

PSSA Practice   Directions: Read each question. Then circle the letter for the best answer.

1. Paul drew this pair of lines.

What is the **best** description of the lines he drew?

A   parallel

B   perpendicular

C   skew

D   intersecting

2. Miguel is reading streets on a map.

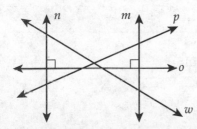

n = North St.   *o* = O'Sullivan Rd.
m = Mystic Ave. *w* = Wall St.
p = Petal Rd.

According to the map, which of the following is a **true** statement?

A   Mystic Avenue is parallel to O'Sullivan Road.

B   Petal Road is perpendicular to Mystic Avenue.

C   North Street is parallel to Wall Street.

D   O'Sullivan Road is perpendicular to Mystic Avenue.

3. Libby is describing parallel lines to her little brother. Which of the following descriptions is correct?

A   two lines that are not in the same plane

B   two lines that intersect to form right angles

C   two lines that never meet and travel in exactly the same direction

D   two lines that cross but do not form right angles

4. Which two lines pictured at the right are perpendicular?

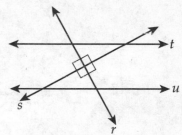

A   *r* and *s*   B   *r* and *t*

C   *t* and *u*   D   *s* and *u*

5. Clara is using a software program to practice geometry. She creates the following diagram. Plane *ABC* is parallel to plane *DEF*. Both *ABC* and *DEF* are crossed by plane *XYZ*.

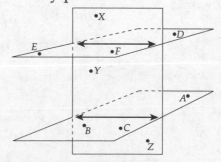

What type of lines are shown?

A   skew lines

B   perpendicular lines

C   intersecting lines

D   parallel lines

Focus on the Pennsylvania Academic Standards

Lesson 46 | Identify Congruent Figures

Assessment Anchors/Eligible Content: M7.C.1.2.1 Identify and/or use polygons that are similar and/or congruent, given either measurements or tick and angle marks.

M7.C.1.2.2 Identify corresponding sides and/or angles of congruent or similar polygons.

Academic Standards: 2.9.8.F, 2.9.8.K

Two polygons are **congruent** if their corresponding angles and their corresponding sides are congruent. **Congruent angles** are angles that have the same measure. **Congruent sides** are line segments that have the same measure. The symbol ≅ means *congruent to*.

Look at each pair of corresponding angles and each pair of corresponding sides.

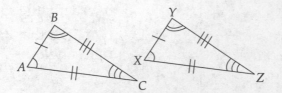

Matching tick marks tell you that $\overline{AB} \cong \overline{XY}$, $\overline{AC} \cong \overline{XZ}$, and $\overline{BC} \cong \overline{YZ}$.

Matching angles arcs tell you that ∠A ≅ ∠X, ∠B ≅ ∠Y, and ∠C ≅ ∠Z
So △ABC ≅ △XYZ

Guided Instruction

Problem

Mr. Tolman is building the rectangular gate shown at the right. To brace it, he added $\overline{NL}$. Is △KLN ≅ △MNL? Explain how you know.

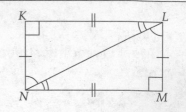

Step 1   Use the tick marks to find congruent segments.

$\overline{NK} \cong$ _____

$\overline{KL} \cong$ _____

$\overline{NL} \cong$ _____

Step 2   Use the angle arcs to find congruent angles.

∠NKL ≅ ∠ _____

∠KNL ≅ ∠ _____

∠KNL ≅ ∠ _____

Is △KLN ≅ △MNL? Explain how you know.

_____

Solution

_____

_____

_____

Tell why the triangles in each pair are congruent.

1.

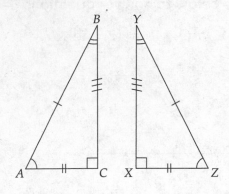

_____

_____

2.

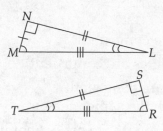

_____

_____

Triangle _PQR_ is congruent to triangle _GHJ_. Complete each statement.

3. ∠Q ≅ _____

4. ∠P ≅ _____

5. If ∠R measures 40°, then ∠J measures _____.

6. If $\overline{PR}$ measures 5 inches, then $\overline{GJ}$ measures _____.

7. If $\overline{QR}$ is 4 inches long, then _____ is also 4 inches long.

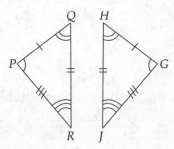

The diagram at the right shows a signal flag.
In the diagram, △_RST_ ≅ △_TWR_. Solve each problem.

8. What is the measure of ∠_SRT_? Explain.

_____

_____

9. What is the length of $\overline{WR}$? Explain.

_____

_____

PSSA Practice   Directions: Read each question. Then circle the letter for the best answer.

1. Which statement is true?

   A   All squares are congruent.

   B   All right triangles are congruent.

   C   If two angles are congruent, then they have the same measure.

   D   If two line segments are congruent, then they have different lengths.

2. An angle has measure $2x$. An angle congruent to it has measure $3x - 40$. What is the measure of each angle?

   A   8°   B   40°

   C   80°   D   160°

Use the figure below to answer questions 3–4.

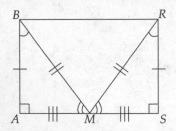

3. Which angle corresponds to $\angle RMS$?

   A $\angle RSM$ B $\angle BMR$

   C $\angle ABM$ D $\angle BMA$

4. Which triangles are congruent?

   A $\triangle BAM$ and $\triangle BMR$

   B $\triangle BAM$ and $\triangle RSM$

   C $\triangle BMR$ and $\triangle RSM$

   D $\triangle RMS$ and $\triangle BMR$

Use the figure below to answer questions 5–6.

$\triangle KLM \cong \triangle PRQ$, $ML = 12$, and $KL = 11$

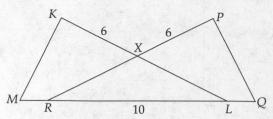

5. What is the measure of $\overline{LQ}$?

   A   2

   B   4

   C   10

   D   12

6. What is the measure of $\overline{XR}$?

   A   4

   B   5

   C   8

   D   12

7. Point Y is the midpoint of $\overline{AB}$. Which statement is true?

   A $AY = 0.5(YB)$

   B $AY = 2(YB)$

   C $\overline{AY} \cong \overline{YB}$

   D $\overline{AY} \cong \overline{AB}$

Lesson 47 Identify Similar Figures

Assessment Anchors/Eligible Content: M7.A.2.2.6 Use proportions to find the missing length of a side in similar figures.
M7.C.1.2.1 Identify and/or use polygons that are similar and/or congruent, given either measurements or tic and angle marks.
M7.C.1.2.2 Identify corresponding sides and/or angles of congruent or similar polygons.
Academic Standards: 2.9.8.F; 2.9.8.K

Two figures are **similar** if they have exactly the same shape, but may or may not have the same size. Similar figures have corresponding angles of equal measure, and corresponding sides that are proportional. The symbol ~ means *similar to*.

Look at each pair of corresponding angles and corresponding sides.

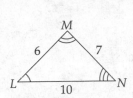
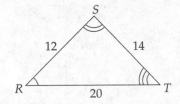

Matching angles arcs tell you that
$\angle M \cong \angle S$, $\angle N \cong \angle T$, and $\angle L \cong \angle R$.

Compare the corresponding sides to see that each are in proportion.

$\frac{LM}{RS} = \frac{6}{12} = \frac{1}{2}$; $\frac{MN}{ST} = \frac{7}{14} = \frac{1}{2}$; $\frac{NL}{TR} = \frac{10}{20} = \frac{1}{2}$

So $\triangle MNL \sim \triangle STR$.

Guided Instruction

Problem

Douglas draws the figure to the right.
Is triangle *ABE* similar to triangle *ACD*?
Explain your answer.

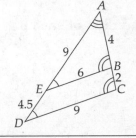

Use what you know about similar figures to solve the problem.

Step 1 Identify the angles that have equal measure. Matching angle arcs show that angles have equal measure.

$\angle EAB \cong \angle$_____

$\angle ABE \cong \angle$_____

$\angle BEA \cong \angle$_____

Step 2 Determine if each pair of corresponding sides is in proportion. Write the ratios of the corresponding lengths in simplest form.

$\frac{AB}{AC} = \frac{4}{4 + 2} = \frac{4}{6} = $_____

$\frac{BE}{CD} = \frac{6}{9} = $_____

$\frac{EA}{DA} = \frac{9}{9 + 4.5} = \frac{9}{13.5} = $_____

So triangle *ABE* is _____ triangle *ACD*.

Is triangle *ABE* similar to triangle *ACD*? Explain your answer.

Solution

_____

_____

_____

Determine whether each pair of figures is *similar* or *not similar*. If possible, write the ratio of the similar figures.

1.

_____

2.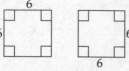

_____

3.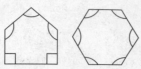

_____

4.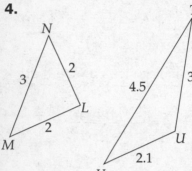

_____

5.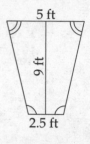

_____

Find the ratio of each pair of similar figures.

6.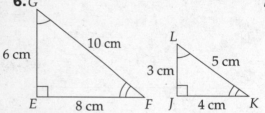

_____

7.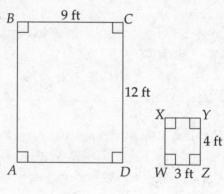

_____

8.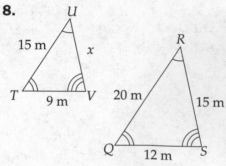

_____

Solve each problem.

9. Kai and Julie each have a notebook. Kai's notebook is 20 centimeters wide and 28 centimeters long. Julie's notebook is 15 centimeters wide and 21 centimeters long. Based on these measures, are both notebooks similar? If they are, write their ratio.

_____

_____

_____

_____

_____

PSSA Practice

Directions: Read each question. Then circle the letter for the best answer.

1. John draws a parallelogram with sides of 6 inches and 5 inches. Which of the following parallelograms could be similar to the one he drew?

   A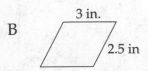
   2.5 in.
   1.5 in

   B
   3 in.
   2.5 in

   C
   2 in.
   6 in

   D
   5 in.
   5.5 in

2. Using the problem above, what is the ratio formed between the parallelogram John drew and the similar parallelogram?

   A   2:1

   B   3:1

   C   4:1

   D   6:5

Use the figures below to answer questions 3–4.

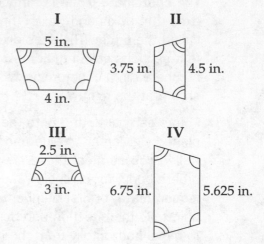

I
5 in.
4 in.

II
3.75 in.   4.5 in.

III
2.5 in.
3 in.

IV
6.75 in.   5.625 in.

3. Which of the following figures is similar to the others?

   A   Figures I and II

   B   Figures III and IV

   C   Figures I, II, and III

   D   Figures II, III, and IV

 4. Which of the following ratios describes the relation between two of the similar figures above?

   A   2:1

   B   3:2

   C   4:3

   D   8:5

Focus on the Pennsylvania Academic Standards

Lesson 48 Plot Points on the Coordinate Grid

Assessment Anchors/Eligible Content: M7.C.3.1.1 Plot and/or identify ordered pairs on a coordinate plane (all four quadrants).
M7.C.3.1.2 Identify Quadrants I, II, III, IV, the *x*- & *y*-axes and the origin on a coordinate plane.
Academic Standards: 2.8.5.H

The **coordinate plane** is formed by two coordinate axes (the *x*-axis and *y*-axis) that cross at a point called the **origin**. The axes divide the plane into four sections called **quadrants,** which are numbered in a counterclockwise direction as shown at the right.

Points can be plotted onto the coordinate plane by giving an *x*-value and a *y*-value. Called **coordinates,** these are written as an ordered pair, for example (3, −4). The ***x*-coordinate,** or first number of the ordered pair, tells the direction and number of units to move horizontally from the origin. The ***y*-coordinate**, or second number of the ordered pair, tells the direction and the number of units to move vertically from the origin.

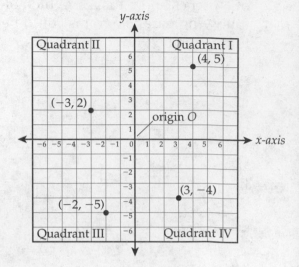

Guided Instruction

Problem

Greta plots two points on a coordinate plane. If the third point is 8 units from each plotted endpoint and is in Quadrant III, what are the coordinates of point *C*? What are the coordinates of the other points? If she connects all three points, what figure has she formed?

Use what you know about the coordinate plane to solve the problem.

Step 1 What are the coordinates of point *A*? _____

What are the coordinates of point *B*? _____

Step 2 Draw a line segment to connect points *A* and *B*. If point *C* is 8 units from each vertex, which points could be point *C*? _____

Step 3 Find Quadrant III. Which of these points is in Quadrant III? _____

Label and plot point *C* on the coordinate plane. Then draw a line segment from it to points *A* and *B*.

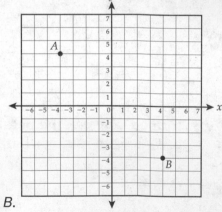

Solution

What are the coordinates of point *C*? _____

What are the coordinates of the other points? _____

What figure has she formed? _____

Apply the Pennsylvania Academic Standards

Write the quadrant for each point.

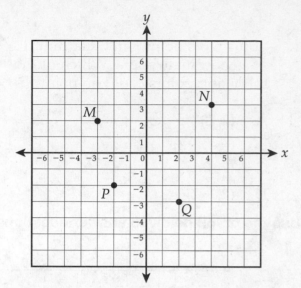

1. (3, 3) _____

2. (3, −1) _____

3. (−1, 2) _____

4. (−1, −5) _____

Write the ordered pair for each point.

5. M _____

6. N _____

7. P _____

8. Q _____

Plot each ordered pair

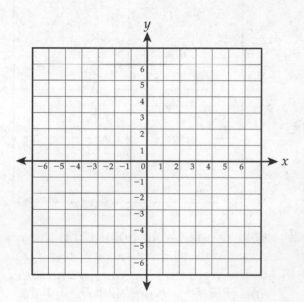

9. A(−3, 4)

10. B(1, 4)

11. C(1, 0)

12. Plot point D, so that points A, B, C and D form a square.

Solve each problem.

13. Julie starts at the origin on a coordinate plane. She moves 4 units to the left, up 3 units and plots point Z. What are the coordinates for point Z? Explain your answer.

_____

_____

_____

14. Melvin starts at point (−1, −1) on a coordinate plane. He moves 7 units to the right, 5 units down, and draws point X. In which quadrant is point X? Explain your answer.

_____

_____

_____

PSSA Practice   Directions: Read each question. Then circle the letter for the best answer.

1. Louis plots point *F* in Quadrant II of a coordinate plane. Which of the following points could be point *F*?

   A   (2, 2)

   B   (−4, −2)

   C   (−3, 1)

   D   (2, −2)

Use the graph below to answer questions 2–3.

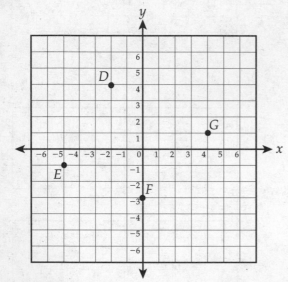

2. Beverly started at point *D* on the coordinate plane. She counted 5 units to the right and 3 units down from *D* and plotted a point that she labeled *A*. What are the coordinates of point *A*?

   A   (−7, 1)

   B   (3, 7)

   C   (−7, 7)

   D   (3, 1)

3. Eric plotted point *F* on the coordinate plane. What are the coordinates of point *F*?

   A   (0, −3)

   B   (−3, 0)

   C   (3, 0)

   D   (0, 3)

4. Tim plots point *R* in quadrant IV of a coordinate plane. Which of the following points could be point *R*?

   A   (−3, 5)

   B   (5, 1)

   C   (4, −3)

   D   (−2, −4)

Use the graph below to answer questions 5–6.

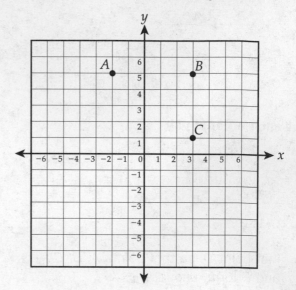

5. Using the points *A*, *B*, and *C*, which point would form a parallelogram?

   A   (−2, 1)

   B   (1, 2)

   C   (−1, −2)

   D   (2, −1)

6. In which quadrant is point *B* located?

   A   Quadrant I

   B   Quadrant II

   C   Quadrant III

   D   Quadrant IV

Assessment Anchors/Eligible Content: M7.A.2.2.6 Use proportions to find the missing length of a side in similar figures.

M7.C.1.2.1 Identify and/or use polygons that are similar and/or congruent, given either measurements or tick and angle marks.

M7.C.1.2.2 Identify corresponding sides and/or angles of congruent or similar polygons.

Academic Standards: 2.9.8.F; 2.9.8.K

When solving problems involving similar figures, it can help to create models or drawings and label them with the numbers given in the problem.

Guided Instruction

Problem

A flagpole is sitting on a level field. The pole casts a shadow on the ground that is 16 feet long, creating a right triangle. A student standing near the flagpole has a height of 5 feet and casts a shadow that is 2 feet long, creating a similar right triangle. What is the height of the flagpole?

Step 1 Understand the problem.

What do you need to find? _____

Step 2 Draw a picture of the similar triangles to help set up a proportion between corresponding sides. Label each side with the correct length.

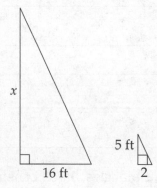

x

16 ft

5 ft

2

Write a proportion to solve for x. $\frac{2}{16} = $ _____

Step 3 Solve the proportion.

_____ = 2x

Cross multiply to solve for x.

$\frac{\_\_\_}{2} = \frac{2x}{2}$

_____ = x

Step 4 Determine if your answer is reasonable.

$\frac{5}{40} \overset{?}{=} \frac{2}{16}$

$5 \cdot 16 \overset{?}{=} 40 \cdot 2$

$80 = 80 \checkmark$

So your answer is reasonable.

Solution

What is the height of the flagpole? _____

Solve each problem. Draw a picture to help solve the question.

1. A flagpole on a level field is 30 feet tall. A flagpole casts a shadow on the ground that is 18 feet long. A building near the flagpole casts a shadow on the ground that is 15 feet long. What is the height of the building?

2. Paolo has a rectangular garden with a length of 8 feet and a width of 6 feet. This summer, he plans on expanding his garden, so that it will have a width of 9 feet. If he intends to extend the garden proportionally, what will be the length of his new garden?

3. Jae has constructed a parallelogram with a base of 16 inches and a height of 8 inches as a prop for a school play. If he needs to make the prop smaller so that it now has a base of 4 inches, how many square inches of material does Jae need to remove? Explain your answer.

4. Using a square and two congruent triangles, Jared constructed triangle *ABC*, to the right. Are triangles *AED* and *EBF* similar to triangle *ABC*? Explain your answer.

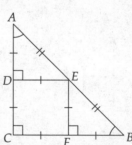

1. The front of Harry's tent is shaped like the triangle below.

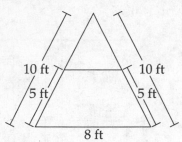

10 ft   10 ft
5 ft   5 ft
8 ft

As pictured, a line splits the triangle into two parts. What is the length of the line?

A   2 feet

B   4 feet

C   5 feet

D   8 feet

2. The shadow of a building measures 198 feet. A stick with a height of 25 inches is placed near the building. It casts a shadow with a length of 16.5 inches. What is the height of the building?

A   130.7 ft

B   156.5 ft

C   206.5 ft

D   300 ft

3. A 250-foot building casts a shadow that is 40 feet. A woman stands on the top of a ladder nearby. Together, the woman and the ladder form a shadow that is 2 feet long. If she is five feet six inches tall, what is the height of the ladder?

A   4 ft   B   5 ft

C   6 ft   D   7 ft

4. Dominique drew two similar right-angled triangles. If the legs of the bigger triangle are 6 inches and 8 inches, and one leg of the smaller triangle is 3 inches, what could be the size of the other leg of the smaller triangle?

A   2 in.

B   4 in.

C   6 in.

D   12 in.

5. Juan is plotting similar triangles on the coordinate plane below.

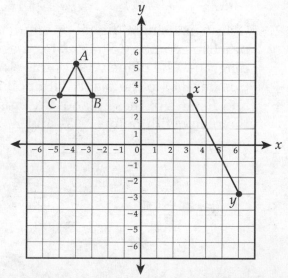

If triangle *ABC* is similar to triangle *XYZ*, which could be the coordinates of point *Z*?

A $(-3, 3)$

B $(-3, 0)$

C $(0, -3)$

D $(3, -3)$

Directions: Read each question. Then circle the letter for the best answer.

1. Adam has a hot tub in his backyard. The hot tub is similar to the backyard. Using the figures below, what is the value of x?

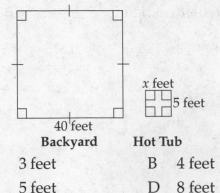

40 feet
Backyard

x feet
5 feet
Hot Tub

A   3 feet

B   4 feet

C   5 feet

D   8 feet

2. Celeste is using a digital program to practice geometry. She creates the following diagram. The plane with points A, B, and C is parallel to the plane with points D, E, and F. Both of these planes are crossed by the plane with points X, Y, and Z.

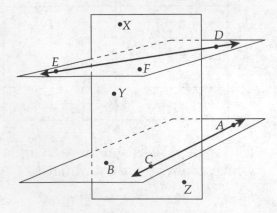

What is the **best** description of lines ED and CA?

A   skew lines

B   perpendicular lines

C   intersecting lines

D   parallel lines

3. Jaime plotted three points in the coordinate graph below.

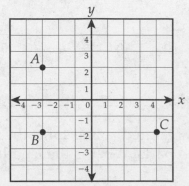

She wants to create a rectangle. If the missing point is in Quadrant I, what could be the coordinates of the missing point?

A $(-2, -4)$

B $(2, 4)$

C $(4, 2)$

D $(-4, -2)$

4. Plot the points $A(-2, 4)$, $B(-1, -1)$, and $C(4, -1)$ on the coordinate graph, below.

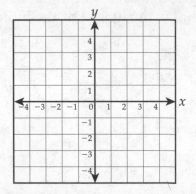

If Derek wants to form a parallelogram from the points plotted, where must he plot point D?

A $(-4, 2)$

B $(1, 1)$

C $(2, -4)$

D $(3, 4)$

Use the following diagram to answer questions 5–8.

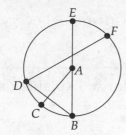

Point *A* is the center of the circle.

5. Which line segment is a chord, and **not** a diameter?

   A $\overline{AC}$

   B $\overline{BA}$

   C $\overline{DF}$

   D $\overline{EB}$

6. Which line segment is the radius?

   A $\overline{AC}$

   B $\overline{BD}$

   C $\overline{DF}$

   D $\overline{EB}$

7. Which line segment is the diameter?

   A $\overline{AC}$

   B $\overline{BD}$

   C $\overline{DF}$

   D $\overline{EB}$

8. If the length of $\overline{AE}$ is 5 feet, what is the diameter of the circle?

   A   5 ft

   B 10 ft

   C 15 ft

   D. 20 ft

9. Katie built a tennis court that has a length of 81 feet and a width of 54 feet. Which of the rectangles below is similar to Katie's tennis court?

A
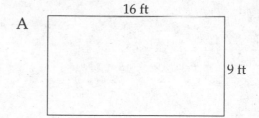
16 ft / 9 ft

B
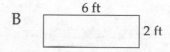
6 ft / 2 ft

C
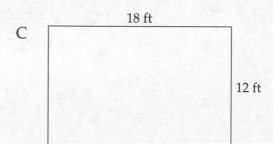
18 ft / 12 ft

D
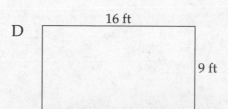
16 ft / 9 ft

Open-Ended Items

10. During the summer, Matt rides his bike from his house to the town pool every day. The wheels on Matt's bike have a 10-inch diameter.

A. What is the circumference of Matt's wheel? Use 3.14 for π. Explain your answer.

B. Matt estimates that, during his trip to the pool, his wheels spin 2,520 times. To the nearest tenth of a mile, how many miles is the pool from the house? Explain your answer. (Remember, 1 mile = 5,280 feet.)

10. *Continued.*

C. Suppose Matt gets a pair of 16-inch wheels for his birthday. Each wheel has a diameter of 16 inches. How many spins will each wheel on Matt's bike now make on trip from Matt's house to the town pool? Use 3.14 for π. Explain your answer.

11. On a sunny day, an electrician uses a cherry picker to raise him to the top of a damaged telephone pole to repair its wires. The shadow formed by the man in the cherry picker measures 40 feet. See the figure below.

40 ft

A. If the electrician is 6 feet 3 inches tall, and a tree nearby has a height of 6 feet and a shadow with a length of 8 feet, how far off the ground is the electrician?

B. If a building nearby has a 120-foot shadow, how tall is the building? Explain your answers.

Assessment Anchors/Eligible Content: M7.E.2.1.1 Identify/calculate the mean (average), median, mode or range of a set of data.

Academic Standards: 2.5.8.A, 2.6.8.A

You can use the mean, median, mode, and range to describe a set of data.

The **mean**, or average, is found by adding the numbers in a set of data and then dividing the sum by the number of addends.

The **median** is the middle number or the average of the two middle numbers in a group of numbers listed from least to greatest.

The **mode** is the number or numbers in a set of data that occur most frequently.

The **range** is the difference between the greatest and least numbers in a set of data.

Guided Instruction

Problem

Mr. Torres is looking for a case to hold his handheld computer. At one computer store, he found cases priced at $32, $70, $32, $40, $47, $19, $42, and $55. What is the mean price of a case? What is the median price? Which price is the mode? What is the range of case prices?

Find the mean, median, mode, and range of the prices.

Step 1 Find the mean price. Divide the sum of the prices by the total number of prices. Then round to the nearest whole number.

$$\frac{32 + 70 + 32 + 40 + 47 + 19 + 42 + 55}{8} = \frac{337}{8} \approx \underline{\hspace{1in}}$$

Step 2 Find the median price. List the prices in order from least to greatest. The middle number is the median. When there are two middle numbers, find their average.

19 32 32 | 40 42 | 47 55 70

$$\frac{(40 + 42)}{2} = \underline{\hspace{1in}}$$

Step 3 Find the mode, or the price that occurs most frequently. There may be no mode, or 1 or more modes. Which price is the mode? _____

Step 4 Find the range of case prices. Arrange the prices in order from least to greatest. Subtract the least price from the greatest price.

19 32 32 40 42 47 55 70

70 − 19 = _____

Solution

What is the mean price of a case? _____

What is the median price? _____

Which price is the mode? _____

What is the range of case prices? _____

Apply the Pennsylvania Academic Standards

Find the mean, median, mode, and range of each set of data.

1. (3, 5, 7, 1, 3, 7, 1, 2, 6, 5, 5, 5, 3, 3) mean_____median_____mode_____range_____

2. (2.8, 1.6, 4.5, 3.9, 2.2) mean_____median_____mode_____range_____

3. (68, 72, 77, 48, 57, 33, 68, 72, 44, 72) mean_____median_____mode_____range_____

4. (488, 392, 715, 233, 555) mean_____median_____mode_____range_____

Use the information below to solve problems 5–7.

Each time Ms. Serna visits the gas station, she records her odometer reading, the number of miles traveled since last visit, the number of gallons purchased, and her mileage per gallon. Complete the table.

Ms. Serna's Driving Log

Date	Odometer Reading	Miles Traveled	Gallons Purchased	Miles per Gallon
Feb. 10	18,873	263	10	26.3
Feb. 24	19,013		6	
Mar. 7	19,224		8.9	
Mar. 28	19,530		11.5	
Apr. 11	19,784		10	

5. What is the range of miles per gallon? _____

6. What is the median number of miles per gallon? _____

7. About how many miles per gallon does Ms. Serna's car average?

_____

Solve each problem using the following set of data.

34   26   14   22   60   55   36   20 | ? |

8. If the mode of the set of data is 14, what is the missing number? _____

9. If the range of the set of data is 51, what could be the missing number? _____

10. If the mean of the set of data is 32, what is the missing number? _____
Explain your reasoning.

_____

_____

PSSA Practice **Directions: Read each question. Then circle the letter for the best answer.**

1. An ornithologist counted the eggs in several blue jays' nests: 4, 4, 3, 5, 2, 4, 4, 5, 6, 5, 5, 4. What is the median number of eggs in a nest?

   A   2

   B   3

   C   4

   D   5

2. William bought books for $22, $12, $18, $28, and $16. What is the mean price he paid for a book?

   A $18.00

   B $19.20

   C $20.80

   D $23.30

3. There is only one mode in Andrea's data, 17. Which set of data is Andrea's?

   A   34, 16, 27, 37, 15, 17, 17, 23, 44, 1

   B   19, 17, 17, 24, 19, 24, 21, 13, 27, 24

   C   17, 18, 29, 31, 26, 26, 36, 14, 27

   D   12, 12, 16, 27, 38, 13, 26, 37, 17

4. When Jorge's height is added to this set of data, the mean height will be 66 inches. What is Jorge's height?

Name	Height (in).
Brad	70
Leticia	62
Mira	67

   A   64 in.   B   65 in.

   C   66 in.   D   68 in.

5. Danny jogs x miles on the first day, y miles on the second day, and z miles on the third day. Which expression represents the average number of miles per day that Danny jogs?

   A xyz

   B $x + y + z$

   C $\dfrac{xyz}{3}$

   D $\dfrac{x + y + z}{3}$

6. There are 12 students on a swim team. Their ages are 16, 13, 15, 17, 16, 17, 12, 16, 12, 15, 16, and 16 years. What is the median age?

   A   13

   B   14

   C   15

   D   16

Focus on the Pennsylvania Academic Standards

Lesson 51 Select the Appropriate Statistical Measure

Assessment Anchors/Eligible Content: M7.E.2.1.1 Identify/calculate the mean (average), median, mode or range of a set of data.

M7.E.2.1.2 Decide/choose which measure of central tendency (mean, median, mode or range) would be most appropriate for a given situation.

Academic Standards: 2.5.8.A, 2.6.8.A

You can represent data numerically or graphically.

Hours of Television A Day

Hours	Tally
1	IIII IIII IIII I
2	IIII IIII III
3	IIII IIII I
4	IIII
5	IIII
6	I
7	
8	I

Guided Instruction

Problem

Victoria made the tally chart to the right to record the number of hours she watches television each day. Which measure of central tendency, mean, median, or mode, best describes the number of hours Victoria watches television on a daily basis?

Find the mean, median, and mode. Then select the number that best describes the data.

Step 1 Find the mean.

$$= \frac{(16 \times 1) + (13 \times 2) + (11 \times 3) + (4 \times 4) + (4 \times 5) + (1 \times 6) + (1 \times 8)}{50}$$

$$= \frac{16 + 26 + 33 + 16 + 20 + 6 + 8}{50} = \underline{\hspace{2cm}}$$

Step 2 Find the median. There are 50 numbers, so the 25th and 26th numbers are the middle numbers. The median is _____.

Step 3 Find the mode. The number of hours with the greatest number of tally marks is the mode. The mode is _____.

Step 4 Evaluate the effectiveness of the different representations.

The mean is not effective because it is being influenced by _____ hours and _____ hours of television.

The median is _____ because most of the numbers are close to it.

The mode is _____ because about two thirds of the numbers are greater.

Generally, the middle value of the measures of central tendency (mean, median, and mode) best describes a set of data.

Step 5 Decide which number best describes the data in the chart.

Is 2.5 hours, 2 hours, or 1 hour the best description of the number of hours Victoria watches television on most days? _____

Solution

Which measure of central tendency best describes the number of hours Victoria watches television on a daily basis? _____

Measuring Up® to the Pennsylvania Academic Standards

Apply the Pennsylvania Academic Standards

Use the bar graph below to solve Problems 1–5 and justify your answers. The graph below shows the number of siblings for each student in a class.

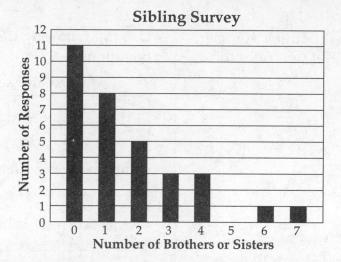

1. The most common number of siblings is _____

2. A little more than half the students have fewer than _____ siblings.

   _____

3. The range of the number of siblings is _____.

4. The mean number of siblings that each student has is _____.

   _____

5. The measure of central tendency that best describes the number of siblings that each student has is the _____.

   _____

Solve each problem.
List the measure of central tendency that justifies your solution for problems 6–7.

6. Prices for the main entrees at Fast Feast are:
   $18, $16, $25, $27, $19, $26, $16
   On average, how much can a customer expect
   to pay for an entree at Fast Feast? _____

7. Iku made the following points during a school basketball game:
   2, 2, 3, 2, 2, 2, 1, 2, 2, 1, 1, 2, 2, 2, 2, 3
   About how many points did Iku score each time he made a basket? _____

8. Use the data in the table at the right. Who is the better player? Explain.

   _____

   _____

   _____

Player	Game Scores
Tania	325, 317, 335, 325, 320
Leticia	426, 120, 250, 426, 172

Directions: Read each question. Then circle the letter for the best answer.

1. Blueberries are the most popular summer fruit. Which measure **best** describes this fact?

   A   Mean

   B   Median

   C   Mode

   D   Range

2. Half of the seventh graders are 12 years old or less. Which measure **best** describes this fact?

   A   Mean

   B   Median

   C   Mode

   D   Range

3. Alvin wants to assure his family that he is passing history. Suppose passing is 70% and above and his teacher plans to use his scores equally to calculate his final grade. Which measure of central tendency should he use to describe his grades?

   History Grades

Test Date	Grade
Jan. 21	73%
Feb. 1	60%
Feb. 10	74%
Apr. 6	65%
May 2	72%

   A   Mean

   B   Median

   C   Mode

   D   Range

Use the following data below to answer questions 4–6.

Ocean Kayak Store Prices

Store	Store Manager	Prices of Selected Models
Ship Shop	Elena	$315, $609, $591, $699, $545, $429, $429
Outpost	Lahar	$579, $519, $679, $430, $489, $309, $579

 4. Which measure of central tendency should Elena use to show that Ship Shop has lower prices?

   A   Mean

   B   Median

   C   Mode

   D   Range

 5. Which measure of central tendency should Lahar use to show the variety of outpost's prices?

   A   Mean

   B   Median

   C   Mode

   D   Range

 6. Which measure of central tendency indicates that the prices at both stores are about the same?

   A   Mean

   B   Median

   C   Mode

   D   Range

Assessment Anchors/Eligible Content: M7.E.1.1.1 Analyze data and/or answer questions pertaining to data represented in histograms, double bar graphs, multiple line graphs or stem-and-leaf plots.

M7.E.4.1.1 Formulate predictions and/or draw conclusions based on data displays (bar graphs, circle graphs or line graphs) or probability.

Academic Standards: 2.4.8.F, 2.6.8.F

You can make inferences and draw conclusions by analyzing data presented in graphs. Three kinds of graphs you can use to analyze data are bar graphs, line graphs, and circle graphs.

Bar graphs use bars to compare data.

Line graphs show changes, trends, or developments over a period of time.

Circle graphs shows how parts of a whole compare, using a circle.

Guided Instruction

Problem

The editors of a magazine conducted a survey to find out which topics readers liked the most. The results of the survey are shown in the bar graph. Which topics should the editors of the magazine feature most frequently in their articles?

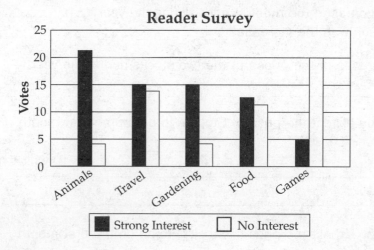

Use the graph to compare data.

Step 1   Eliminate choices, if possible.
Which topic can be eliminated because few people had *strong interest* and many people had *no interest*? _____

Step 2   Consider the remaining topics.
Which topic shows a greater number of readers with *strong interest* compared to the number of readers with *no interest*? _____

Solution

Which topic should the editors of the magazine feature most frequently in their articles? _____

Use the graph below to solve questions 1–5.
The graph shows the change in price of two stocks during one year.

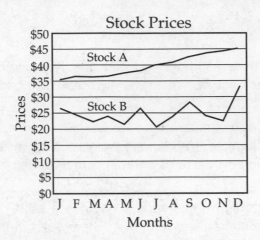

Stock Prices

1. Which stock had the greatest one-month increase? _____
   When did the increase occur? _____

2. Which stock increased the most in price during the year? _____
   About how much was the increase? _____

3. Compare the range of the prices of the two stocks during the year.

   _____

4. What would you expect the price of Stock A to be on the first month
   of the new year? Explain.

   _____

   _____

5. What would you expect the price of Stock B to be on the first month
   of the new year? Explain.

   _____

   _____

Use the graph to solve problems 6–7.
The circle graph shows Maria's monthly budget.

6. What are Maria's greatest and least
   budgeted items each month?

   _____

7. If Maria gets $100 for her birthday, how much
   of it would you expect her to spend on books?
   Explain your reasoning. _____

   _____

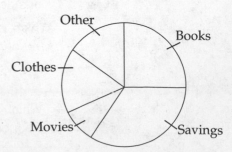

Monthly Budget

 Measuring Up® to the Pennsylvania Academic Standards

PSSA Practice

Directions: Read each question. Then circle the letter for the best answer.

Use the graph below to answer questions 1–3.

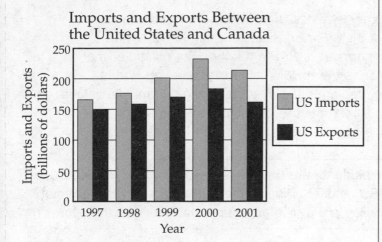

Imports and Exports Between the United States and Canada

3. During which year were imports and exports between the United States and Canada at their highest?

A   1998

B   1999

C   2000

D   2001

 1. Which conclusion can be drawn from the graph?

A   Exports to Canada remained constant.

B   Imports have increased more than exports.

C   The United States exports more than it imports from Canada.

D   Both imports and exports continue to increase each year.

4. Which graph suggests that Ms. Forester will narrowly win the election?

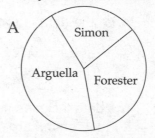

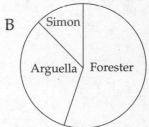

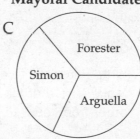

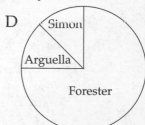

 2. Which statement can be inferred from the graph?

A   Imports were less than $150 billion in 2002.

B   Imports were greater than exports in 2002.

C   Imports did not reach $150 billion prior to 1997.

D   Exports were greater than imports in 1995.

Focus on the Pennsylvania Academic Standards

Lesson 53   Stem-and-Leaf Plots

Assessment Anchors/Eligible Content: M7.E.1.1.1 Analyze data and/or answer questions pertaining to data represented in histograms, double bar graphs, multiple line graphs or stem-and-leaf plots.

Academic Standards: 2.4.8.F, 2.6.8.F

You can display collected data in a stem-and-leaf plot to identify the median, mode, and range of the data.

A **stem-and-leaf plot** displays data in order by place-value. Each **stem** represents the place values to the left of the rightmost digit. For example, the number 103 has a stem of 10. Each **leaf** represents the rightmost digit of a number. For example, the number 103 has a leaf of 3. The **median** is the middle value in a data set. When there is an even number of values, the median is the average of the two middle values of the set. The **mode** is the value that occurs most frequently in a given set of data. The **range** is the difference between the greatest and least values in a data set.

Guided Instruction

Problem

Science test scores for 17 students are 65, 80, 90, 85, 85, 70, 75, 80, 80, 60, 95, 100, 75, 80, 95, 80, and 75. Display the data in a stem-and-leaf plot. Using the organized data, what is the median, mode, and range of the scores?

Create a stem-and-leaf plot of the data.

Step 1   Write the data in order from least to greatest.

60, 65, _____

Step 2   The data includes numbers from 60 to 100. So their stems are 6 through 10. Write these numbers vertically from least to greatest in the plot to the right.

Stem	Leaf
6	
7	

Step 3   Write each leaf to the right of its stem. Make sure that leaves are listed in order from least to greatest.

Stem	Leaf
6	0
7	
8	
9	
10	

Step 4   Provide a key for your plot that explains how to read the data.

Key: 6|0 means 60

Step 5   Interpret the data.

The mode is _____. The median is _____. The range is _____.

Solution

What is the median test score? _____

What is the mode test score? _____

What is the range of the test scores? _____

Apply the Pennsylvania Academic Standards

Use the data found in the stem-and-leaf plot below to solve problems 1–4.

1. The stem-and-leaf plot at the right shows the weights, in pounds, of 13 high school students. List all of the weights shown in the stem-and-leaf plot in order from least to greatest.

_____

Stem	Leaf
15	4 6 8
16	2
17	4 5
18	1 3
19	0 0
20	6 8 9

Key: 18|1 means 181

2. What is the median weight? _____

3. What is the mode weight? _____

4. What is the range of weights? _____

Use the organized data to solve each problem.

5. Complete the stem-and-leaf plot using the information in the table below.

Monthly High Temperatures for Amarillo, Texas (°F)

Jan.	Feb.	Mar.	Apr.	May.	June	July	Aug.	Sept.	Oct.	Nov.	Dec.
76	76	80	88	99	92	103	105	96	90	83	77

6. How many months had a high temperature greater than 80°F?

_____

Stem	Leaf
7	
8	
9	
10	

Key: 9|0 means 90

7. What is the range of high temperatures?

_____

8. What is the mode high temperature for the 12 months?

_____

9. What is the median high temperature for the 12 months?

_____

Explain how you found your answer.

_____

_____

_____

Directions: Read each question. Then circle the letter for the best answer.

Use the stem-and-leaf plot below to answer questions 1–3.

Stem	Leaf
45	0 2 3 7
46	1 1 5 5
47	
48	8 9
49	4 5 6

Key: 45|0 means 450

1. Which number is shown in the stem-and-leaf plot?

   A   53

   B   461

   C   470

   D   484

 2. Which statement below is NOT true?

   A   The range of the data is 46.

   B   The median number is 465.

   C   The mode number is 463.

   D   There are no numbers from 470 to 479.

 3. Which number, if added to the stem-and-leaf plot, requires adding a new stem?

   A   503

   B   493

   C   477

   D   451

 4. Which stem-and-leaf plot correctly displays the data below?

Bowling Scores
155, 206, 162, 193, 173, 164, 201, 180, 155, 171, 174, 195, 177, 160, 199

A

Stem	Leaf
15	5 5
16	2 4
17	1 3 4 7
18	
19	3 5 9
20	1 6

Key: 15|0 means 155

B

Stem	Leaf
15	5 5
16	0 2 4
17	1 3 4 7
18	0
19	3 5 9
20	1 6

Key: 15|0 means 155

C

Stem	Leaf
15	5 5
16	0 2 4
17	1 3
18	4 7
19	3 5 9
20	1

Key: 15|0 means 155

D

Stem	Leaf
15	5 5
16	0 2
17	1 3 4 4 7
18	3 5
19	9
20	1 6

Key: 15|0 means 155

Focus on the Pennsylvania Academic Standards

Lesson 54 Use Graphs to Display Data

Assessment Anchors/Eligible Content: M7.E.1.1.1 Analyze data and/or answer questions pertaining to data represented in histograms, double bar graphs, multiple line graphs or stem-and-leaf plots.

Academic Standards: 2.4.8.F, 2.6.8.F

When you use a graph to display data, such as a histogram, you can quickly see where there are a number of clusters and gaps. A **histogram** is a special type of bar graph that shows the frequency of data with equal intervals.

Guided Instruction

Problem

Students at a summer camp are divided into groups according to their ages. The tally chart below shows the number of students in each age group. Draw a histogram to display the data. Where is there a gap in the data?

Age	Tally Marks	Frequency
4–6	ЖЖ	5
7–9		0
10–12	ЖЖ IIII	9
13–15	ЖЖ I	6
16–18	II	2

Step 1 Draw and label a horizontal axis to represent the age groups. Draw and label a vertical axis to represent the frequencies.

Step 2 Draw a bar over each age group. Use the bar height to represent frequency.

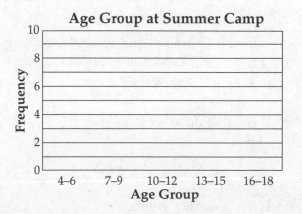

Age Group at Summer Camp

Step 3 Look for an age group that has no bar.

There is a gap at _____.

Solution

Where is there a gap in the data? _____

Use the data found in the double bar graph below to solve questions 1–5.

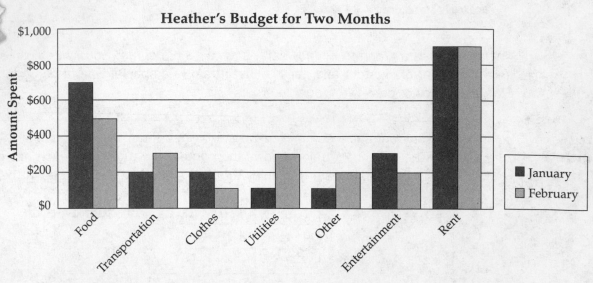

Heather's Budget for Two Months

1. What is Heather's total budget for each month? _____

2. Which expense increased the most between January and February? _____

3. Which expense remained the same between January and February? _____

4. In January, how much money did Heather spend altogether on transportation, clothes, and entertainment? _____

5. How much money did Heather spend on utilities for both months? _____

Use the information below to solve problems 6–8.

As part of a science experiment, Desmond and Sharon each recorded the height of a plant over a five-week interval. The double line graph at the right displays their data.

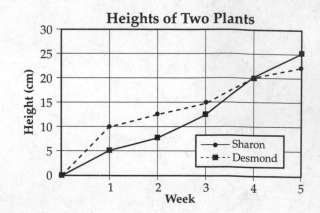

Heights of Two Plants

6. During which interval did Desmond's plant grow the fastest?

_____

7. During which interval did Sharon's plant grow the fastest?

_____

8. When were Desmond's and Sharon's plants the same height?

_____

PSSA Practice

Directions: Read each question. Then circle the letter for the best answer.

Use the data below to answer questions 1–2.

Florence surveyed eighth and ninth grade students at her school about their favorite types of novels. The double bar graph below displays her results.

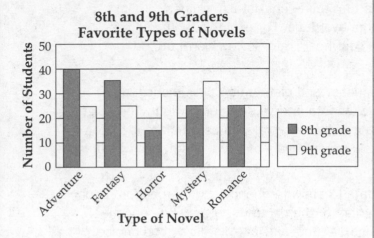

1. What percent of the 8th grade students chose Fantasy as their favorite type of novel?

   A   13%   B   18%

   C   21%   D   25%

2. Altogether, how many students chose Mystery and Romance as their favorite type of novel?

   A   50   B   60

   C   110   D   120

3. Which two types of novel received the same total number of votes?

   A   Adventure and Fantasy

   B   Fantasy and Mystery

   C   Fantasy and Romance

   D   Mystery and Romance

4. Which histogram correctly displays the data listed below?

Heights of 15 Students (in.)
66, 60, 58, 72, 70, 59, 65, 67, 57, 62, 64, 69, 67, 60, 70

A

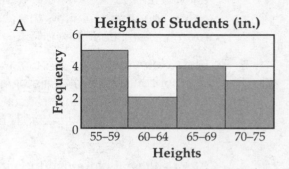

B

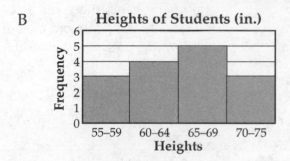

C

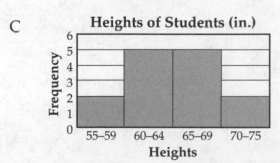

D

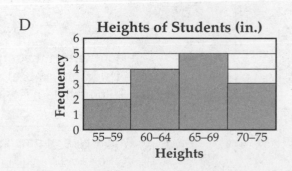

Focus on the Pennsylvania Academic Standards

Lesson 55 | Choose the Appropriate Representation

Assessment Anchors/Eligible Content: M7.E.1.1.1 Analyze data and/or answer questions pertaining to data represented in histograms, double bar graphs, multiple line graphs or stem-and-leaf plots.

Academic Standards: 2.4.8.F, 2.6.8.F

To represent data effectively, you need to select an appropriate representation.

Bar graphs use bars to show amounts or numbers. The bars show comparisons between groups of data. For example, you could use a bar graph to graph the number of students in the fifth, sixth, seventh, and eighth grades.

Line graphs use lines to connect points that represent data. The lines show changes, trends, and developments over time. For example, you could use a line graph to show the change in your heart rate as you warm up, exercise, and cool down.

Histograms use bars to display the frequency and distribution of numerical data. The horizontal axis of a histogram is broken into intervals of equal width. The height of a bar represents the frequency of data in that interval. Histograms are ideal for displaying data that can easily be broken into intervals of equal width, such as heights, weights, or ages.

Stem-and-Leaf plots use the digits of data to show frequency and distribution. Each stem represents the place values to the left of the rightmost digit, while each leaf represents the rightmost digit of a number. A stem-and-leaf plot is a good choice for showing data with two or three digits, such as test scores, temperatures, or prices.

Guided Instruction

Problem

Which type of graph would most effectively represent the data in the table?

Population of Summerville

Year	1960	1970	1980	1990	2000
Population	15,256	17,004	18,936	22,419	28,377

Use what you know about graphs.

Step 1 Examine the data.
What does this data show?

_____

_____

Step 2 Select a graph that effectively represents the data.
Which graph will best show the change in the population
of Summerville over time? _____

Solution Which type of graph would most effectively represent the data
in the table? _____

Apply the Pennsylvania Academic Standards

Name a graph that could best represent the given data. Justify your selection.

1. The number of men and number of women working in each of five different professions

   _____

   _____

2. The test scores of students in a math class

   _____

   _____

3. The change in the number of people who have cell phones over a ten-year period

   _____

4. The weights of eight different animals

   _____

5. The daily high temperature each day in August

   _____

Use the information below to solve problems 6–7.

The tables at the right show how much money Federico and Samantha each spent on different parts of their gardens.

6. Explain why a double bar graph is appropriate for displaying the data shown in the tables. What would you put on each axis of the graph?

   _____

   _____

   _____

7. Could a double line graph be used to represent the data in the tables? Explain why or why not.

   _____

   _____

Federico's Spending

Fertilizer	$40
Seeds	$10
Plants	$35
Tools	$15
Soil	$100

Samantha's Spending

Fertilizer	$40
Seeds	$10
Plants	$60
Tools	$55
Soil	$35

PSSA Practice Directions: Read each question. Then circle the letter for the best answer.

1. Which graph would **best** represent the weights of two growing puppies over a six-month period?

   A double bar graph

   B double line graph

   C stem-and-leaf plot

   D histogram

2. A stem-and-leaf plot would **best** represent which of the following sets of data?

   A the results of a survey on favorite movies

   B water levels in a reservoir over a 10-day period

   C high temperatures for the month of August

   D colors of cars in a parking lot

3. The bar graph shown below would **best** represent which of the following sets of data?

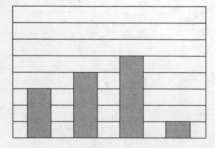

   A wins, losses, ties and total games played by teams in a soccer league

   B populations of four different cities every ten years over a 50-year period

   C the growth of a tadpole over one day

   D number of days of rain in four different cities in one month

4. Why is the line graph below a good representation of the data?

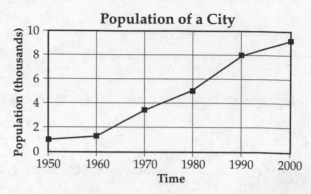

   A The graph shows a change over time.

   B The graph compares two sets of data.

   C The line is easy to draw.

   D The data shown is linear.

5. The results of a customer survey are shown in the table below.

   Customer Satisfaction Survey

Very Satisfied	750
Satisfied	150
Unsatisfied	60
Very Unsatisfied	40

   Which graph would **best** represent the data?

   A bar graph

   B double bar graph

   C line graph

   D double line graph

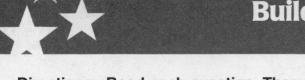

Directions: Read each question. Then circle the letter for the best answer.

1. Twyla bought movies for $17, $12, $26, $22, $16, and $9. What is the mean price she paid for a movie?

   A $12.60

   B $15.40

   C $17.00

   D $19.30

2. John has a table with the total United States population for every decade from 1900 to 2000. Which representation would **best** display the data?

   A Circle graph

   B Bar graph

   C Line graph

   D Stem-and-leaf plot

3. Which of the following statements about the stem-and-leaf plot below is **not** true?

Stem	Leaf
3	1 1 3
4	0 0 0 6
5	4
6	0

   Key: 5|4 = 54.

   A The range of the data is 29.

   B The median number is 40.

   C The mode number is 40.

   D The stem 6 has no leaves.

Use the information below to answer questions 4–6.

Coach Simonson decides to use a stem-and-leaf plot to show the heights of each player in his basketball team.

Stem	Leaf
7	2 3 4 6 6 6 8 8 9
8	0 0 1

Key: 7|2 = 72.

4. In the athletic program, the height of each basketball player is listed in inches. What is the approximate mean height of a basketball player on the team?

   A 74.86 in.

   B 75.34 in.

   C 76.92 in.

   D 78.46 in.

5. What is the mode of the set of data?

   A 73 in.

   B 76 in.

   C 78 in.

   D 80 in.

6. What is the median height of the basketball team?

   A 80 in.

   B 79 in.

   C 78 in.

   D 77 in.

Use the table below to answer questions 7–8.

Athlete	100-meter Time (seconds)
Renee	12.89, 14.22, 13.46, 15.01, 14.74, 13.51, 13.89
Chimere	12.98, 13.01, 12.98, 15.12, 13.23, 14.03, 12.98

 7. Which of the following does **not** show that Chimere has better times than Renee?

    A   Mode

    B   Mean

    C   Median

    D   Range

8. Which of the following should Chimere use to show that she is a more consistent runner than Renee?

    A   Mode

    B   Mean

    C   Median

    D   Range

 9. Which representation would **best** display the standardized-test scores, for males and females, for grades 5 through 12?

    A   Double-bar graph

    B   Double-line graph

    C   Circle graph

    D   Histogram

Use the graph below to answer questions 9–10.

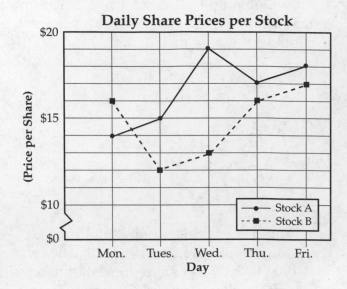

10. During which day did the share prices for Stock A have the **greatest** increase?

    A   Monday

    B   Tuesday

    C   Wednesday

    D   Thursday

11. What is the range in price for Stock B?

    A $4

    B $5

    C $6

    D $17

Open-Ended Items

12. Carly asked her classmates to pick a number between 10 and 80. She got the following responses: 48, 27, 66, 16, 28, 37, 40, 40, 24, 36, 35, 11, 72, 38, 15, 28, 48, 40, 16, 27, 56, 50, 30, and 56.

A. Create a stem-and-leaf plot from the set of data.

B. Create a histogram from the set of data.

---

12. *Continued*

C. Find the measures of central tendency: mean, median, and mode. Round each measure to the nearest tenth, as necessary. Show your work.

D. Which measure of central tendency best describes the set of data? Explain your answer.

13. Yvonne has been keeping track of her test scores throughout the semester for Science class. The scores are shown in the table below.

Test Number	Test Score
1	67
2	82
3	93
4	98
5	81
6	76
7	97
8	93

A. What are the mean, median, and mode of the set of data? Explain your answer.

B. Which of measure of central tendency best describes Yvonne's scores? Explain your answer.

Chapter 10
Focus on the Pennsylvania Academic Standards
Lesson 56 — Find the Probability of Simple Events

Assessment Anchors/Eligible Content: M7.E.3.1.1 Find the theoretical probability of a simple and/or compound event (answer written as a fraction in lowest terms – any compound events should be independent).

M7.E.3.1.2 Find the theoretical probability of an event not occurring (e.g., what is the probability of not rolling a 1 on a number cube).

Academic Standards: 2.4.8.B, 2.7.5.E, 2.7.5.G, 2.7.5.J, 2.7.8.E

You can determine the probability of an event occurring by writing the ratio of favorable outcomes to possible outcomes.

Probability tells the likelihood that an event will occur.

It is expressed by this ratio: $\dfrac{\text{number of favorable outcomes}}{\text{number of possible outcomes}}$.

A **sample space** lists all the possible outcomes of an event.
Possible outcomes are the possible results in an experiment.
Favorable outcomes are the results you want.

Guided Instruction

Problem

Bob is flipping a coin once and spinning a spinner. Bob earns a point if he tosses heads and spins an odd number. What is the probability that Bob will not earn a point?

Make a tree diagram to construct the sample space.

Coin	Spinner	Outcomes
	1	Heads, 1
Heads	___	___
	___	___
	___	___
	1	Tails, 1
	___	___
	___	___
	___	___
	___	___

Step 1 Complete the diagram. There are a total of _____ possible outcomes.

Step 2 How many outcomes will earn Bob a point? _____

Write the probability of this event.

$\dfrac{\text{number of favorable outcomes}}{\text{number of possible outcomes}} = $ _____

Step 3 To find the probability that Bob will not earn a point, find the difference of 1 minus the probability that he will earn a point.

1 − *probability Bob earns a point* = 1 − _____ = _____

Solution   What is the probability that Bob will not earn a point? _____

Apply the Pennsylvania Academic Standards

Use the items below to solve problems 1–5.

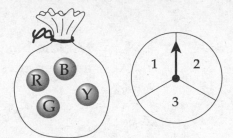

1. What is the sample space for drawing one marble from the bag? _____

2. What is the sample space for spinning the spinner one time? _____

3. Make a tree diagram to construct the sample space for drawing a marble from the bag and then spinning a number one time.

4. How many possible outcomes are there for drawing a marble from the bag and then spinning a number one time?

   _____

5. What is the probability of:

   a. drawing a red marble and spinning a 1?

   _____

   b. drawing a green marble and spinning an odd number?

   _____

   c. drawing any marble and not spinning an even number?

   _____

Use the items to the right to solve each problem.

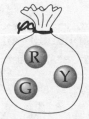

6. What is the probability of flipping a head and then spinning a 3? _____

7. What is the probability of not spinning a 5 and then drawing a red marble? _____

8. What is the probability of flipping a tail, spinning a 2, and then drawing a blue marble? _____
   Explain your answer.

   _____

   _____

PSSA Practice

Directions: Read each question. Then circle the letter for the best answer.

Use the spinners below to answer questions 1–3.

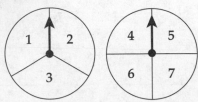

1. How many possible outcomes are there for spinning each spinner one time?

   A 4
   B 6
   C 8
   D 12

2. What is the probability of spinning two even numbers when you spin each spinner one time?

   A $\frac{1}{2}$
   B $\frac{1}{3}$
   C $\frac{1}{6}$
   D $\frac{5}{12}$

3. What is the probability of **not** spinning two even numbers, when you spin each spinner once?

   A $\frac{1}{4}$
   B $\frac{1}{3}$
   C $\frac{1}{2}$
   D $\frac{3}{4}$

Use the box with letter blocks below to answer questions 4–6.

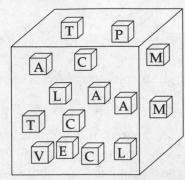

4. Vowels are the letters A, E, I, O, and U. What is the probability of picking a vowel?

   A $\frac{1}{5}$
   B $\frac{4}{15}$
   C $\frac{4}{11}$
   D $\frac{1}{3}$

5. What is the probability of **not** picking an M?

   A $\frac{13}{15}$
   B $\frac{1}{2}$
   C $\frac{1}{3}$
   D $\frac{2}{15}$

6. What is the probability of **not** picking the letters C or E?

   A $\frac{1}{15}$ B $\frac{4}{15}$
   C $\frac{4}{11}$ D $\frac{11}{15}$

Lesson 57 Experimental Probability

Assessment Anchors/Eligible Content: M7.E.3.1.3 Use data displayed in charts, graphs or tallies to find experimental probability.
M7.E.4.1.1 Formulate predictions and/or draw conclusions based on data displays (bar graphs, circle graphs or line graphs) or probability.
Academic Standards: 2.7.8.B, 2.7.8.D, 2.7.8.E

You can use experimental results to make predictions about future events.

Guided Instruction

Problem 1

Kenny and his father are counting the types of birds that arrive at a thistle feeder in the park. What is the experimental probability that the next bird to arrive at the feeder will be a goldfinch?

Birds at the Thistle Feeder

Type	Goldfinch	Pine Siskin
Tally	卌 卌 卌 卌 l	卌 ll

Use the probability formula: $P(\text{event}) = \dfrac{\text{number of favorable outcomes}}{\text{number of possible outcomes}}$.

Step 1 Find the total number of possible outcomes.
What is the total number of birds that arrived at the feeder? _____

Step 2 Find the number of favorable outcomes.
How many of the birds were goldfinches? _____

Step 3 Write the formula. Simplify the ratio, if possible.

$$P(\text{goldfinch}) = \dfrac{\text{number of goldfinches}}{\text{total number of birds}} = \underline{\hspace{3cm}}$$

Solution

What is the probability that the next bird that arrives at the feeder will be a goldfinch? _____

Problem 2

Based on the data in Problem 1, how many of the next 100 birds that arrive at the feeder will be pine siskins?

Write and solve a proportion.

$$\dfrac{\text{number of pine siskins}}{\text{total number of birds}} = \dfrac{\text{number of pine siskins}}{\text{total number of birds}}$$

$$\dfrac{7}{28} = \dfrac{p}{100}$$

$$28p = \underline{\hspace{1.5cm}}$$

$$p = \underline{\hspace{1.5cm}}$$

Solution

How many of the next 100 birds that arrive at the feeder will be pine siskins? _____

Another Example

A bag contains six green marbles and seven red marbles. Yolanda picks one marble from the bag and returns it. Then Martin picks from the bag. What is the probability that Martin's marble will be red, if Yolanda picked a green marble?

There are six green marbles and 7 red marbles. So the probability that Yolanda picks a green marble is $\frac{6}{13}$. If her marble is returned, the probability that Martin picks a red marble is $\frac{7}{13}$.

Apply the Pennsylvania Academic Standards

Use the table below to answer questions 1–5.

A spinner is marked green, yellow, red, and blue. What is the experimental probability that the spinner will stop on each of the following?

Results	Tally
Green	卌 卌 卌 卌 卌 卌 卌 I
Yellow	卌 卌 I
Red	II
Blue	I

1. on blue _____

2. not on blue _____

3. on green or yellow _____

4. If the spinner is spun 500 times, how many times would you expect to spin red? _____

5. What percent of the spins would you expect to stop on green? _____

Solve each problem.

6. Frank dropped a coin on the floor. What are the possible outcomes of how the coin landed? _____

7. What is the probability of each of the possible outcomes of Problem 6? Write each probability as a fraction.

   _____

8. A bag contains 10 tiles numbered 1–10. Without looking, Miranda picks one tile from the bag and returns it. Then Brianna picks a tile without looking, as well. What is the probability that Miranda's tile will be 2? What is the probability that Brianna's tile will be 7 after Miranda picks 2?

   _____

9. A bag contains 14 tiles. Each tile is either green, red, blue or yellow. Based on the information in the table below, how many tiles of each color are likely to be in the bag? Explain.

Results	Green	Red	Blue	Yellow
Tally	卌 卌 卌 卌 I	III	卌 I	卌 卌 II

   _____

   _____

   _____

PSSA Practice

Directions: Read each question. Then circle the letter for the best answer.

Use the graph below to answer questions 1–2.

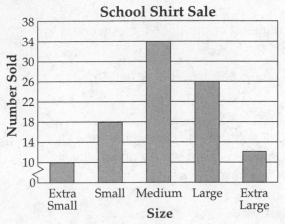

School Shirt Sale

1. What is the experimental probability that the next shirt sold will be either large or extra large?

   A $\frac{7}{25}$

   B $\frac{17}{50}$

   C $\frac{19}{50}$

   D $\frac{19}{25}$

2. If the school secretary orders 300 **more** shirts, how many additional shirts should be large?

   A   54

   B   78

   C   104

   D   211

3. Dana found that seven out of sixteen brands of toothpaste carried by a local store have fluoride. Based on her data, what percent of all brands of toothpaste have fluoride?

   A   about 17%

   B   about 44%

   C   about 56%

   D   about 86%

4. Based on observation, Sara predicted that $\frac{3}{5}$ of the students at her school wear jeans on any given day. Which of the following tables reflects Sara's prediction?

A
Jeans	60
Shorts	21
Chinos	14
Other	5

B
Jeans	58
Shorts	40
Chinos	32
Other	10

C
Jeans	39
Shorts	42
Chinos	31
Other	18

D
Jeans	40
Shorts	36
Chinos	40
Other	3

5. A bookstore has a box of magazines, each with a cardboard insert for a different magazine. There are 9 inserts for computer magazines, 8 for sports magazines, 10 for gardening magazines, 8 for art magazines, 6 for home improvement magazines, 16 for health magazines, 8 for business magazines, and 14 for puzzle magazines. Which of the following predictions can you make based on this data?

   A   A customer will probably get a sports magazine insert.

   B   The probability that a customer will get a business magazine insert is about $\frac{1}{5}$.

   C   It is just as likely that a customer will get a health magazine insert as it is that he or she will get either a sports or business magazine insert.

   D   A customer is least likely to get an art magazine insert.

Focus on the Pennsylvania Academic Standards

Lesson 58 · Find the Probability of Independent Events

Assessment Anchors/Eligible Content: M7.E.3.1.1 Find the theoretical probability of a simple and/or compound event (answer written as a fraction in lowest terms – any compound events should be independent).

M7.E.3.1.2 Find the theoretical probability of an event not occurring (e.g., what is the probability of not rolling a 1 on a number cube)

M7.E.3.1.3 Use data displayed in charts, graphs or tallies to find experimental probability.

Academic Standards: 2.4.8.B, 2.7.5.E, 2.7.5.G, 2.7.5.J, 2.7.8.E

You can make a list or draw a tree diagram to find all of the possible outcomes for two independent events.

Two events are **independent** if the outcome of one event does not affect the outcome of the other event.

Guided Instruction

Problem

George has red and blue baseball caps. He has red, blue, and white T-shirts. If George chooses a cap and a shirt without looking, what is the probability that both will have the same color?

Match each possible outcome of the first event with each possible outcome of the second event.

Step 1 List all of the possible outcomes for each event.

What are the possible outcomes for choosing a cap? _____

What are the possible outcomes for choosing a shirt? _____

Step 2 Make a list or draw a tree diagram. List red cap along with each possible shirt color. List blue cap along with each possible shirt color.

Cap	Shirt
Red	Red
Red	Blue
Red	White
Blue	_____
Blue	_____
Blue	_____

Cap   Shirt

Red < Red
        Blue
        White

Blue < _____
         _____
         _____

Step 3 Use the probability formula, $P(\text{event}) = \frac{\text{favorable outcomes}}{\text{possible outcomes}}$.

Count to find the total number of color combinations and the number of same color combinations.

$$P(\text{same color}) = \frac{\text{same color combinations}}{\text{total combinations}}$$

$P(\text{same color}) = $ _____

Solution

What is the probability that George will choose a cap and shirt that have the same color? _____

Apply the Pennsylvania Academic Standards

Write each probability as a fraction.

1. If you toss two coins, what is the probability that one will land on heads and one will land on tails?

   _____

2. If you toss 3 coins, what is the probability that one will land on heads and two will land on tails?

   _____

3. If you pick a letter from each box, what is the probability that you will pick two vowels?

   _____

Use the information below to answer questions 4–10.

Laura tossed a number cube and flipped a coin at the same time. She tallied the results of flipping the coin next to the results of tossing the cube.

Number Cube	Heads	Talls
1	卌 I	卌 I
2	卌 IIII	卌
3	III	卌 卌
4	I	卌 I
5	卌 IIII	卌 III
6	卌 I	卌 IIII

4. How many times did the coin land on heads? on tails?

   _____

5. How many times did Laura do the experiment?

   _____

6. Based on the chart, what is the experimental probability that the number cube will land on 5 and the coin will land on heads?

   _____

7. What is the theoretical probability that the number cube will land on 5? _____

8. What is the theoretical probability that the coin will land on heads? _____

9. You can find the theoretical probability that the number cube will land on 5 and the coin will land on heads at the same time by multiplying the probability of one event by the probability of the other event. What is the theoretical probability of the cube landing on 5 and the coin landing on heads?

   _____

10. Is the experimental probability and the theoretical probability of rolling a 5 and flipping heads the same? If they are different, explain why.

    _____

    _____

Directions: Read each question. Then circle the letter for the best answer.

 1. If you pick one ball and one block, what is the probability that **at least** one of them will have stripes?

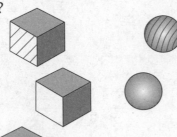

A $\frac{1}{3}$

B $\frac{2}{5}$

C $\frac{1}{2}$

D $\frac{2}{3}$

2. If you spin this spinner twice, what is the probability that you will get **two consonants?**

A $\frac{8}{9}$

B $\frac{2}{3}$

C $\frac{4}{9}$

D $\frac{1}{3}$

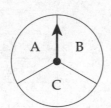

3. What is the probability of **not** picking a consonant and flipping tails?

A 0

B $\frac{1}{8}$

C $\frac{3}{8}$

D $\frac{5}{8}$

4. If a red and a blue number cube each labeled 1 through 6 are tossed, what is the probability that the sum of the two numbers will **not** be 2?

A $\frac{1}{36}$

B $\frac{1}{18}$

C $\frac{1}{12}$

D $\frac{35}{36}$

5. Michelle tossed three coins 50 times. She recorded in the table below the number of coins that came up heads each time.

Heads	Tally
0	JHT
1	JHT JHT JHT I
2	JHT JHT JHT JHT I
3	JHT III

What is the experimental probability of tossing **fewer** than 2 heads?

A $\frac{1}{5}$

B $\frac{21}{50}$

C $\frac{21}{29}$

D $\frac{4}{5}$

 Measuring Up® to the Pennsylvania Academic Standards

Directions: Read each question. Then circle the letter for the best answer.

Use the picture below to answer questions 1–3.

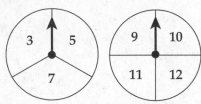

1. What is the probability of spinning two odd numbers when you spin each spinner one time?

    A   0

    B $\frac{1}{4}$

    C $\frac{1}{3}$

    D $\frac{1}{2}$

2. What is the probability of spinning two even numbers when you spin each spinner one time?

    A   0

    B $\frac{1}{4}$

    C $\frac{1}{3}$

    D $\frac{1}{2}$

3.   What is the probability of spinning a multiple of 3 on each spinner when you spin each spinner one time?

    A   0

    B $\frac{1}{6}$

    C $\frac{1}{3}$

    D $\frac{1}{2}$

Use the information below to answer questions 4–6.

A spinner is divided into four equal sections green, yellow, red, and blue. The results are shown below.

Results	Tally
Green |卌 卌 卌 卌 |||
Yellow	卌 卌 ||||
Red	卌 ||
Blue	卌	

4.   What is the experimental probability of landing on blue or yellow?

    A $\frac{12}{25}$

    B $\frac{2}{5}$

    C $\frac{7}{25}$

    D $\frac{3}{25}$

5. What is the theoretical probability that the spinner will land on green?

    A $\frac{1}{2}$

    B $\frac{23}{50}$

    C $\frac{1}{4}$

    D $\frac{1}{50}$

6.   If the spinner is spun 600 times, how many times would you expect to spin red?

    A   108   B   84

    C   76   D   42

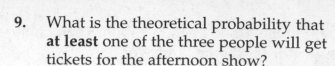

Use the information below to answer questions 7–9.

Tomas, Carrie, and Sam are part of a group waiting to get tickets for a nusical ahow. The tickets are assigned randomly to each person. To find the probability that at least one of the three friends will get tickets for the afternoon show, they flip three coins 180 times. The results are shown below.

Results	Tally
HHH	卌 卌 卌 卌 II
HHT	卌 卌 卌 卌 卌 I
HTH	卌 卌 卌 IIII
HTT	卌 卌 卌 卌 卌 II
THH	卌 卌 卌 卌 III
THT	卌 卌 卌 IIII
TTH	卌 卌 卌 卌 卌
TTT	卌 卌 卌 IIII

H = evening show

T = afternoon show

7. What is the experimental probability that **at least** one of the three will get tickets for the afternoon show?

A $\frac{19}{180}$ B $\frac{11}{90}$

C $\frac{67}{180}$ D $\frac{79}{90}$

8. What is the experimental probability that two friends will get tickets for the afternoon show?

A $\frac{17}{45}$ B $\frac{81}{180}$

C $\frac{99}{180}$ D $\frac{28}{45}$

9. What is the theoretical probability that **at least** one of the three people will get tickets for the afternoon show?

A $\frac{1}{8}$ B $\frac{1}{4}$

C $\frac{7}{8}$ D $\frac{9}{10}$

10. Marcela counted the vehicles going past her house on a one-way street. She counted 50 cars, 30 trucks, and 10 motorcycles. What is the probability that the next vehicle will **not** be a truck?

A $\frac{1}{9}$ B $\frac{1}{3}$

C $\frac{4}{9}$ D $\frac{2}{3}$

11. Javier and Francis used the circle graph below to record the total number of times each letter was drawn from a box.

Experimental Probability of Choosing W, X, Y, or Z

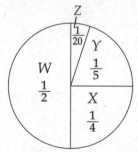

If Javier and Francis drew from the box 80 times, which of the following is **not** true?

A   They drew W 40 times.

B   They drew Y 20 times.

C   They drew X 20 times.

D   They drew Z 4 times.

Open-Ended Items

12. Marcus rolls two number cubes labeled 1 through 6.

A. How many possible outcomes are there? Explain your answer.

12. *Continued.*

B. What is the theoretical probability of rolling a sum of 7?

C. What is the probability of not rolling an even number on the first number cube, and on the second number cube, rolling a number with two factors: itself and 1?

13. Lisa experimented by rolling a number cube labeled 1 through 6 and then tossing a coin. The results of Lisa's experiment can be found below.

Number Cube	Heads	Tails
1	卌 卌 卌 卌 l	卌 卌 卌 lll
2	卌 卌 卌 lll	卌 卌 ll
3	卌 卌 卌 llll	卌 卌 卌 llll
4	卌 ll	卌 卌 卌
5	卌 卌 卌 lll	卌
6	卌 卌 ll	卌 卌 卌 l

A. What is the experimental probability of a rolling a 3 and tossing tails?

B. If Lisa repeated this experiment 600 times, how many times would you expect her to roll a 2?

Directions: Read each question. Then circle the letter for the best answer.

1. The large square below has a side of 20 centimeters. Which is the **best** estimate of the area of the shaded region?

A   246 cm²

B   286 cm²

C   356 cm²

D   396 cm²

2. A bottle of soda has a capacity of 16 fluid ounces. What is the capacity of sixteen bottles of soda?

A   2 gallons 4 ounces

B   2 gallons

C   7 pints 6 ounces

D   1 gallon 14 ounces

3. Grace is running in a 26-mile marathon. If there are 5,280 feet in 1 mile, how long is the marathon in yards?

A   44,520 yd

B   44,680 yd

C   45,760 yd

D   46,290 yd

4. Tiffany plotted two points, as shown below. She wants to create a right triangle with the missing vertex in the first quadrant. Which of the following coordinates could be the missing vertex?

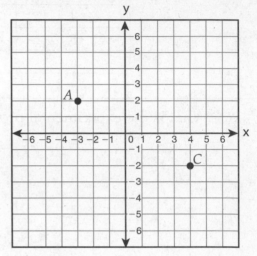

A   (−3, 5)

B   (−2, 4)

C   (3, −2)

D   (4, 2)

5. Taylor bought video games for $37.30, $40.70, $36.50, $42.10, $31.25, $34.63, and $35.12. What is the mean price he paid for a video game?

A $34.76

B $36.80

C $38.25

D $41.35

6. In the athletic program, the height of each player on the women's soccer team is listed in inches. What is the mean height of a soccer player on the team?

Stem	Leaf
5	5, 6, 6, 7
6	3, 4, 4, 4, 4, 5, 6, 6, 6, 8, 9
7	0, 1, 2, 2, 3

Key: 6|3 = 63

A 60.05 in.

B 62.25 in.

C 65.05 in.

D 66.25 in.

7. Burt conducted a survey asking students for their favorite color. Which display would **best** represent how parts of the data relate to the whole?

A circle graph

B bar graph

C line graph

D stem-and-leaf plot

8. How can you define diameter in terms of radius?

A The diameter is 2 more than the radius.

B The diameter is twice the radius.

C The diameter is half the radius.

D The diameter is 2 less than the radius.

9. Mr. Handler surveyed 300 college freshmen to find out what major they plan to pursue. The results are shown in the graph below. Which conclusion can be drawn from the graph?

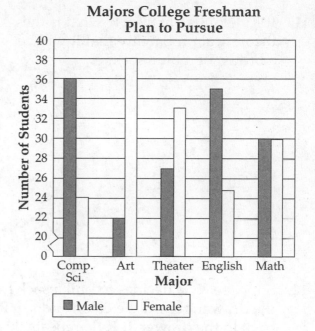

A More students plan to pursue an art major than an English major.

B Computer science is pursued by more females than by males.

C The same number of males and females will pursue a math major.

D Theater has the biggest difference between males and females.

10. Which display would **best** represent the growth in height of a 14-year-old over the course of one year?

A circle graph

B bar graph

C line graph

D stem-and-leaf plot

Use the following information to answer questions 11–12.

In his dresser drawer, Kyle has 12 pairs of white, 7 pairs of blue, 9 pairs of black, and 2 pairs of brown socks.

11. If Kyle pulls out a sock, what is the theoretical probability that it will be a brown or a blue sock?

   A $\frac{1}{30}$

   B $\frac{1}{15}$

   C $\frac{3}{10}$

   D $\frac{7}{70}$

12. Suppose Kyle decides to pull a sock from the drawer, record the color, and put it back in the drawer. If Kyle repeats this experiment 100 times, how many socks will Kyle have pulled out that are **not** white?

   A 20

   B 40

   C 50

   D 60

13. Mr. O'Neil is 85 inches tall. How tall is he in feet and inches?

   A 6 ft 7 in.

   B 6 ft 11 in.

   C 7 ft 1 in.

   D 8 ft 5 in.

Use the figure below to answer questions 14–15.

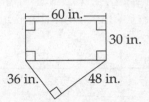

14. What is the perimeter of the figure?

   A 184 in.

   B 192 in.

   C 204 in.

   D 264 in.

15. What is the area of the figure?

   A 864 in.^{2}

   B 1,044 in.^{2}

   C 1,800 in.^{2}

   D 2,664 in.^{2}

16. A fruit salad contains 24 ounces of pineapple, 16 ounces of apples, 30 ounces of melon, 8 ounces of grapes, and 14 ounces of strawberries. How many pounds of fruit does the salad contain?

   A 5.57 lb

   B 5.75 lb

   C 7.57 lb

   D 7.75 lb

17. Adam has a patio in his backyard that is similar to the shape of the backyard. Using the drawing below, what is the value of x?

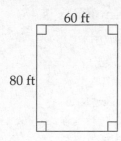

60 ft

80 ft

x

12 ft

A   6 ft

B   8 ft

C   10 ft

D   16 ft

18. A pizza shop will donate a pizza for the school raffle. The shop sells the following types of pizzas: small, medium, large, and extra large. Each type of pizza is available with one topping: ham, mushroom, olive, peppers, pepperoni, pineapple, and sausage. What is the probability that the pizza donated will be a medium sausage?

A $\frac{1}{28}$

B $\frac{1}{24}$

C $\frac{1}{7}$

D $\frac{1}{4}$

Use the information below to answer questions 19–21.

A spinner has four sections. Each is labeled LEFT, RIGHT, UP, or DOWN. Kamel spun the spinner and recorded the number of times each section came up in the tally chart below.

Results	Tally
Up	ЖЖ ЖЖ ЖЖ ЖЖ ЖЖ ЖЖ I
Down	ЖЖ ЖЖ ЖЖ ЖЖ ЖЖ III
Left	ЖЖ ЖЖ ЖЖ ЖЖ ЖЖ ЖЖ IIII
Right	ЖЖ ЖЖ ЖЖ ЖЖ ЖЖ II

19. What is the experimental probability of landing on RIGHT or DOWN?

A $\frac{11}{24}$

B $\frac{1}{2}$

C $\frac{2}{5}$

D $\frac{7}{30}$

20. If the spinner is spun 360 times, how many times would you expect to spin UP?

A   116

B   104

C   93

D   75

21. What is the theoretical probability that the spinner will **not** land on LEFT?

A $\frac{4}{5}$ B $\frac{43}{60}$

C $\frac{3}{4}$ D $\frac{17}{30}$

Use the information below to answer questions 22–23.

Mr. Young gave a 50-question pop quiz to his class. The test results were: 35, 36, 38, 39, 40, 42, 42, 44, 45, 45, 47, 48, 50, 50, 50, and 50.

22. If Mr. Young decided to use a stem-and-leaf plot to display the data, which of the following is correct?

A

Stem	Leaf
3	5, 6, 8, 9
4	0, 2, 2, 4, 5, 5, 7, 8
5	0, 0

Key: 4|0 = 40

B

Stem	Leaf
3	5, 6, 8, 9
4	0, 2, 2, 4, 5, 5, 7, 8
5	0, 0, 0

Key: 4|0 = 40

C

Stem	Leaf
3	5, 6, 8, 9
4	0, 2, 2, 4, 5, 5, 7, 8
5	0, 0, 0, 0

Key: 4|0 = 40

D

Stem	Leaf
3	5, 6, 8, 9
4	0, 2, 2, 5, 5, 6, 7, 8
5	0, 0, 0

Key: 4|0 = 40

23. Which of the following statements is true?

A   The range of the data is 29.

B   The median number is 45.

C   The mode number is 50.

D   The mean is 43.

24. Lucy flew on a flight from Seattle, Washington to Tokyo, Japan. If her flight was 15 hours 7 minutes, how many seconds long was it?

A   54,420 sec

B   60,780 sec

C   62,700 sec

D   65,520 sec

25. Evan jogs 3.1 kilometers each day from Monday through Friday. He jogs 5.4 kilometers on Saturday. If he does not run on Sunday, how many meters does he run each week?

A   20,900 m

B   2,090 m

C   20.9 m

D   2.09 m

Use the following diagram to answer questions 26–28.

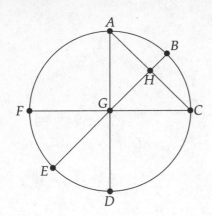

26. Which line segment is **not** a radius?

    A $\overline{AG}$

    B $\overline{BH}$

    C $\overline{CG}$

    D $\overline{DG}$

27. Which line segment is a chord?

    A $\overline{AC}$

    B $\overline{BH}$

    C $\overline{DG}$

    D $\overline{EH}$

28. If the length of $\overline{AD}$ is 20 feet and the length of $\overline{HG}$ is 8 feet, what is the length of $\overline{BH}$?

    A 1 ft

    B 2 ft

    C 3 ft

    D 4 ft

Use the table below to answer questions 29–31.

Athlete	1000-meter Freestyle Time (in seconds)
Monisha	10.89, 11.22, 13.89, 10.74, 13.46, 11.22, 12.01
Marjorie	13.28, 12.12, 10.84, 11.22, 12.98, 11.22, 11.98

29. Which of the following measures of central tendency for Monisha and Marjorie are equal?

    A mean

    B median

    C mode

    D mean and median

30. Which measure(s) of central tendency should Marjorie use to show that she is a **better** freestyle swimmer than Monisha?

    A mode

    B mean

    C median

    D mean and median

31. Marcela counted the birds eating at the bird feeder in her backyard. She counted 26 robins, 14 blue jays, and 10 finches. What is the probability that the **next** bird will be a finch?

    A $\frac{1}{5}$ B $\frac{1}{4}$

    C $\frac{7}{25}$ D $\frac{13}{25}$

Use the information below to answer questions 32–33.

Devin, Erin, and Holly are part of a group waiting to get tickets to go to a new water park. Half of the group members will get tickets for Saturday and half will get tickets for Sunday. The tickets are assigned randomly to each person. To find the probability that at least one of the three friends will get tickets for Saturday, they flip 3 coins 150 times. The results are shown below.

Result	Tally
HHH	＝＝＝＝ ||
HHT	＝＝＝＝	
HTH	＝＝＝ ||
HTT	＝＝＝	
THH	＝＝＝ |||
THT	＝＝＝ ||||
TTH	＝＝＝ |||
TTT	＝＝＝ ||||

H = Saturday   T = Sunday

H = Saturday

T = Sunday

32. What is the experimental probability that all three will **not** get tickets for the same day?

A $\frac{109}{150}$

B $\frac{41}{150}$

C $\frac{1}{4}$

D $\frac{1}{8}$

33. What is the theoretical probability that all three will **not** get tickets for the same day?

A $\frac{1}{8}$

B $\frac{1}{4}$

C $\frac{3}{4}$

D $\frac{7}{8}$

34. Mr. Dawson drew the figure below on the board in his Math class.

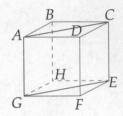

If figure *ACEG* forms a parallelogram, what can you say about line segments *AC* and *GE*?

A The line segments are perpendicular.

B The line segments are skewed.

C The line segments intersect.

D The line segments are parallel.

Use the figure below to answer questions 35–37.

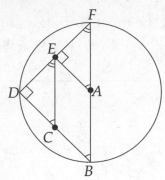

$\overline{DB}$ = 6 cm

$\overline{BA}$ = 5 cm

$\overline{FE}$ = 4 cm

Point *A* is the center of the circle.

35. What is the perimeter of triangle *FDB*?

   A   8 cm

   B   10 cm

   C   12 cm

   D   24 cm

36. Which are the correct area **and** perimeter of parallelogram *EABC*?

   A   12 cm and 6 cm^2

   B   24 cm and 24 cm^2

   C   16 cm and 12 cm^2

   D   12 cm and 16 cm^2

37. What is the circumference of circle *A*?

   A   31.4 cm

   B   17.7 cm

   C   78.5 cm^2

   D   39.25 cm^2

38. Which graph would **best** represent the annual rainfall for Akron, Trenton, and Erie?

   A   circle graph

   B   double line graph

   C   stem-and-leaf plot

   D   histogram

39. What is the probability of each spinner landing on the same number when you spin each spinner one time?

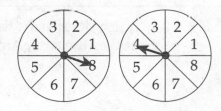

   A $\frac{1}{64}$

   B $\frac{1}{32}$

   C $\frac{1}{16}$

   D $\frac{1}{8}$

Open-Ended Items

40. Jeb, Angela, and Lloyd were arguing about who studied the most each day. Lloyd studies 150 minutes per day, Jeb studies 5,400 seconds per day, and Angela studies 2 hours per day.

A   Who studies the most each day? Explain your answer.

B   How much does each student study, in hours, from Monday through Thursday if each studies the same amount of time each day? Explain your answer.

41. Find the area of the shaded region. Use 3.14 to approximate π.
Explain how you found your answer.

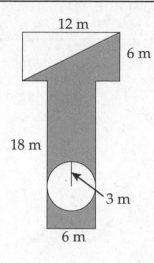

12 m

6 m

18 m

3 m

6 m

42. A tall statue and its shadow form the legs of a right triangle. On a sunny day, Paul and his shadow form the legs of a similar right triangle. If Paul is 5 feet tall and his shadow is 12 feet long, how tall is the statue if it casts a 60-feet long shadow? Explain your answer.

43. Clive brings a bag of clothes to the laundromat. The bag has 5 dark shirts, 6 pairs of light pants, 9 pairs of white socks, 4 pairs of white underwear, and 7 pairs of dark shorts. Suppose each pair of socks was separated before Clive went to the laundromat. They should be counted as two socks.

A If Clive begins sorting his clothes in darks, lights, and whites, what is the probability that the first item he picks without looking is not white? Show your work.

B What is the probability that Clive picks a pair of pants or shorts? Show your work.

End-of-Book

Building Stamina®

The end-of-book **Building Stamina®** is a

comprehensive review of the

Pennsylvania Academic Standards and Assessment Anchors

covered in the lessons.

By practicing with these challenging,

broad-based, higher-level thinking questions,

you will build up your stamina

to succeed on the PSSA

and in other academic endeavors

that require higher-level thinking.

Directions: Read each question. Then circle the letter for the best answer.

1. What is the area of the shaded figure?

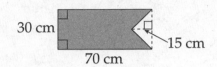

30 cm
70 cm
15 cm

A   1,875 cm²

B   2,100 cm²

C   2,875 cm²

D   4,100 cm²

2. Phillip is playing a game with a number cube labeled 1 through 6. If a 1 comes up, he loses a point. If a 2, 3, 4, or 5 comes up, he gains a point. If a 6 comes up, he gains 2 points. What is the probability that Phil gains a point?

A $\frac{1}{6}$

B $\frac{1}{3}$

C $\frac{1}{2}$

D $\frac{2}{3}$

3. What is the value of the following expression?

$$21 + (12 - 4)^2 \div 4$$

A   23

B   29

C   37

D   54

4. Darryl had a spinner with sections marked blue, red, green, yellow, and orange. He spun the spinner 1,500 times and recorded which section the spinner landed on each time. The table below shows his results.

Color	Frequency
blue	389
red	273
green	378
yellow	172
orange	288

According to Darryl's results, what is the experimental probability that the spinner lands on green?

A   20.0%

B   25.2%

C   37.8%

D   41.56%

5. Derrick had m candies in a box. Then he gave 27 candies to his friends. If 3 candies were left, what is the value of m?

A $m = 3$

B $m = 9$

C $m = 27$

D $m = 30$

6. Marvin spins both of the spinners shown below.

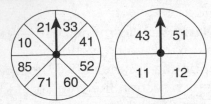

What is the probability that both spinners land on an even number?

A $\frac{3}{32}$

B $\frac{3}{8}$

C $\frac{5}{8}$

D $\frac{29}{32}$

7. Alice, Gary, and Martin are baking cakes for a wedding party. Alice has $2\frac{1}{4}$ cups of flour, Gary has $2\frac{1}{2}$ cups of flour, and Martin has $1\frac{7}{8}$ cups of flour. Altogether, they need $7\frac{3}{4}$ cups of flour. How much more flour do they need?

A $\frac{3}{8}$ cup

B $\frac{3}{4}$ cup

C $1\frac{1}{8}$ cups

D $1\frac{3}{4}$ cups

8. If 15, −5, 10, 5 and −1 are all plotted on a number line, which will appear farthest to the **left**?

A −1   B −5
C 15   D 10

9. The figure below shows a right triangle.

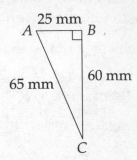

Which triangle below is similar to triangle ABC?

A

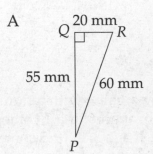

B

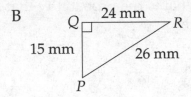

C

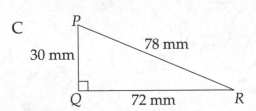

D

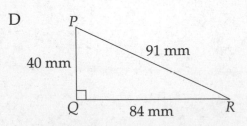

10. Both Jackie and Bruce ran in a race. Jackie finished the race in 3 fewer minutes than Bruce. Bruce finished the race in 12 minutes. In how many minutes did Jackie finish the race?

   A   3 min   B   4 min
   C   9 min   D   15 min

11. Which list shows the ratios ordered from **least** to **greatest**?

   A $0.79, \frac{7}{9}, 75\%$

   B $0.79, 75\%, \frac{7}{9}$

   C $75\%, 0.79, \frac{7}{9}$

   D $75\%, \frac{7}{9}, 0.79$

12. A number cube with sides labeled 1 through 6 is rolled once, and then it is rolled a second time. What is the probability that the number cube shows a 5 on the first roll, but does **not** show a 5 on the second roll?

   A $\frac{1}{36}$ B $\frac{1}{6}$

   C $\frac{5}{36}$ D $\frac{5}{6}$

13. The scale on a blueprint of a house is 2 inches : 5 feet. In the blueprint, the living room has a length of 5.5 inches, and a width of 8 inches. What is the area of the actual living room?

   A   110 square feet
   B   275 square feet
   C   440 square feet
   D   550 square feet

14. A chord $\overline{AB}$ is drawn at random through a circle with center O, as shown in the figure below.

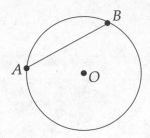

   Which of the following **cannot** be true?

   A   The length of the chord is less than the radius of the circle.
   B   The length of the chord is less than the diameter of the circle.
   C   The length of the chord is greater than the radius of the circle.
   D   The length of the chord is greater than the diameter of the circle.

15. Which of the addition expressions below is equivalent to the following expression?

$$-20 - (-15)$$

   A $-20 + 15$
   B $-20 + (-15)$
   C $20 + 15$
   D $20 + (-15)$

16. The histogram below shows data about the ages of visitors at an art gallery during one day.

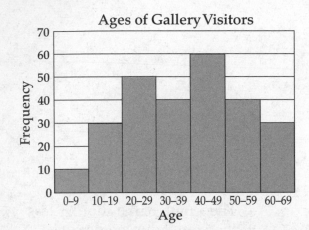

Ages of Gallery Visitors

According to the histogram, how many visitors were less than 30 years old?

A   40
B   50
C   80
D   90

17. What is the area of the shape shown below?

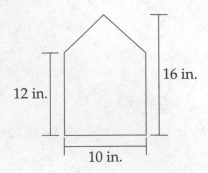

16 in.

12 in.

10 in.

A   60 square inches
B   80 square inches
C   140 square inches
D   200 square inches

18. Gerald has plotted points P and Q on the coordinate grid below.

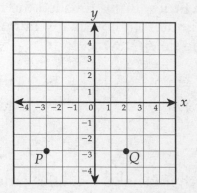

He would like to add another point R to the **second** quadrant so that all three points will form a right triangle with an area 15 square units. Where should Gerald plot point R?

A $(-3, 3)$ B $(-3, 0)$
C $(2, 2)$ D $(2, 5)$

19. Which list shows only equivalent fractions?

A $\frac{27}{36}, \frac{36}{48}, \frac{48}{96}$

B $\frac{10}{15}, \frac{15}{25}, \frac{25}{45}$

C $\frac{24}{27}, \frac{48}{54}, \frac{64}{72}$

D $\frac{3}{15}, \frac{4}{20}, \frac{10}{45}$

20. Which of the following is a true statement?

A $\frac{4}{5} < 1.3 < \frac{9}{4}$

B $\frac{9}{4} < 1.3 < \frac{4}{5}$

C $3.055 < 3.55 < 3.505$

D $3.505 < 3.55 < 3.055$

21. Frederick is creating number patterns for a math class. Which rule best describes the following number pattern?

$$2, 4, 16, 256, \ldots$$

A double the previous number

B square the previous number

C add 2 to the previous number

D add the previous two numbers

22. Four figures have been drawn on the grid below.

For which figure is the number of units for the perimeter equal to the number of square units for the area?

A Figure 1

B Figure 2

C Figure 3

D Figure 4

23. The table below shows the number of birds that Wilbur observed at the bird feeder in his yard each day during one week.

Day	Number of Birds Observed
1	35
2	48
3	33
4	51
5	40
6	39
7	48

What was the mean number of birds that Wilbur observed each day?

A 40

B 42

C 48

D 49

24. Peter divided 30 stickers evenly among c of his friends. Each person got 6 stickers. Which equation represents this situation?

A $30 + c = 6$

B $30 - c = 6$

C $\frac{30}{c} = 6$

D $\frac{c}{30} = 6$

25. Which decimal is between $\frac{9}{10}$ and $\frac{11}{12}$?

A   0.90   B   0.91

C   0.92   D   0.93

26. If $x = 8$ and $y = 3$, what is the value of the expression $xy + 2(x - y)^2$?

A   22   B   31

C   74   D   98

27. Which expression is **not** equivalent to $4x + 12y + 3z$?

A $2(2x + 6y) + 3z$

B $3(z + 4y) + 4x$

C $3(x + 4y) + 3z$

D $4(x + 3y) + 3z$

28. Alejandro has a recipe for fruit punch that calls for $2\frac{1}{2}$ cups of pineapple juice. This recipe yields enough punch to serve 8 people. If Alejandro wants to make enough punch to serve 30 people, how many cups of pineapple juice will he need?

A $3\frac{3}{4}$ cups

B $5\frac{5}{8}$ cups

C $6\frac{1}{4}$ cups

D $9\frac{3}{8}$ cups

29. The figure below shows a semicircle inscribed within a rectangle.

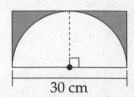

30 cm

What is the approximate area of the shaded portion of the figure? Use 3.14 as an approximation for π, and round to the nearest tenth.

A   96.8 cm^2

B   193.1 cm^2

C   273.3 cm^2

D   546.6 cm^2

30. Which of the following is **not** equivalent to $\frac{4}{7}$?

A $\frac{12}{21}$

B $\frac{16}{28}$

C $\frac{28}{49}$

D $\frac{32}{63}$

31. If $k = 12$, then what is the value of $12(k - 3) + 2$?

A   110

B   132

C   143

D   165

32. Consider the rectangular prism shown in the figure below.

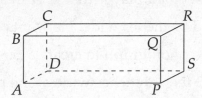

Suppose that a line is drawn through the vertices B and R, and that another line is drawn through the vertices D and P. Which of the following will **best** describe the relationship between these two lines?

A   intersecting

B   parallel

C   perpendicular

D   skew

33. An essay is p pages long and contains a total of w words. Which expression represents the average number of words per page for this essay?

A wp

B $\dfrac{w}{p}$

C $\dfrac{p}{w}$

D $w + p$

34. The figure below shows a circle inscribed in a square.

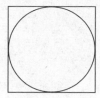

The **area** of the square is 36 square inches. What is the **radius** of the circle?

A   3 in.

B   6 in.

C   9 in.

D   18 in.

35. The surface of Lake Assal in Djibouti is 512 feet below sea level. The peak of Mount Kilimanjaro in Tanzania is 19,340 feet above sea level. Which equation shows the difference in elevation between the peak of Mount Kilimanjaro and the surface of Lake Assal?

A $19,340 - 512 = 18,828$ ft

B $19,340 - (-512) = 19,852$ ft

C $-19,340 - 512 = 19,852$ ft

D $-19,340 - (-512) = 18,828$ ft

Use the figure below to answer questions 36–37.

25 feet

Marcie has a circular swimming pool in her backyard. The diameter of her swimming pool is 25 feet, as shown in the figure.

36. If tarps come in sizes with radii of 13 feet, 16 feet, and 20 feet, what is the **least** area of the tarp she could buy, to the nearest foot? Use a calculator.

   A   531 ft²

   B   804 ft²

   C   1,031 ft²

   D   1,257 ft²

37. To secure the tarp, Marcie needs a length of twine that will completely wrap around the circumference of the pool. To the nearest foot, what is the smallest length of a string that completely wraps around the circumference of Marcie's pool?

   A   32 ft

   B   47 ft

   C   79 ft

   D   157 ft

38. Ned has a photograph of a famous basketball player that is 11 inches long and $8\frac{1}{2}$ inches wide. He wants to enlarge this photograph to create a poster that is 2 feet 10 inches wide at the base. What will be the length of Ned's poster?

   A   2 feet 2 inches

   B   2 feet 7 inches

   C   3 feet 6 inches

   D   3 feet 8 inches

39. Gaetano works Mondays, Wednesdays, and Fridays at his part-time job. This week, Gaetano worked 9.5 hours on Monday, 8 hours on Wednesday, and 9 hours on Friday. Altogether, he earned $304.75 from working these three days. How much is Gaetano paid per hour at his job?

   A $11.00

   B $11.50

   C $11.75

   D $12.50

40. Which of the following gives a product that is **less than** 1?

   A $\frac{4}{3} \cdot \frac{3}{4}$

   B $\frac{4}{3} \cdot \frac{6}{4}$

   C $\frac{5}{4} \cdot \frac{6}{7}$

   D $\frac{4}{5} \cdot \frac{6}{5}$

41. A machine at a factory assembles 84 mechanical dolls in 2 hours and 20 minutes. What is the unit rate of dolls assembled per hour?

A   36 dolls per hour

B   38 dolls per hour

C   40 dolls per hour

D   42 dolls per hour

42. The figure below shows two similar rectangles that share a common side.

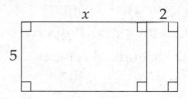

What is the value of x?

A   10

B   12.5

C   15

D   17.5

43. What is the **next** number in this pattern?

10.25, 11.50, 12.75, 14.00, _____

A   15.25

B   15.75

C   16.25

D   16.50

44. Nia and Sonja each recorded the number of points that they scored in several basketball games. The table below shows their results.

Game	Nia's Points	Sonja's Points
1	15	14
2	25	17
3	26	18
4	12	14
5	12	19
6	12	14

Which measure(s) should Nia use if she wants to convince her coach that she is a more skilled player than Sonja?

A   mean

B   median

C   median and mode

D   mode

45. Using his riding mower, Evan can mow 1 acre in 50 minutes. Working at this same rate, how many acres can Evan mow in 3 hours and 15 minutes?

    A   2.1 acres

    B   3.1 acres

    C   3.9 acres

    D   4.7 acres

46. Frank has a portrait of his father that is 24 inches long and 20 inches wide. He would like to make a wallet-sized version of this portrait that is 3 inches long and $2\frac{1}{2}$ inches wide. What scale factor should Frank use in making the reduction?

    A $\frac{1}{9}$

    B $\frac{1}{8}$

    C $\frac{5}{6}$

    D $\frac{6}{5}$

47. A horse ran 810 yards around a racetrack in 45 seconds. What was the horse's average speed in feet per second?

    A   6 feet per second

    B   18 feet per second

    C   54 feet per second

    D   72 feet per second

48. Which property allows you to conclude that $(2x + 3) + y$ is equivalent to $y + (2x + 3)$?

    A   Associative Property

    B   Commutative Property

    C   Distributive Property

    D   Inverse Property

49. The table below shows ticket sales for three different events at a certain arena.

Event	Tickets sold
rock concert	23,121
football game	19,949
baseball game	21,042

Which is the **best** estimate of total ticket sales for all three events?

    A   50,000

    B   60,000

    C   65,000

    D   70,000

50. The graph below shows the total distance traveled by a man walking along a nature trail.

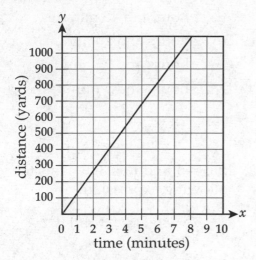

If the man continues walking at the same rate without breaks, how many minutes will have elapsed when his total distance along the trail is 1,600 yards?

A   10 minutes

B   12 minutes

C   15 minutes

D   20 minutes

51. Hannah is 4 feet 11 inches tall. Her father is 6 feet 2 inches tall. How much taller is Hannah's father?

A   1 foot 3 inches

B   1 foot 9 inches

C   2 feet 3 inches

D   2 feet 9 inches

52. According to a census, 27,598 people live in a county that occupies 4,057 square miles. Which is the **best** estimate of the people per square mile of this county?

A   7 people per square mile

B   8 people per square mile

C   70 people per square mile

D   80 people per square mile

53. Which phrase **best** represents the inequality $9x - 7 \leq 2$?

A   The difference between 9 times a number x and 7 is less than 2.

B   The difference between 9 times a number x and 7 is no more than 2.

C   A number x minus 7 times 9 is less than 2.

D   A number x minus 7 times 9 is no more than 2.

54. Guillermo needs $5\frac{1}{3}$ cups of water for a certain recipe, but he only has a $\frac{2}{3}$-cup measure. How many times must Guillermo fill the $\frac{2}{3}$-cup measure in order to get $5\frac{1}{3}$ cups of water?

A 5

B 6

C 7

D 8

55. A motorcyclist took $\frac{1}{4}$ hour to complete 23 laps around a $\frac{1}{2}$-mile dirt racetrack. What was the motorcyclist's average speed, in miles per hour?

A 32 miles per hour

B 43 miles per hour

C 46 miles per hour

D 50 miles per hour

56. Which of the following is a true statement?

A $|15| + |-15| = 0$

B $|15| - |-15| = 30$

C $15 - (-15) = 0$

D $15 - (-15) = 30$

57. Alice fell asleep at 4:50 P.M. She woke up for dinner at 7:15 P.M. How long was Alice's nap?

A 1 hour and 45 minutes

B 2 hours and 20 minutes

C 2 hours and 25 minutes

D 3 hours and 5 minutes

58. If $m = 1$ and $n = 3$, what is the value of the following expression?

$$2(3m + 4n) + 5$$

A 20

B 22

C 31

D 35

59. Which of the following is **not** equivalent to 250%?

A $\frac{5}{3} + \frac{5}{6}$

B $2 + \frac{1}{5}$

C $6.5 \div 2.6$

D $3\frac{1}{2} \div 1\frac{2}{5}$

Open-Ended Items

60. Jamar surveyed his class to discover the range in heights in inches. He got the following heights: 60, 66, 59, 59, 67, 62, 63, 59, 57, 59, 59, 58, 62, 57, 56, 62, 62, 60, 62, 59, 59, 62, 55, 59.

Create a frequency table from the set of data. Use the table to create a histogram. Explain your answer.

61. Miriam is designing square bathroom floor tiles. Four square-tiles are pictured below. The side of each tile is 3 inches.

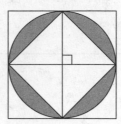

A. What is the area of the square inside the circle as formed by the four tiles?

B. What is the area of the shaded portion of **one** of Miriam's tiles, to the nearest inch? Use a calculator. Explain your work.

62. On August 15, 2006, the space probe Voyager 1, a space probe launched 30 years ago, reached a distance of 100 Astronomical Units (AU) from the Sun. 1 AU is approximately 150 million kilometers. It is the distance from the Earth to the Sun. The graph below shows the progress Voyager 1 has made in the last 30 years.

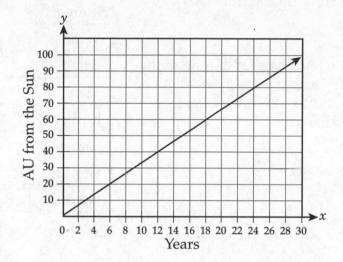

A. What is the approximate speed of the probe in kilometers per year? Explain your answer.

62. *Continued.*

B. The table to the right shows the approximate distance each planet is from the Sun, in Astronomical Units (AU).

Using the table and the graph, how many years ago did Voyager 1 reach the planet Neptune? Round to the nearest year. Explain your answer.

Planet	Approximate Distance from the Sun (in AU)
Mercury	0.4
Venus	0.7
Earth	1
Mars	1.5
Jupiter	5.2
Saturn	9.5
Uranus	19.2
Neptune	30.1

Problem-Solving Guide

To solve some mathematics problems you need to think about the question in a different way. You need to use special problem-solving skills like the ones below. You can use these four steps to solve any problem. Just follow the steps one at a time. Now you're on your way to becoming a good problem solver.

Step 1	**Understand the problem.** Think about what you need to do to solve the problem. • Read the problem carefully. • What does the problem ask you to find? • What information do you need to solve the problem?
Step 2	**Make a plan.** Choose a strategy that works best for the problem. • Draw a picture • Act it out • Look for a pattern • Make a table • Guess and check • Use logical reasoning
Step 3	**Solve the problem.** Follow your plan to solve the problem. • How can you use the strategy to help solve the problem? • Think about the steps you need to follow. • Show all your work. • Record your answer.
Step 4	**Check your answer.** • Look back at the problem. • Did you answer the question that the problem asks? • Does your answer make sense? • How else could you solve the problem? Do you get the same answer?

Use the chart on page 276 to organize your thinking while solving problems.

Use this problem-solving organizer to help you solve problems.

Step 1 Understand the problem.
Write what the problem asks you to find.

Step 2 Make a plan.
Write the steps you'll take to solve the problem.

Step 3 Solve the problem.
Show your work and record your answer.

Step 4 Check your answer.
Explain why your answer makes sense.

General Scoring Guidelines
for Open-Ended Mathematics Items

General Description of Scoring Guidelines

4 — **The response demonstrates a *thorough* understanding of the mathematical concepts and procedures required by the task.**

The response provides correct answer(s) with clear and complete mathematical procedures shown and a correct explanation, as required by the task. Response may contain a minor "blemish" (e.g., missing $) or omission in work or explanation that does not detract from demonstrating a ***thorough*** understanding.

3 — **The response demonstrates a *general* understanding of the mathematical concepts and procedures required by the task.**

The response and explanation (as required by the task) are mostly complete and correct. The response may have minor errors or omissions that do not detract from demonstrating a ***general*** understanding.

2 — **The response demonstrates a *partial* understanding of the mathematical concepts and procedures required by the task.**

The response is partially correct with ***partial*** understanding of the required mathematical concepts and/or procedures demonstrated and/or explained. The response may contain some work that is incomplete or unclear.

1 — **The response demonstrates a *minimal* understanding of the mathematical concepts and procedures as required by the task.**

0 — **The response has no correct answer and *insufficient* evidence to demonstrate any understanding of the mathematical concepts and procedures as required by the task for that grade level.**

Response may show only information copied from the question.

Special Catagories within zero reported separately:
BLK—Blank, entirely erased or written refusal to respond
OT—Off Task
IL—Illegible
LOE—Response in a language other than English

Pennsylvania Mathematics Reference Sheet

Formulas that you may need to work the questions are found below.
You may use calculator π or the number 3.14.

 $A = s \cdot s$

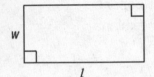 $P = 2l + 2w$
$A = lw$

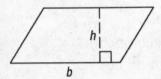 $A = bh$

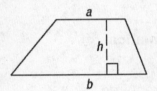 $A = \frac{h}{2}(a + b)$

 $A = \frac{1}{2}bh$

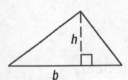 $C = 2\pi r$
$A = \pi r^2$

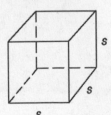 $V = s \cdot s \cdot s$

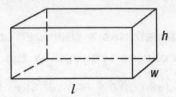 $V = lwh$

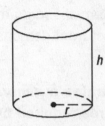 $V = \pi r^2 h$

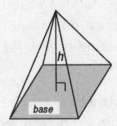 $V = \frac{1}{3}$ (Area of the base) × (h)

Customary Conversions :

1 yard (yd) = 3 feet (ft)
1 foot = 12 inches (in.)

1 pound (lb) = 16 ounces (oz.)

1 gallon (gal) = 4 quarts (qt)
1 quart = 2 pints (pt)
1 pint = 2 cups (c)
1 cup = 8 fluid ounces

1 day = 24 hours (hr)
1 hour = 60 minutes (min)
1 minute = 60 seconds (sec)

Metric Conversions :

1 millimeter = 0.001 meter
1 centimeter = 0.01 meter
1 decimeter = 0.1 meter
1 meter
1 dekameter = 10 meters
1 hectometer = 100 meters
1 kilometer = 1000 meters

     Measuring Up® to the Pennsylvania Academic Standards

Glossary

A

absolute value   a number's distance from zero on the number line. (Lesson 16)

area   the number of square units inside a figure. (Lesson 39)

associative property   changing how numbers are grouped does not change the sum or product. (Lesson 22)

Addition: $(a + b) + c = a + (b + c)$
Multiplication: $(ab)c = a(bc)$

B

bar graphs   a method of displaying and comparing data using the height of bars to represent numbers. (Lessons 52, 55)

C

chord   a line segment that connects two points on the circle. It does not have to pass through the center point. (Lesson 44)

circle graphs   a method of comparing parts of the set of data to the whole using a circle. (Lesson 52)

circumference   the distance around a circle. (Lessons 42, 44)

coefficient   the number by which a variable is multiplied. (Lesson 20)

commutative property   changing the order of the numbers does not change the sum or product. (Lesson 22)

Addition: $a + b = b + a$
Multiplication: $a \times b = b \times a$

compatible numbers   numbers that are close to the actual numbers but are easier to divide. (Lesson 6)

congruent angles   are angles that have the same measure. (Lesson 46)

congruent sides   line segments that have the same measure. (Lesson 46)

constant   a symbol or number whose value does not change. (Lesson 20)

coordinate plane   a plane formed by two coordinate axes (the x-axis and y-axis) that cross at a point called the origin. (Lesson 48)

coordinates   the x- and y-values used to plot a point, which are written as an ordered pair (x, y). (Lesson 48)

cross products   multiplication on the diagonals of a proportion to determine equality. (Lesson 30)

D

diameter   a line segment connecting two points on a circle and passing through the center. (Lessons 42, 44)

distributive property   If one factor is a sum, multiplying before adding does not change the result. (Lesson 22)

$a(b + c) = ab + ac$

E

equation   a mathematical sentence with an equal sign. (Lesson 23)

equivalent fractions   fractions that name the same number. (Lesson 8)

equivalent ratios   different ratios that have equal values. (Lesson 28)

estimation helps determine whether an answer to a problem is reasonable. The best estimate is usually one that is close to the exact answer. (Lessons 3,6)

exponent the number of times the base is used as a factor. (Lesson 21)

expression a mathematical phrase that may include constants, variables, and operation symbols. (Lesson 20)

F

favorable outcomes the result being looked for in a probability experiment. (Lesson 56)

G

greatest common factor (GCF) the greatest factor that two or more numbers share. (Lesson 8)

H

histogram a special type of bar graph that shows the frequency and distribution of data with equal intervals. (Lessons 54, 55)

I

identity property adding zero or multiplying by one does not change a number. (Lesson 22)

improper fraction a fraction that has a numerator greater than or equal to its denominator. (Lesson 9)

independent events when the outcome of one event does not affect the outcome of the other event. (Lesson 58)

inequality a mathematical sentence with one of these symbols: $<$, $\leq$, $\geq$, or $>$. (Lesson 23)

intersecting lines when two lines meet at a point or cross each other. They occupy the same plane and meet at only one point. (Lesson 45)

inverse property adding a number's opposite equals zero. Multiplying by a number's reciprocal equals 1.

Addition: $a + (-a) = 0$
Multiplication: $a \times \frac{1}{a} = 1$
The number 0 does not have a multiplicative inverse. (Lesson 22)

L

least common denominator (LCD) the least common multiple of the denominators. It is the least multiple that two or more numbers share. (Lessons 9, 11)

line graphs a method that uses lines to connect the data. These graphs show changes, trends, and developments over time. (Lessons 52, 55)

M

mean the average of a set of data found by adding the numbers in a set of data and then dividing the sum by the number of addends. (Lesson 50)

median the middle number or the average of the two middle numbers in a group of numbers listed from least to greatest. (Lessons 50, 53)

mixed numbers fractions that have a whole number part and a fraction part. (Lesson 9)

mode the value that occurs most frequently in a given set of data. (Lessons 50, 53)

N

negative integers whole numbers to the left of zero on a horizontal number line. They are less than zero and must be written with the negative sign (−). (Lessons 2, 15)

O

opposite a number that is the same distance from zero on a number line as a given number, but in the opposite direction. (Lesson 18)

origin the point at which the *x*-axis and *y*-axis cross. It has the coordinates (0, 0). (Lesson 48)

P

parallelogram a quadrilateral with parallel opposite sides. (Lesson 40)

parallel lines lines that extend forever in both directions in the same plane and never intersect. (Lesson 45)

pattern the rule that an ordered set of terms follows. (Lesson 26)

percent is a special kind of ratio that compares a number to 100. (Lesson 33)

perimeter the distance around a figure. (Lesson 41)

perpendicular lines when two lines intersect and form 4 right angles. (Lesson 45)

pi, or π the ratio of a circle's circumference to its diameter. The decimal 3.14 and the fraction $\frac{22}{7}$ are approximations of pi. (Lesson 42)

positive integers whole numbers that lie to the right of zero on a horizontal number line. They are greater than zero, and may be written with or without the positive sign (+). (Lesson 15)

possible outcomes all possible results in an experiment. (Lesson 56)

power an expression of the form x^n. (Lesson 21)

probability likelihood that an event will occur. (Lesson 56)

proportion an equation stating that two ratios are equal. (Lesson 30)

Q

quadrants the four sections of a coordinate plane, formed by the crossing of two coordinate axes. Quadrants are numbered in a counterclockwise direction. (Lesson 48)

R

radius half the diameter of a circle. It connects the center point of the circle to a point on the circle. (Lesson 44)

range the difference between the greatest and least values in a data set. (Lesson 53)

rate a ratio that compares quantities involving two different units. (Lessons 28, 34)

ratio a comparison between two numbers called terms. (Lesson 28)

reciprocals two numbers that have a product of 1. For example, the reciprocal of $\frac{2}{3}$ is $\frac{3}{2}$ because $\frac{2}{3} \cdot \frac{3}{2} = 1$. (Lesson 13)

rectangle a special parallelogram with four right angles. (Lesson 40)

round one way to estimate a product. (Lesson 6)

S

sample space   lists of all the possible outcomes of an event. (Lesson 56)

scale   the ratio of the measurements of a drawing, a model, a map, or a floor plan to the actual size of the objects or locations. (Lesson 31)

scale factor   the ratio that describes an enlargement or reduction. A scale factor between 0 and 1 represents a reduction of the original. A scale factor greater than 1 represents an enlargement of the original. (Lesson 32)

sequence   an ordered set of terms. (Lesson 26)

similar   two figures with exactly the same shape that may or may not have the same size. Similar figures have corresponding angles of equal measure, and corresponding sides that are proportional. (Lesson 47)

simplest form   for fractions, when the numerator and the denominator have no common factors other than 1; for ratios, when its terms have no common factors other than 1. (Lessons 8, 28)

skew lines   a pair of lines that are not parallel but never intersect. They occupy two different planes. (Lesson 45)

square   a special parallelogram with four right angles and four sides of equal length. (Lesson 40)

stem-and-leaf plots   a method that uses the digits of data to show frequency and distribution. Each stem represents the place values to the left of the rightmost digit, while each leaf represents the rightmost digit of a number. (Lessons 53, 55)

T

term   a number, a variable, or a product of numbers and/or variables. (Lesson 26)

U

unit rate   when the second term of a rate is 1. A unit rate often includes the word per. (Lesson 29)

V

variable   a letter or symbol that represents a quantity. (Lesson 20)

volume   the measure of space inside a solid figure. (Lesson 43)

X

x-coordinate   the first number of the ordered pair that tells the direction and number of units to move horizontally from the origin. (Lesson 48**)**

Y

y-coordinate   the second number of the ordered pair that tells the direction and the number of units to move vertically from the origin. (Lesson 48)

Copy Master 1
Number Lines

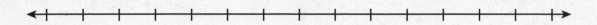

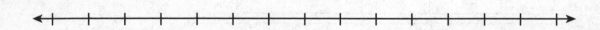

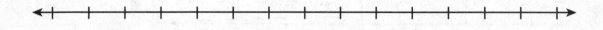

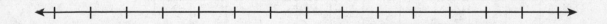

Name _____

Copy Master 2
Fraction Bars

Copying is illegal.

Copy Master 3
Line Graphs

Title: _____

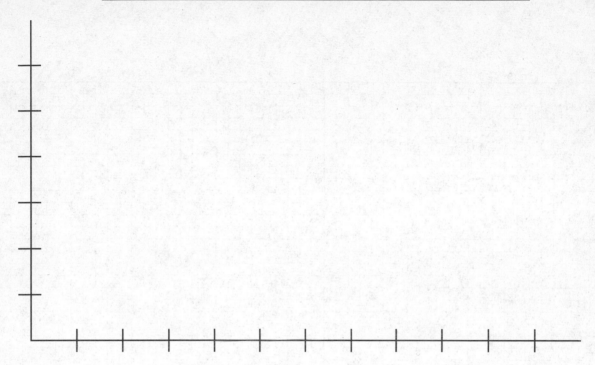

Title: _____

Name _____

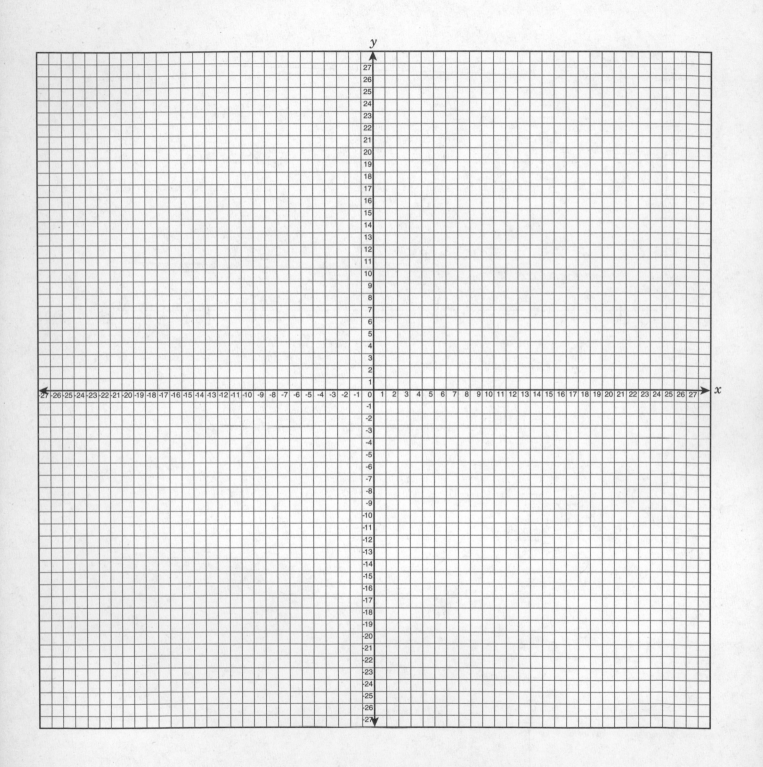

Measuring Up® to the Pennsylvania Academic Standards